THE
GARDEN
RAILWAY
MANUAL

THE GARDEN RAILWAY MANUAL

A step-by-step guide to building and operating an outdoor model railway

C.J. FREEZER

PSL

Patrick Stephens Limited

AN IMPRINT OF HAYNES PUBLISHING

Also by C. J. Freezer, in the same series:

The Model Railway Design Manual
How to plan and build a successful layout

The Model Railway Manual
A step-by-step guide to building a layout

Cover illustrations
Front, main picture and top left: The 19mm gauge, live steam garden railway of Stephen and Janet Dolby of Esholt, West Yorkshire. Located in the garden of a former weaver's cottage, just 50 yards from the original 'Woolpack' of Emmerdale fame. *(Linda Viney)*
Left, middle: Battery-powered narrow gauge diesel locomotives on James Slater's SM32 garden railway. *(Courtesy Railway Modeller)*
Left, bottom: Lawnton station on the Trepolpen Valley Light Railway. *(Courtesy Peter Denny)*
Back: A Lancashire & Yorkshire saddle tank heads a mixed goods across an impressive viaduct in a garden setting. *(Brian Monaghan)*

First published in 1995
Reprinted 1998, 1999, 2001 and 2002

British Library Cataloguing-in Publication Data:
A catalogue record for this book is available from the British Library

ISBN 1 85260 465 4

Patrick Stephens Limited is an imprint of
Haynes Publishing, Sparkford, Yeovil,
Somerset BA22 7JJ, UK

Tel: 01963 442030   Fax: 01963 440001
Int. tel: +44 1963 442030   Int. fax: +44 1963 440001

E-mail: sales@haynes-manuals.co.uk
Web site: www.haynes.co.uk

Typeset by J. H. Haynes & Co. Ltd.
Printed in Great Britain by J. H. Haynes & Co. Ltd.

Contents

Introduction

I approached this book with a certain amount of trepidation since, although I have often enjoyed operating garden railways, my own practical experience in the field has been limited to some abortive experiments in the 1940s. I do have one advantage, though: my interest in this facet of the hobby began before the modern garden railway theme had begun to gain ground. Indeed, when I was in my teens, laying tracks on or near the ground was strictly for the toy train fraternity; real enthusiasts erected proper waist-height baseboards. As with many aspects of the hobby, the 'correct' way to undertake modelling usually means the currently fashionable approach. Therefore I have made frequent reference to the currently outmoded high-level outdoor baseboard, since I believe that it is particularly suited to a OO gauge extension to a shed-housed main station. This is, I consider, the only way most 4 mm scale workers can enjoy the spectacle of a scale-length express running under clear signals over a long stretch of main line.

Although most scale/gauge combinations have been used out of doors, most workers adopt one of three gauges, 16.5, 32 or 45 mm. These are, of course, those used for OO and HO, O and 1 with standard gauge prototypes, but they are also employed for railways based on narrow gauge practice. In recent years the abominable American solecisms, OO scale, HO scale, O scale, etc., have come into use in Britain. Of course, these symbols refer to the *gauge*, which is the most important practical measurement for railway operation. Stock of different scales happily operate over the same gauge tracks, most markedly with G gauge, where one can have models for 2 ft, 60 cm, 3 ft and 1 m gauges running over the same track. For this reason I have to a very large extent avoided the use of these terms. It has long been my belief that, in the interests of accuracy, it is necessary to specify gauge according to either of the two international conventions, imperial and metric, and to be very careful to make sure your reader knows which one you are using. For this reason you will find references to 16.5, 32 and 45 mm gauges, and where scales are mentioned they are given in the two accepted formats, the equivalent of a foot and the much more convenient ratio. As a matter of interest, all drawings have been prepared by CAD using metric standards.

With much of the current thrust in the garden being oriented towards live steam operation, the impression is growing that garden railways are a rich man's hobby. Insofar as a building plot now costs considerably more than a house did 50 years ago, there is a modicum of truth in this. Far from the railway itself costing a fortune, several of the earliest essays in 32 mm gauge garden railways began as shoestring projects, using old Hornby clockwork mechanisms gleaned from broken toy trains. Whilst this source is no longer economic, old clockwork toys having become collector's items, one can still build a narrow gauge garden railway almost entirely from scrap, with rail, wheels, gears and motors being the only parts that cannot be produced in a basic home workshop with simple hand tools. Indeed, 16 mm scale on 32 mm narrow gauge tracks is primarily a scratchbuilder's gauge, where a scale half-inch is clearly visible to the naked eye and you can incorporate as much detail as you want whilst building a robust model that does not need to be kept in a glass case.

I would like to conclude by thanking the many friends and acquaintances who have provided advice and help with this project. The most important fact I have discovered during my investigations is that garden railway builders are a friendly group, happy to pass on information to others and, above all, intent on having fun from their hobby. I can't think of a better recommendation.

C.J. Freezer
Hemel Hempstead 1995

Chapter 1

The Joys of the Garden

There are few things in life that can give greater all-round pleasure than a well-conducted garden railway, combining as it does two excellent hobbies, model railways and gardening. It has been around in various forms for a long time, and although the genre appeared to have gone into a decline during the 1950s and '60s, when it was believed that the then predominant size, OO gauge, was unsuited to outdoor operation, it has since undergone a complete transformation.

The 1930s were the heyday of the outdoor railway. This was very much a matter of necessity, since O gauge was the order of the day and there was rarely enough room for a decent-sized 7 mm scale layout inside the usual suburban semi-detached home. Gardens, on the other hand, were quite large: a 75–100 ft (23–30 m) deep plot was not unusual even on low-priced speculative estates. For most of the inter-war period model railways in the garden were described as outdoor layouts. They were normally built on waist-level baseboards and frequently covered much of the garden to create an elaborate system with numerous stations.

The delights of clockwork

Clockwork was the preferred motive power, and many people relied on the better Hornby O gauge models, for one needed a fairly deep pocket to afford the superior Bassett-Lowke, Milbro or Leeds Model Co. products. The more serious modeller often built his own locomotives around a clockwork mechanism, frequently adapting the dimensions to fit the fixed wheelbase of the commercial unit. Bodies were generally made from tin plate, an admirable material which provided a strong incentive to complete the job as rapidly as possible. It was also very cheap, and once the body was finished, as the saying goes, "a coat of paint could hide a multitude of tins".

Clockwork drive is very much a thing of the past, which in a way is a great pity. Forget the fact that it was associated with the child's train set; in experienced hands the better quality spring-drive mechanisms were, indeed still are, remarkably effective motive power for an intensively operated model railway system. They do not require a mass of wires, a battery of switches and a source of electricity, and they operate with equal unconcern on clean or dirty track.

Clockwork mechanism was almost perfect for the garden railway, but it did mean that each locomotive got a good deal of handling, and as a result, fine detail was ruled out. The main failing with spring drive, however, was that at low temperatures mainsprings became brittle and could be easily broken. This was not quite so serious as it seems, since most outdoor operation ceases over the winter months.

For all that, solemn warnings were given in the model railway press: the late Ernest F. Carter, founder of *Model Railway Constructor* and a knowledgeable authority on O gauge practice, was almost vehement on this point. One wonders if he had had a very unfortunate experience one cold winter.

Problems with electric traction

In the inter-war heyday of the outdoor model railway, electricity was looked on as somewhat unreliable. There were good and proper reasons for this. For a start, the standard voltage was low, a mere 6v, while the power of many electric mechanisms was dubious. For much of the time, the so-called permanent magnets, forged from high-carbon steel, lost their magnetism for any one of a dozen reasons or, as often as not, for no clear reason at all. Then, although by the early thirties most urban homes had an electricity supply, there was no really effective means of rectifying the 3-4 amp supply most O gauge locomotives needed at that time. Metal rectifiers were only just emerging from the experimental stage, and employed copper oxide as the barrier. At current flows measured in milliamps, with ample ventilation, they were reliable, but at higher ratings they teetered on the borderline. The most popular power supply was the car starter battery, which could be trickle-

The fascination of the garden railway. A group of boys watch intently as an O gauge GWR Mogul heads a typical between-the-wars GWR semi-fast.

charged in the house. This is why 6v was so common, since it was only in the late 1930s that cars switched to 12v starters.

Before I leave this subject, I should mention that in his definitive book *Garden Railways*, Ray Tustin states categorically that two-rail out of doors is impractical. We have to remember he was writing around 1947–8, at a time when many established modellers considered that two-rail was unreliable under any circumstances. Knowing from personal experience what little equipment we had at the time, I can fully understand this point of view. Not to put too fine a point on it, two-rail pickup, taken for granted today, was only just out of the experimental stage and a lot of equipment was basically three-rail oriented, with a two-rail jury rig tossed in for those brave souls who wanted to eliminate the obtrusive third rail. However, we're getting ahead of the story.

Until the late 1930s the majority of outdoor railways were virtually identical to their indoor equivalents, in that only the bare minimum of buildings were provided and all tracks were laid directly onto a flat baseboard. Unfortunately, in those days baseboard design was very hit and miss, the few textbooks available giving only the sketchiest of guidance. Even Henry Greenly failed to give timber sizes in his otherwise informative 1924 book *Model Railways*. This surprising omission arose, I suspect, because he took it for granted that the task of baseboard erection would be farmed out to a jobbing carpenter. This failure to provide adequate advice led to many enthusiasts building flimsy structures and ignoring the potential for rot out of doors. By the late 1930s enough had been said in *Model Railway News* to point people in the right direction, but then, as now, not everyone subscribed to a magazine.

Enter the ground-level railway

The problems of building a reliable outdoor baseboard led several enthusiasts to think of a ground-level line. This had two advantages: the main constructional material was

Gauge 1 is big – until it is set in the garden. This lavish station at Bekonscot, based on the nearby Great Western–Great Central Joint line, doesn't appear to be anything out of the ordinary, yet it occupies more space than many small-scale indoor layouts.

immediately to hand, and it also allowed the railway to blend into the garden. Actually, this was not an altogether novel idea, since Bekonscot, the pioneer miniature town, had its Gauge 1 railway down on the ground from the outset. However, it was not until the late thirties that the principle caught on among individual enthusiasts, but once the advantages had been demonstrated, many turned their thoughts to this type of layout

At this point the Second World War brought the hobby to a near stop. It didn't happen at once: during the phoney war of 1939–40 there was still a good deal of activity, but by the end of 1940 most railway modellers were in the Forces and those in reserved occupations were working a 60-hour week. Manufacture of such frivolous things as toy trains (for officialdom made no distinctions) was halted. For the next four years the hobby had to live on its reserves.

When production resumed, O gauge in general and outdoor railways in particular received a body blow. Meccano Ltd effectively abandoned 7 mm scale, the only post-war O gauge products coming out of Binns Road being tin-plate toy trains and a limited range of four-wheeled locos and stock. Bassett-Lowke was still functioning much as before, but the other pre-war O gauge manufacturers did not survive long into the post-war period. If anyone doubts the importance to the hobby of a low-cost, ready-to-run system that is widely available through High Street retailers, just look at the rapid decline of O gauge that took place between 1939 and 1950.

Of course, garden railways did not disappear altogether, but with OO in better supply, coupled with

an intensive drive to popularize compact layouts based on branch line practice, they became very much a minority interest. In direct contrast to the situation before the war, when almost every issue of *Model Railway News* featured outdoor lines in one way or another, in the 1950s it proved difficult to get a description of one respectable garden railway a year. Indeed, Jack Ray's 'Crewchester' was for a long time the major focus of attention for outdoor O gauge.

Narrow gauge in the garden

Meantime, in a small village by the Tamar, Peter Denny was at work on the Tamar Valley Light Railway. Working in ⅜in scale on O gauge track, using Hornby O gauge clockwork mechanisms as a starting point, he created a freelance 3 ft 6 in gauge railway in the garden of his home in Harrowbarrow. By the mid-1950s the line was in full working order and a new era had dawned.

Although one would be stretching a point to suggest that Peter Denny pioneered narrow gauge in the garden, his layout, now in its third and, in all probability, final form, has been working continuously for over 40 years and is still as much fun today as it was when it first turned a wheel all those years ago.

Fun is perhaps the most significant feature of the garden railway. A lot of work being done today on indoor layouts is deadly serious. Not only are scale dimensions quoted in microns, but arcane matters of prototype practice are treated with the reverence more properly associated with Holy Writ. It is held in some circles that a serious railway modeller should be just that; having fun is not in good taste.

This does not apply in the garden. One reason is that exposure to the elements makes many of the quirks of modern exact scale modelling either irrelevant or even counter-productive. Then the

Priestfield Station on P.D. Hancock's Torlum Hill Light Railway, his ground-level SM32 (16 mm scale, 32 mm gauge) garden railway, a comparatively new development for the pioneer OO9 narrow gauge modeller. (P.D. Hancock)

mere act of going outdoors, for most people, brings a sense of freedom from petty restrictions. But perhaps the most significant factor is that, on a garden railway, there is far less need for simulation. This is particularly so with the ground-level line, where civil engineering is for real. Operationally, matters are better balanced, with a much greater proportion of plain track to station complexes, the antithesis of the somewhat artificial terminus/fiddle yard, where most of the train working takes place in the imagination. In even a modest-sized garden it is possible to provide sufficient main line to allow one the pleasure of seeing a scale-length express train thundering along at full speed between stations.

All this, and seasons too

Above all, the garden railway is subject to the seasons. On most models, the period from late spring to early autumn is mainly spent operating the line, coupled with day-to-day maintenance. As autumn shades towards winter, running ceases, the more vulnerable parts of the model are dismantled, and wood preservatives are applied to ensure that timber will over-winter without serious damage. During the winter, repairs, replacement and new construction occupy one's leisure hours until spring returns once more and the line can be brought back into operation.

Operation is, of course, subject to the vagaries of the weather.

On a warm summer's evening, it can be a positive delight. With the heat of the day spent, an hour or two pottering around the garden running trains is a wonderful way to relax after a hard, overheated day's toil. A short running session after rain is equally delightful, for the air will be fresh and the scents of the garden more pronounced. Of course, should you enjoy battling with the elements, then the normal British year provides ample opportunity to defy the worst weather without being obliged to carry on beyond the point where personal discomfort overrides the exhilaration.

Although it is claimed that real model railwaymen ignore the elements, I have to say that all the garden operators I know who run trains regardless of weather conditions do so from the cosy comfort of a garden shed! Indeed,

A TEE express – technically an RA Be EC – speeds through on the extensive rail network at Swissminatur, Melide, Tichino, Switzerland.

Garden O gauge at ground level. Long trains and sweeping curves, difficult to achieve indoors, add to the effect provided by the small plants in the foreground and the dry stone retaining wall behind the railway. (Brian Monaghan, courtesy Railway Modeller*)*

accommodate more than four operators, and then only at the expense of crowding. Many established garden railways routinely play host to ten or more fellow enthusiasts without seriously stretching the household facilities.

The ideal situation is for entire families to come together around a model railway. When this occurs, it is nothing short of idyllic, and the hobby is enjoyed at its highest level. Unfortunately, this is not an idyllic world, and sometimes being able to separate a group of visitors from the intimate side of the family makes it easier to tolerate individuals. On such occasions the 'my house, your garden' syndrome is inevitable.

Above all, garden railways are spacious. It is no longer necessary to decide which of two equally attractive features you will incorporate into the model: you can not only usually have both, there is frequently room for more. Equally, because you do not have initially to work close to the physical limits of the site, there is far greater scope for development once the basic system is complete. Above all, for the majority of railway modellers, the garden is the only place large enough to allow one to accommodate scale-length trains and still provide enough unencumbered track to display them in action.

on a well-organized garden railway you can enjoy all the pleasant features of a rainstorm without having to suffer the worst of the unpleasant side-effects. Of course, the trains will get wet, but so do their prototypes!

Hospitality out of doors

Garden railways are more hospitable than their indoor equivalents. This is mainly a function of space, for few indoor layouts can comfortably

Chapter 2

Gauges and Scales for Outdoor Use

It would be a more courageous man than I who said that any particular scale/gauge combination was impractical for outdoor use. Were he to say it in the presence of any of the more determined members of the hobby, it could well be taken as a challenge. Agreed, I have yet to learn of a Z gauge outdoor layout, but N gauge in the garden is certainly a practical proposition. Bert Groves built just such a line and it worked – for him. He not only demonstrated this to me, he insisted that it was weatherproof and doused the entire main line with a bucketful of water to prove it.

N gauge!

To the best of my knowledge, no-one has repeated the experiment. Certainly modern N gauge track will withstand the rigours of the British climate and the locomotives and rolling stock are unlikely to suffer from the effects of a sudden, heavy downpour, so the primary conditions for outdoor operation can be met. There is, however, another important factor to consider. An indoor layout is housed and operated in a controlled environment. Agreed, the degree of control can vary enormously, but the owner can usually keep dirt, dust and other deleterious materials away from the actual models.

It is essential to remember at all times that a garden railway is operating in the real world.

Bert Groves preparing his N gauge ground-level garden railway for operation.

Although the models will be built to a specific scale, you are in practice operating a real railway whose gauge is expressed in millimetres. Scale is, in my opinion, of secondary importance. However, if you disagree, consider this. The wind can easily lift and carry a piece of grit 1 mm wide. In N gauge this is a scale-sized boulder. However, the main reason that N gauge can be discounted for garden use is that to move it out of doors strips it of its main advantages, whilst conferring few if any benefits in return.

OO gauge

OO gauge is a different proposition, for although the smaller models are more susceptible to outdoor hazards than the more usual larger sizes, the garden provides the 4 mm scale worker in a normal-sized home with the opportunity to enjoy the sight of full-length main line trains running around curves which are not too obviously under scale. With the easy availability at very affordable prices of ready-to-run models of most diesel-era locomotives and coaches, as well as a good selection of later steam-age prototypes, there is no inherent difficulty in collecting enough stock to be able to operate accurate replicas of main line trains. The problem is finding the space to accommodate these indoors, hence in recent years there has been a tendency to regard the branch or minor cross-country route as the norm for the private individual and leave the more exciting main line models to clubs.

An alternative is to follow the example of the pre-war O gauge modeller, move out of doors and enjoy the thrill of watching a 12-coach express roaring round large sweeping curves. This is an aspect of the garden railway that is easily overlooked. Indoors, a 1 m (3 ft) radius curve is regarded as an ideal not easily achieved. In the garden, it is perfectly possible to have a minimum radius of 1.5 m (5 ft) or even 2 m (6½ ft) without in any way cramping the rest of the model. Likewise, gradients can be more in accordance with prototype practice: 1 in 80 can be the ruling grade on most outdoor systems.

OO gauge, even in a small garden, offers considerable scope for an interesting layout, though very few modellers have so far exploited its full potential, preferring to enjoy the sight of scale-length trains running for up to 1 scale km (0.6 miles) between stations. Generally speaking, the tendency is to enclose the main station in a shed so that the stock can be quickly run under cover. This is an important consideration since OO gauge not only gives ample scope for extensive trackwork, it also allows one to amass a large locomotive stud, several rakes of 10-12 coaches and enough goods stock to run 40+ wagon trains as well. The possibility of creating a complex system operated by a group of enthusiasts has hardly been considered and, in the one case I have encountered, the garden

Figure 2.1 Comparison of size for the three main outdoor standard gauges, 1, O and OO (45, 32 and 16.5 mm gauge). No attempt has been made to show narrow gauge profiles, since the prototype loading gauges are so divergent that comparison is misleading.

aspect was only of a limited nature.

Although I do know of one case where EM gauge was used out of doors, no suitable mass-produced track is available. The case in point was laid with OO gauge Streamline slit down the middle and pinned to the base, which to my mind completely negates the main purpose of EM, which is the improved appearance of the track. P4, with its fine flanges and close tolerances, is probably out of the question, since the shallow flanges would not have the tolerance needed to cope with the inevitable grit on the rail head.

Needless to say, the other scales running on 16.5 mm gauge track are also suited to outdoor use. From a mechanical standpoint, HO gauge is identical to OO (wind, rain and weather do not recognize the concept of scale), and 16.5 mm gauge narrow gauge is another possibility.

16.5 mm gauge tracks have been laid at ground level with considerable success. However, the happiest arrangement for this size is undoubtedly to house the principal station within a garden shed, or even along one side of the garage, and extend running

lines into the garden, where sweeping curves, prototypical gradients and ample main line runs are easily achieved. Barring a fortuitous arrangement of ground level, this would involve high-level baseboards for the external sections.

O gauge

Between the wars, when Gauge O was the preferred choice of the serious modeller, a high proportion of layouts were housed in the garden, since there was clearly no expectation of there ever being enough room in the normal suburban house for anything but a very abbreviated 7 mm scale model. The normal practice was to erect the layout on raised baseboards with little regard for the overall appearance. Wherever possible, the main station was under cover and provided dry and fairly secure stock storage as well.

Then, as now, most modellers began with Hornby models. However, the pre-war Hornby O gauge has no connection, apart from the name, with the modern OO system. Manufactured by Meccano Ltd, Hornby O gauge was mainly aimed at the toy end of the market, using traditional tin-plate track. This was completely unrealistic, with widely spaced, pressed tin-plate sleepers and a round-headed, flat-bottomed rail that was very much over scale. The wheels were equally crude, with very deep flanges. Locomotives had cast-spoked wheels, usually whitemetal, but latterly mazak. Rolling stock normally came with two-part tin-plate wheels loose on their axles, though a 'superior' pattern with a solid wheel was available as a replacement.

So-called 'scale' track, with solid-drawn bullhead rail in sheradized steel or brass and cast

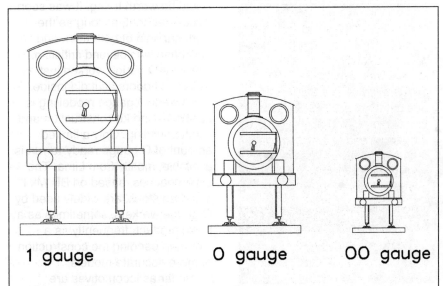

1 gauge   O gauge   OO gauge

The approach to Manchester Central station on Bob Ledger's O gauge garden railway.
(R.A. Loynds)

whitemetal slide-on chairs which were pinned to wooden sleepers, was provided by several manufacturers. In point of fact this too was very much over scale and was more correct for Gauge 1. The reason for this is historical; it continued in use partly through inertia but mainly because it would take the deep flanges of Hornby models. One firm, Bonds o' Euston Road, advertised it in *Hobbies*

Weekly and several magazines for boys as a low-cost alternative to Hornby tin-plate track.

The 'scale' O gauge market also used over-scale wheel profiles to match this track. Whilst not as coarse as the Hornby pattern, they had very deep flanges and wide treads. From a scale model aspect this was deplorable; from the operational aspect it was considered desirable.

Ground-level O gauge in action. A GWR 14xx class 0-4-2T is coupled to a Southern Railway coach.
(Author's collection)

These old, superseded standards had one great bonus: they had very wide tolerances. Although they were not quite 'to the nearest quarter inch', you could be a sixteenth of an inch astray on most dimensions without any serious consequences. The trains might lurch a bit here and there, but they usually stayed on the rails. To modern enthusiasts, this seems horribly casual, but there was a very good reason. Ready-made track was expensive, so most modellers laid their own, *whether or not they were capable of accurate tracklaying.*

The steamroller wheel had another advantage when used out of doors. Dust and dirt are the traditional enemies of good running, but in the garden there is no way of preventing the track getting its due share of flying debris. Deep flanges and wide treads were believed to be best able to deal with this situation. So when commercial finescale track and wheels became available in the late 1930s, the cry went up, 'You'll never be able to use those in the garden!' While this was widely accepted as sound common sense, a couple of maverick modellers thought it would be worth trying. It was soon discovered that, so long as the workmanship of both track and trackbase was beyond criticism, finescale O gauge worked just as well out of doors as it did inside.

Current O gauge modelling is based around kit construction and scratchbuilding. Only a limited amount of O gauge ready-to-run is available, mostly from Lima. The Lima coaches, based on BR Mk I standard stock, are widely used by O gauge workers, sometimes as a basic product, frequently as a stop-gap pending the construction of more accurate models.

So far as locomotives are

Geoff Bigmore's O gauge Ivatt Atlantic at the head of a train of Gresley wood-bodied LNER coaches passes his North London 0-6-0 and typical rake of North London four-wheeled coaches.

concerned, the O gauge worker has a respectable range of kits on offer. In the main the emphasis is on etched brass and prices are, not surprisingly, much higher than for the 4 mm scale equivalents. However, for the garden railway, scratchbuilding is a very attractive proposition, provided one important point is grasped. Garden railways are normally viewed from a distance of at least 2 m (6½ ft) where a lot of the fine detail now associated with high-class 7 mm scale models will be almost indistinguishable. A model built to pre-war 'superdetail' standards will more than meet the needs of the outdoor operator.

Moreover, coaches and wagons can be assembled or scratchbuilt during the winter. A wide selection of 7 mm scale coach and wagon kits is available. They are straightforward to assemble and have all the detail one could wish for. More

specialized stock is produced as etched brass kits. However, as the basic essentials – wheels, axleguards, brake gear, buffers and couplings – are in good supply, scratchbuilding O gauge wagons presents no particular difficulty.

1 gauge

It is a little difficult to believe that, in the early days of the hobby, Gauge 1, then the most popular size, was considered ideal for an indoor layout. There is a simple explanation: the hobby was then very much a middle- and upper middle-class affair and a fair proportion of its active workers had large houses with big lofts where a simple but satisfying Gauge 1 layout could be housed. Even so, there were just as many modellers laying their 1¾in gauge tracks in their gardens.

The track components which were over-size for O gauge were reasonably accurate when used for the larger scale. By the same token, the wheel standards could be closer to scale without sacrificing any of the ruggedness then considered essential for reliable operation. Most important of all, accurate, reliable Gauge 1 steam locomotives are a practical proposition.

Indeed, Gauge 1 is the size where railway modelling merges seamlessly into model engineering. This, I should hasten to add, is not the view of many model engineers. It is sufficient to say that a Gauge 1 locomotive can come very close to the true

Gauge 1 at Bekonscot, with GWR steam railcar and trailer entering one of the stations. The buildings here are in proportion with the railway and to a smaller scale than other structures in this pioneering miniature village.

Live steam 2-6-2 tank on Bob Symes's Gauge 1 Onslow Railway. (Author)

arrangement of its prototype, electric stock can have individually powered axles, and the current can be generated in the locomotive with an internal combustion engine. On the steam side, a working de Glenn compound is a possibility, even though it would fully live up to G.J. Churchward's classic description of the prototype as 'watchmaker's work'.

Although technically obsolescent for many years, Gauge 1 remained a force in the land. Its popularity on the Continent stemmed from a belief that it is inherently superior, a sentiment that all British members of the Gauge 1 Association will endorse. There is little doubt that their stalwart work has ensured that 45 mm gauge has remained a viable proposition, though it is largely a scratchbuilder's scale. At all events, the size of the models makes scratchbuilding that much easier, since not only are detail parts much easier to fabricate, they are also very much easier to

find when they are dropped on the floor.

Today, not only has Märklin resumed manufacture of Gauge 1 models, but a goodly array of specialist manufacturers are providing components and even kits for the scale. While it is not a gauge one can lightly adopt, it has much going for it.

We can now consider two gauges which do not feature in recent books on model railways.

2 gauge

One of the more intriguing mysteries of the hobby is how 2 gauge (2 in gauge, 7/16 in scale) ever came into existence, since it is only fractionally larger than Gauge 1. The only explanation I can offer is that, a century ago, it seemed like a good idea.

3 gauge

Although until recently, 3 gauge was known only to historians, in its other guise – 2½ in gauge – it enjoyed considerable popularity among model engineers. Much of this was due to the stalwart work of L.E. 'Curly' Lawrence, more widely known by his pen-name

'LBSC'. A former engine driver and largely self-taught engineer, he built and described a series of live steam locomotives, mainly, but not exclusively, in the columns of *Model Engineer*. Most of these were for 3 gauge, but as model engineers have always distanced themselves from railway modelling proper, they preferred to quote the gauge in inches. In many ways this is an admirable practice, as it leaves no room for error.

Although the passenger-hauling potential of 2½ in gauge locomotives has been frequently demonstrated, this is severely limited, with the result that in recent years the emphasis has been on 3½ in, 5 in and 7¼ in gauges. This move has been accelerated by the judging rules applied by model engineers which take into account the work put into the model. As this is difficult, if not downright impossible, to gauge from the finished model, size and complexity have been taken as a rough guide. This left 2½ in gauge out in the cold, but as coal firing and full working valve gear are a straightforward proposition in this size, the advent of radio control, which allows a steam locomotive to be driven from the lineside, has brought 3 gauge back into the realms of railway modelling proper.

Clearly 3 gauge requires a large garden for even a modest circuit and, in the main, most of the models will need to be scratchbuilt, so a well-equipped workshop is an absolute essential. On the other hand, the potential for not only live steam, but real diesel-electric locomotives as well, is considerable. Electric traction through overhead or third rail is possible, but anyone toying with the idea of scaling the prototype 25kv transmission to a mere 240v should think again!

Narrow gauge

Narrow gauge type railways are today the fastest-growing area for the garden railway modeller. In this field, only the gauges are standardized, at 16.5 mm (OO/HO gauge), 32 mm (O gauge) and 45 mm (1 gauge). The scale chosen depends on the prototype gauge followed. As there are plenty to choose from, it is very much a matter for individual choice, and indeed many modellers are perfectly happy to mix the scales in a haphazard fashion. Commercially, the bulk of ready-to-run models are for 45 mm gauge (G gauge) and are available for 1 m, 3 ft 6 in, 3 ft, 760 mm, 2 ft and 600 mm gauge prototypes. More than anything else, this emphasizes that there are few scale fanatics among garden railway modellers, for the devotees of this size persist in describing it as *G scale*, despite the fact that the scale can be almost anything you like and that many workers are perfectly happy to have locomotives and stock of different gauge prototypes operating over their systems, for the good and proper reason that they happen to like them. It has been said that consistency is the mark of a small mind. 45 mm gauge narrow gauge is extremely popular in Europe and is effectively the mainstream garden gauge in the USA.

A limited supply of 1 m gauge models, operating on 22 mm gauge (S gauge) track, has been around for some years, the production moving from one small firm to another. As I write I learn that the range has been taken over by Roco, and is likely to be extended. One should also mention HOm models, again mainly of Swiss prototypes, since these 1:87 scale models on 12 mm gauge track are on the borderline

for outdoor use. The main question mark does not relate to the suitability of the gauge or the stock, but to the flimsy nature of the essential overhead wires on a fully electrified system. Since Rhätian main line trains routinely load 12–14 coaches behind a powerful locomotive, the spatial advantages of outdoors are appealing. I have a feeling that OO9/HOe (9 mm gauge) narrow gauge is unsuited for outdoor use. Most modellers with a yen to create an extensive 2 ft gauge system find the 16 mm scale/32 mm gauge combination of SM32 irresistible.

Whether based on 2 ft, 3 ft 6 in or 1 m gauges, 32 mm gauge narrow gauge is very strong in Britain, where virtually all the pioneer work has been carried out. Initially it was a clockwork/electric system, but in recent years steam power has proved extremely popular. Much of this stems from the establishment of a thriving industry producing steam locomotives for 32 mm and 45 mm gauges in both ready-assembled and kit form. These are not typical ready-to-run products, for they are made in batches rather than mass-produced in their thousands, and

16 mm scale on 32 mm gauge (SM32) is seen at its best at ground level. The large size of the models makes the contrast with the natural vegetation less marked. (Photo courtesy Railway Modeller*)*

SM32 gauge on the outdoor railway at Pecorama, Beer, Devon. The tracks are on raised baseboards surrounded by close-clipped privet hedges, which create the ambience of surrounding fields, so long as you don't look at them closely!

16 mm scale provides ample scope for the scratchbuilder. Here we have Don Boreham's Strider, *a model 2 ft gauge 0-4-2 saddle tank. A member of the Merioneth group, he named his locomotives after characters in Tolkien's* Lord of the Rings.

they are built by engineers. Indeed, it is not too far-fetched to say that these firms are carrying on the traditions of the full-sized narrow gauge locomotive constructors in offering a standard product for different gauges, as well as a degree of customizing to the client's requirements.

Which is best?

I am always conscious that any discussion of scale and gauge must raise more questions than it answers. One question is inevitable: which is the best combination for a garden railway? The plain fact of the matter is that, if there is an answer to that question, I haven't come across it at any time in the past 60 years. So much depends on personal circumstances, individual inclinations and, above all, the availability of equipment at the crucial moment. When it comes to the crunch, the majority of railway modellers adopt a particular scale/gauge combination because, when they begin their model, it happens to be the most convenient option. Perhaps more to the point, whatever scale/gauge combination is used, the constructional details of the garden railway remain the same.

Chapter 3

Surveying and Setting Out

Garden railways are much closer to their prototypes than the indoor variety and, as with full-sized projects, a survey is the first essential. Measuring a garden is a different matter from measuring a room, because the sizes involved are that much greater and the ground surface can be guaranteed not to be absolutely flat. Fortunately, we do not need extreme accuracy for our purposes: the nearest 3 in or 100 mm will do very nicely for the initial proposals. (The more observant reader will notice that I have given different limits for imperial and metric standards. This is to emphasize that the tolerances are really set by the standards used: in one case a quarter foot, in the other the obsolescent decimetre.)

How to measure

The first consideration when you set out to measure anything is not so much the accuracy of your measuring equipment as its ease of use. Provided your measuring equipment is of a reputable make, its accuracy can be taken for granted. Your main worry will always be the errors you introduce.

The fence

First, I am going to point you towards an unconventional measuring instrument which is well worth considering for one simple reason: it's there.

Many gardens are enclosed by

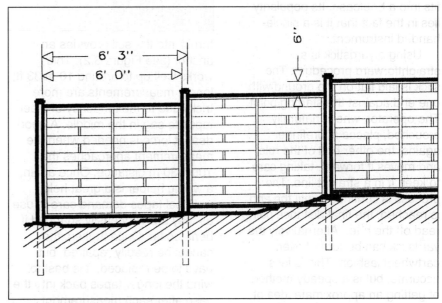

Figure 3.1 *Using the common interwoven wooden boundary fence is a reasonably accurate method of estimating the length of the garden, and getting an idea of the slope of the site.*

prefabricated panel fencing. These come in standard lengths, so you only need make two measurements: the length of the standard panel together with its post and the short end filler (see Figure 3.1). Multiply by the number of panels and you have a fairly accurate idea of the measurements of your garden. The panel fence will also give a very good indication of the inclination of the site, since the posts should be vertical and the panels horizontal – well, as near as makes little practical difference.

Pacing

A very quick method of arriving at the size of a site is pacing. This, the oldest system of survey, is clearly unreliable. There is a very old dodge which involves tying the ankles together exactly 1 yd apart. I've never tried it, for two excellent reasons. The first is an ingrained belief that this is a very good way of tripping oneself up, the second is that I have owned a 100 ft steel tape for over 40 years. However, although long steel tapes are the accepted measuring instruments for this type of survey, it would be wrong to imply that they are essential for a garden railway survey. They fall into the category of luxury tools and moreover require a good deal of care in their handling so, before we come to their proper use, let's look at less costly alternatives.

The yardstick

One measure which is largely ignored by all but professional surveyors is the yardstick. This comes in two forms: the rigid measure, today 1 m long, and the two- or four-fold measure, which is extremely popular with estate agents and surveyors because it fits into a briefcase. Its popularity lies in the fact that it is a single-handed instrument.

Using a yardstick is a straightforward procedure. The stick is laid flat on the ground with one end against the starting point. The operator, who is naturally crouched, places a forefinger against the other end of the rule and moves it forward, taking care to keep it in a straight line. The process is continued until the end is reached, the final distance being read off the rule. Alternatively the yardstick can be turned over, cartwheel fashion. This is less accurate, but is a speedy method of getting an approximate idea of size. The operator now has a measurement in the form 'ten of those and this much', which is readily converted into a more useful figure by simple mental arithmetic.

Steel tapes

The pocket measuring tape, which may be no more than 6 ft/2 m long, is floppy and has a nasty habit of twisting in use. Given a willing assistant, a 3 m, 5 m or better still a 7 m tape is a very useful measuring tool, but unless you have someone at each end, convenience flies over the boundary.

Paradoxically, the longer tapes are easier to use single-handed. This is because they are provided with a loop at the end, rather than a simple hook. A length of ¼ in or 6 mm diameter rod which can be

thrust into the soil provides an anchor (see Figure 3.2). This works well up to around 10 m/33 ft; longer measurements are more tricky due to the tendency of steel tapes to sag in the middle. A good deal of force is needed when the measurement approaches the 100 ft/30 m distance. Once again, a willing helper is a great help.

Steel tapes demand care in use as they are very easily snapped if bent too far. Once broken, they cannot be readily repaired, but have to be replaced. It is best to wind the longer tapes back into the case after each measurement rather than attempt to carry them around the garden. Even if the soil is perfectly dry, it is still advisable to wipe them with a piece of rag as you wind in. A drop or two of oil on the rag is a good idea: a little protection and some lubrication never comes amiss.

'As long as a bit of string'

There is an alternative which is remarkably reliable, based on the principle that 'as long as a piece of string' is a sound measurement if you know precisely how long your piece of string is. Measuring a length of string to the limits suggested is much easier than it might appear, and is demonstrated in Figure 3.3. Two nails driven into a timber batten exactly 1 m or 3 ft apart is all that is needed. A loop is tied at one end of the string and hooked around a nail. The string is

A selection of my measuring tapes. On the left is a 100 ft steel tape in a leather-covered case, by Rabone Chesterman of Sheffield. They don't make cases like this any more, as plastic is now the preferred casing – in this instance, bright red. A 10 m tape is ample for most purposes and, unlike the 100 ft tape, will just go into a trouser pocket. Next there is a 5 m/16 ft Fisco Mark-o-Matic tape, and finally a Stanley 3 m/10 ft tape. The two shorter tapes have belt clips, though in practice I find it easier to slip them into my pocket.

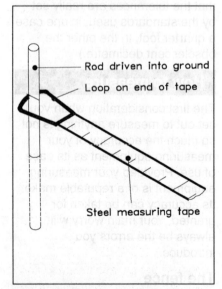

Figure 3.2 *The end of a long steel measuring tape can be hooked over a rod thrust into the ground. A good deal of force is needed to keep the tape approximately straight, so the rod needs to be very firm.*

An aeriel view of the garden O gauge demonstration layout at Pecorama. Although measuring this rectangular site presented no difficulties, setting out the various curves was another story.

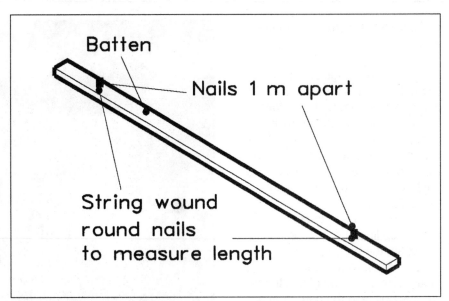

Figure 3.3 *'As long as a piece of string' can be a very useful way of measuring, providing you know how long the string is.*

stretched out and a slip knot tied at the measured distance. This needs to be secure enough not to slip, but easy enough to pull free when the measurement is taken. The string is wound round the nails, the number of turns noted and the extra length measured. Again, it is a case of 'so many of those and that much'.

Whilst this is a primitive system, it has several advantages. Cost is one. Ease of use is another, but most surprising of all is that, providing the two nails are precisely located, it is remarkably accurate since it is relatively easy to stretch the string taut between them.

Obstructions and irregularities

Unless you are dealing with a new garden, there will be numerous fixtures in place. Some can be repositioned, some cannot. Outbuildings and established trees are obvious examples of fixed obstructions. Paths can only be moved around with varying degrees of difficulty, while established trees are best regarded as fixtures since their removal is a major operation. All

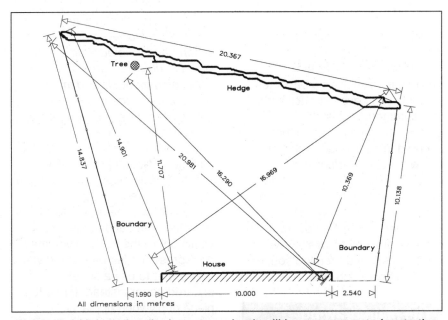

Figure 3.4 *Unless the plot is rectangular, it will be necessary to locate the various points by simple triangulation from a fixed base line – in this case, the rear wall of the house, largely because it is there and is not going to move. Only one internal feature, a tree, is shown to avoid complicating the diagram. (The dimensions were worked out to the nearest millimetre by my CAD program, but nothing like this accuracy is needed or, for that matter, readily achievable by any means available to the majority of garden railway modellers.)*

these features need to be located on your plan.

Apart from this, not every garden is a rectangular plot. While few will be quite as irregular as the one shown in Figure 3.4, it does happen to be the plan of my last garden in Devon, a corner plot in a cul-de-sac. To measure this sort of site and to locate the various obstructions we resort to simple triangulation.

For this we need to set out a fixed base line or datum point – in this case, the back wall of the house. Measurements are then taken from each end of this to the various points in the garden and recorded on a rough plan, or listed in a notebook. The plan is then produced on either a drawing-board or a block of squared paper. The major datum points (fixed starting-points) are, obviously, the extreme corners of the plot and the walls of the house, but the corners of any outbuildings and the trunks of trees can be similarly used. The lines of boundaries and paths will also need noting down.

The preliminary plan

From this rough sketch a preliminary plan is produced on squared paper. There are two types of squared paper. The sort most easily found in Britain is 'graph paper', which is ruled in a precise millimetre grid, with every 10th marking heavier. Not surprisingly, it is fairly expensive. There is another type, very easily found on the Continent, which has uniform 4 mm pitch squares. This can occasionally be found in the better stationers in England. Since discovering this, I have become a convert and make a point of stocking up well on my travels. It is, I find, ideal for sketching and writing. Standard A4 sheets are best for our purpose. The sketch

does not have to be to scale, but it does help if the proportions are approximately correct.

Once you have the rough plan drawn out, it is a straightforward matter to determine which dimensions you need to take. These are then set out on the sketch before you begin to measure on the ground. The reason I advise A4 for the preliminary sketch now becomes obvious: you have to pencil in the measurements whilst in the garden. If your piece of paper is secured to a clipboard, you can do this with ease. Furthermore, you will also need to lay the plan down from time to time. If it is not on a clipboard you will have to remember to weigh it down with a stone to prevent it blowing away. Clipboards, need I remind you, are made to take A4 sheets.

The main drawing

With your dimensioned sketch complete you can now begin work on the main drawing. Here I suggest that it is best to work on an A3 sheet of paper. For utmost convenience, a drawing-board should be used. Modern all-plastic boards with a transparent T-square

This high-level view of James Slater's SM32 narrow gauge layout emphasizes the value of a careful site survey. The formal garden with paving and seats was laid out by the resident professional landscape architect in order to allow the railway to fit into the setting. However, a determined amateur ought to be able to crib some ideas from gardening manuals and in time achieve much the same results. The professional gets it right first time. (Railway Modeller)

running in guides and provided with firm paper clips are one of the few cases where the traditional equipment is so far outclassed that only the hidebound traditionalist would spurn them. However, they do represent a fair outlay and you may prefer to use a sheet of squared paper instead, taped to a piece of plywood or plastic-covered chipboard to keep it flat.

This is not the place for a treatise on drawing office techniques, but a little advice may be in order. You need first of all to decide on a suitable scale. As both the squared paper and the rules on the drawing-board will be in metric, it might seem that you ought not to have measured the garden in feet and inches. However, scales of 10 mm to the foot, or 1 mm to the inch are perfectly suitable, *providing that* you put this essential information down on the sheet before you go any further. It is terribly easy to forget to record this vital piece of information, only to discover some months later that you have forgotten which scale you used. Although it is usually possible to discover this by scaling off a known dimension, it is still a considerable nuisance to have to do this, and a waste of your time.

If the plot is roughly rectangular, you should first set out the main boundaries, either by using the T-square or by taking the squares as a guide. If it is irregular, you will need to triangulate. This can be a little tricky. The classic method is to strike arcs using a pair of compasses, but several of the longer diagonals will be anything up to 400 mm (15½ in) in length. Even a good draughtsman's compass, with extension arm, will not go this far.

There is another way. You will have a rough idea of the angle of the boundary. You should know its length. Using a soft pencil, lightly draw it by guesswork. Now take a long rule, place it on the other end of the main boundary and see how far out you were. Hopefully, it will be within 10 mm (0.4 in), and common sense will show you where to put in the correct spot. Initially you'll probably need a couple of tries to get it right.

Levels

So far I have deliberately ignored the question of levels. The difficulty lies in estimating differences of height, for here the eye is notoriously unreliable. Builders employ a dumpy level, a

simplified theodolite which enables the operator to get a very accurate picture of the vertical displacement of the terrain. Obviously, for most individuals this is an unattainable luxury, but within the relatively small area of a garden, other methods can be used.

For our initial survey, a simple sighting device is adequate. As shown in Figure 3.5, it requires a chequered pole marked off in standard units with contrasting colours and a level sighting board. I have shown a simple wooden T, but if you own a photographer's tripod with pan and tilt head, a flat board fitted to this will be far superior.

The sighting board is placed at the datum point and carefully levelled, and the height from the board to the ground is noted. The assistant now places the chequered pole at the required location and the operator reads off the height. As an alternative, a plain pole is used and the second operator moves a marker (generally his/her thumb) up and down the pole. Once the level is reached, the distance is measured with a pocket tape.

Fortunately, precise levels are not required at the survey stage: a general indication of the main slope over the layout area is enough. More accurate work will be needed when the railway is laid out on the ground.

Setting out

Although the preparation of the overall plan of the railway will be the next stage, this will be covered in the following chapter. As the actual setting out of the line uses many of the techniques we have discussed in this chapter, it is best to deal with that now.

The main consideration is setting the extent of the layout out

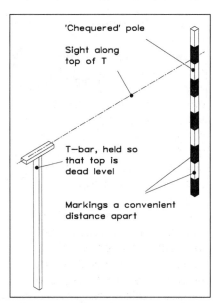

Figure 3.5 The chequered pole used by builders and surveyors is a convenient method of determining the levels of a normal-sized garden. While this is not a precision method, it will give an adequate indication of the rise and fall of the garden sufficient to indicate whether the scheme is practical, and what allowances need to be made.

on the ground. The traditional marker is the peg, a length of wood about 25 mm (1 in) square and 300 mm (1 ft) long, one end of which is provided with a rough point. This is driven into the soil with a hand hammer. The spacing of the pegs will depend on a number of different factors, not the least of which will be the number of pegs you have prepared before you begin marking out. You generally discover you need anything from 50 to 100 per cent more than you thought you did, so this is definitely a case where, within reason, the more, the merrier.

Setting out a straight line of pegs is a very straightforward job. The most satisfactory method is to drive in the first peg, tie a line to it, locate the end point, drive in

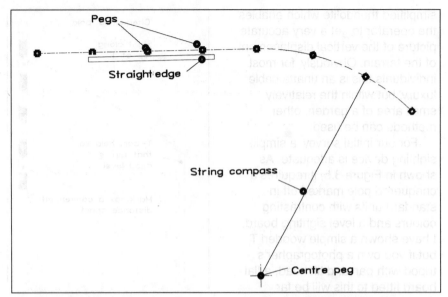

Figure 3.6 Setting out the centre line of the railway by means of pegs. These are driven into the ground at approximately equal intervals, the closer, within reason, the better. For curves, a simple 'compass' using a measured length of string tethered to a post can be used.

another peg and tie the line to that, then set out the intermediate pegs along that line. This neatly skips round the crux of the matter: how do you locate the pegs? This has to be done by first determining the distance the pegs are to be set from the nearest of your datum points.

Arcs are set out as shown in Figure 3.6, by locating the centre point, driving in a peg, tying a line to this and using this line as a simple compass. This only works where first, you can reach the centre of your arc, and second, there is no large obstruction in the way.

You may prefer to set out such curves by eye. So long as they are well in excess of the minimum radius for the stock you will be using, this is acceptable. What you should never do is rely on your eye alone for setting out a right angle.

To set one of these out on the ground, you use a technique older than the pyramids, the 3-4-5 triangle. This is generally associated with lengths of rope, which for very large baseline measurements is to be preferred, but for repeated measurements a wooden square is best. You need two lengths of timber three units and four units long respectively, joined at one corner. The extreme ends are then adjusted until they are exactly five units apart, and a diagonal brace is nailed across to keep the assembly rigid.

Initially, pegs are used to

determine the centre lines of the tracks. It can be useful to lay down the proposed size of the baseboards or railway limits. It will certainly be necessary to set out the sides of any excavations. This last bit sounds simple until you realize that if you simply put a peg into each corner of the hole, they will fall in the moment you begin to dig. The trick is to put in further pegs outside the line of the hole and to string lines from these pegs.

Back to levels

Again, I've left the question of setting out levels to the last. For a start, where the layout is to be laid on high-level baseboards, the levelling is largely carried out by adjustment to the height of the supports and so we are, at this stage, mainly concerned with ground-level layouts. However, we do need first to determine a datum and then establish spot heights around the layout.

Where there are considerable differences in height, it is a good idea to begin by establishing a

Figure 3.7 Levelling the heads of the pegs using a spirit level taped to a straight, stout wooden batten.

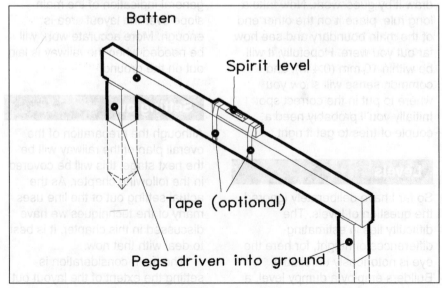

master level and, if practicable, ensure that this cannot be accidentally altered. Similar posts can then be set around the site and the initial levels of the pegs determined from these.

It will be clear that if the pegs are driven into the ground until their tops coincide with the proposed base level for a ground-level layout, it is simply a matter of building the foundations up to the top of the pegs. Once one peg is set to datum level, subsequent pegs are aligned with a spirit level.

The normal spirit level is clearly too short for this job. Builders' levels are much longer and are preferable for outdoor use. The larger DIY stores stock them, but the lengths vary, and although it might seem necessary to get the very largest available, it is a relatively simple matter to span the metre or so between pegs with a stout timber batten and place the level on this (see Figure 3.7). After all, builders' levels aren't exactly cheap.

Gradients

Setting all pegs at one level is simple enough; gradients need a little more forethought. Here the pegs need to be set at one predetermined distance apart, and the difference in height between the pegs arrived at by interposing a standard thickness of packing between the peg and the level at the low end, as shown in Figure 3.8. For a 1 in 100 gradient, a 1 m spacing with a 10 mm spacer is

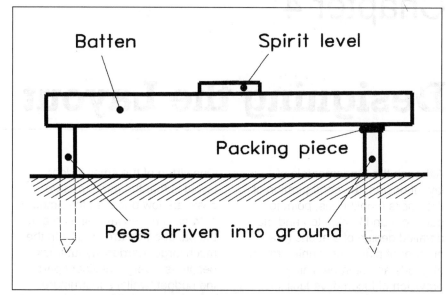

Figure 3.8 *The most straightforward method of setting out a gradient is to interpose a piece of packing between the low end peg and the level. The exact thickness depends on the gradient involved and the spacing of the pegs. The best way to determine this is to standardize on 1 cm thick packing and set the pegs out at a spacing equal to the gradient required in centimetres. With imperial measurements, you either have a very wide peg spacing for an inch of packing, or you use a thinner block and divide the distance accordingly.*

fine. Steeper grades either require a larger spacer or less spacing between the pegs. For a ground-level layout this is quite convenient.

With raised baseboards, where the supports are widely spaced, it will be best to calculate the vertical offset and provide different thicknesses of packing. However, with this system of construction it is customary to carry out fine adjustments when erecting the baseboards proper.

It is not easy to set the gradient of a garden railway to a precise figure, no matter how much care is taken. A nominal 1 in 100 grade can vary between 1 in 90 and 1 in 110. It is, I think, sound practice to take advantage of the greater space available in the garden to use easier gradients than are common on indoor layouts. For this reason I would suggest that nothing steeper than 1 in 80 should be considered during the preliminary planning stage, even though electric and steam power can cope satisfactorily with considerably steeper inclines.

Chapter 4

Designing the Layout

Although the fundamentals of layout design, the configuration of the tracks (continuous, point to point, out and back, etc.) and the detailed design of stations (the number of platforms, configuration of goods and storage sidings, provision of locomotive facilities, etc.) are the same whether the railway is indoors or out, a garden site provides opportunities the normally cramped indoor location cannot offer.

The impact on the garden

Indoors, the actual appearance of the model only matters where it is permanently on view in a living room; where it is located in its own separate area, the builder can close the door and let any disorder remain unseen and uncriticized. A garden railway is difficult to hide. Not only will it be seen by family or friends as a matter of course, it will generally be seen by the neighbours as well. On a reasonably level site, there is no reason why the entire plot cannot be fully taken up with raised baseboards standing on a level concrete base, but this is not going to look good from the living room window. I don't rule out this approach altogether – it was a common arrangement in the 1930s – but with a little forethought the obtrusive impact of this type of layout can be softened.

Cost

There is also the question of cost.

One virtue of the small indoor layout is that the infrastructure costs are low because the amount of track is necessarily limited and the baseboards are small. On the much larger garden layout track becomes a very significant part of the budget, whilst substructure costs, except in the simple case of the layout laid directly onto the ground surface, are also appreciable. It is not unknown for a garden railway to face the same problem that bedevilled many full-sized systems, construction coming to a halt because the money runs out. I'll return to this later on.

Wherever a railway is to be built, it is advisable to consider several alternatives before committing yourself to a master plan. With the garden railway this becomes a necessity because, even with a relatively small plot, many alternative arrangements can be contrived that will satisfy your personal requirements equally well. At the same time, with so much space at your disposal, many factors which loom large in the initial planning stages of an indoor scheme can be deferred until much later.

Track radii and gradients

A vital factor is the minimum radius. Even in a tiny garden, 2 m/6½ ft radius curves do not materially restrict the scope of the design. Gradients are also less of a problem since there is always sufficient length to allow one track

to be carried over another without resorting to rack assistance. Most important of all, you can allocate enough space for stations on the master plan to avoid the need to draw out detailed track plans simply to ensure that you can accommodate the essential facilities. I have followed this practice in the plans which follow since, apart from anything else, the scale to which the plans must be reproduced renders a detailed approach impracticable. The standard practice for these large layouts is to draw the master plan to a small scale and then prepare detailed drawings of the crucial parts to a much larger scale. As a result, the master plan need be little more than a reasonably accurate depiction of the route of the railway.

Most gardens are basically rectangular in plan, the exceptions being mainly confined to corner plots and the rare case of the large house in extensive grounds of an acre or more. Whilst irregular sites are much more interesting to exploit, I will restrict myself to the more usual situations, starting with the old terraced house with a back projection which results in an L-shaped plot (Plan 1). Such gardens are frequently bordered by brick walls and may have a rear access to a communal back alley. The soil is frequently in poor condition through decades of use and, in many cases, outright misuse. With many such gardens, almost any treatment must be an improvement.

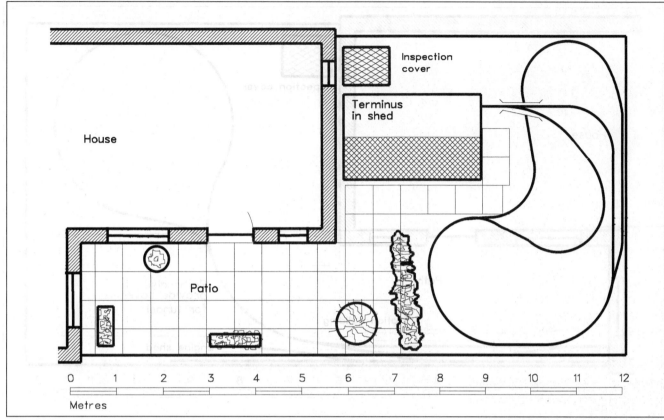

Plan 4.1 *A standard gauge (OO or O) layout on raised baseboards with terminus in shed.*

Hiding a high-level layout

In Plan 1 I have divided the area into two. The narrow portion beside the house is paved and embellished with choice plants grown in containers, effectively dealing with the problem of poor soil whilst reducing maintenance to a minimum. A hedge provides a backdrop: this would be planted in a carefully prepared section of soil and kept well trimmed. The railway occupies most of the remainder of the garden and is assumed to be mounted on waist-level baseboards, with the main terminus located in a wooden shed. It will be seen that building regulations have been quietly ignored by having the shed hard against the house – a detail that might need careful

thought. There is an inspection hatch for the drains hard by, which can hopefully remain undisturbed for years, but this plan is based on a house I once owned where this was very definitely not the case! Inspection covers must be readily accessible at all times.

The layout is assumed to be a standard gauge model, either O or OO gauge. In the former case a branch line theme would be indicated, though the continuous main line could well be double track. In the smaller scale double track would be desirable, and at least one of the connections to the continuous main line could be made into a flying junction.

Two features are missing from the plan: the possible access to a rear alleyway and, more important still, the location of the clothes line. Clearly, if there is a rear access and this is in regular use, either the main line has to be diverted

clear of the path, or sections of the waist-level baseboards must be removable. Where the main use of the rear access is for the weekly dustbin collection, lift-out sections, which can be stored in the shed when the layout is not in use, are a straightforward answer.

We now come to the very important matter of the clothes line. If the width of the patio permits, a rotary line, located in a socket set into the paving, is far and away the most convenient arrangement – it is close to the back door and approached over dry paving. Alternatively, a line could be strung between the house wall and a post in front of the hedge. The layout area is not suitable – waist-level baseboards and clothes lines cannot coexist!

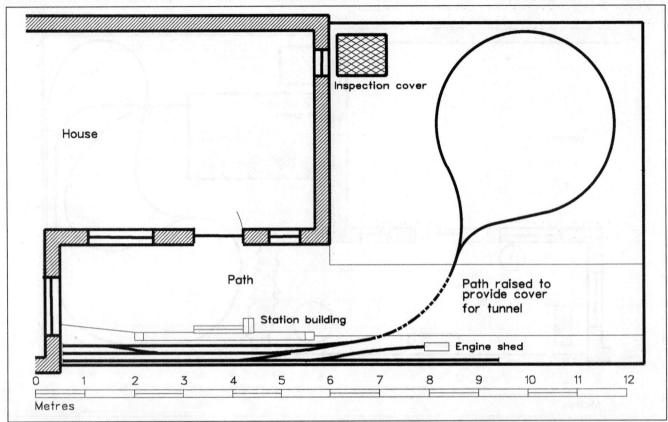

House

Inspection cover

Path raised to provide cover for tunnel

Path

Station building

Engine shed

0 1 2 3 4 5 6 7 8 9 10 11 12

Metres

Ground-level narrow gauge

This problem does not arise with Plan 2. Here we have a ground-level narrow gauge layout on 32 or 45 mm gauge track. This is a very simple scheme that is well suited to a low-cost approach. The tracks would be laid near to ground level on a ballast bed, the only serious problem arising where the track has to cross the path. I have suggested a raised section to form a tunnel; this will be discussed in detail in Chapter 9. It is possible to have a simple level crossing, but this needs to be approached with care. Although one manufacturer has shown an elephant standing on his track, this is a gimmick. While I can't speak for elephants, a fully grown adult can stand on almost any well-made commercial track – only some of the 'finescale' tracks

with very flimsy fixings will object. Walking over ground-level track is another thing altogether, as the rails will then be subject to a sideways thrust rather than a vertical load. I know of no small-scale rail fastening that will stand up to this sort of stress, even when partially buried in concrete. While very substantial steel or brass sections could be so employed, since they will be largely hidden in the path, I cannot help feeling that the raised path is a simpler solution.

As the terminus is close to the house, a removable control centre can be plugged into the mains supply by the simple process of passing the lead through the window opening. As this type of house originally had sash windows, this is a very straightforward proposition. I have much more to say on power supplies in Chapter 15.

Plan 4.2 Ground-level narrow gauge (32 or 45 mm gauge) out-and-back system.

No landscaping is shown. The station occupies most of what was originally the flower bed and the reverse loop runs through the garden proper. Whether this is largely laid to grass, developed with flower beds or simply covered with tarmac depends very much on how you found the back plot when you took over the house and how much work you want to put in.

Live steam operation

This scheme could be run with live steam locomotives, but for this type of motive power a continuous run is preferable. A pleasing arrangement is shown in Plan 3, where the tracks run around the back, mainly on raised beds supported by a dwarf brick wall. Two liftout sections are shown,

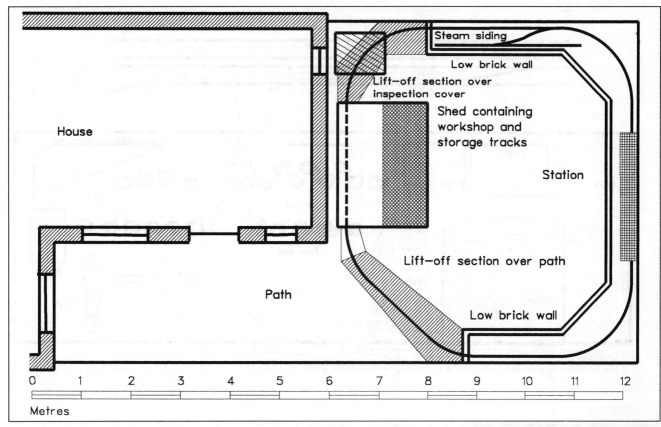

Plan 4.3 *Continuous circuit for live steam-operated line.*

one over the entrance path, one over the inspection hatch. The station is more a scenic feature than an operational unit, reflecting the fact that the fun of steam working lies in the business of raising steam and then controlling the locomotive, either by hand or, as is very much the case today, by radio control.

The most important feature will be the siding along the front of the 'baseboard' for steam raising. So far as the railway is concerned, the shed merely provides stock storage and houses the workshop; it is not a good idea to try to raise steam inside, particularly with butane firing. While flare-ups are rare, they can occur and it is preferable for the operator to have room to step back smartly for at least a metre before reaching for the fire extinguisher.

This is a good point at which to consider another hazard, theft. As intruders have climbed into the grounds of Buckingham Palace, despite police patrols and high brick walls topped with razor wire, we can take it that no garden can be made secure against intruders. Much more to the point, no timber-built shed is thief-proof. As with live steam one is looking at anything from £250 to £5,000 per highly portable locomotive, these should always be stored in the house. As a well-equipped workshop will contain tools worth over £1,000 (more if a lathe, bench drill and grindstone are included), a more secure structure could be worth the investment. A substantial brick or concrete block lean-to building would call for a greater initial investment, but if it could be afforded, it would be money well spent. (I have more to say about sheds in Chapter 6.)

Alongside the fence

In Plan 4 I have taken a fairly typical semi-detached house with a separate garage alongside and a neat rectangular plot behind. The layout is closely based on the late Geoff Bigmore's 'Bigston to Westbridge' O gauge layout, with the two termini housed in wooden sheds at each end of the garden. The railway runs down one side of the garden, but is largely screened from the house and garden proper by extensive rose beds. While this appears a very simple design, its operating potential is high, since with the operators at each end not merely out of sight of each other but, effectively, out of earshot as well, some form of telegraph system is essential. Obviously, a complete block telegraph using prototype instruments is the ultimate in realism. I have incorporated a reverse loop so that

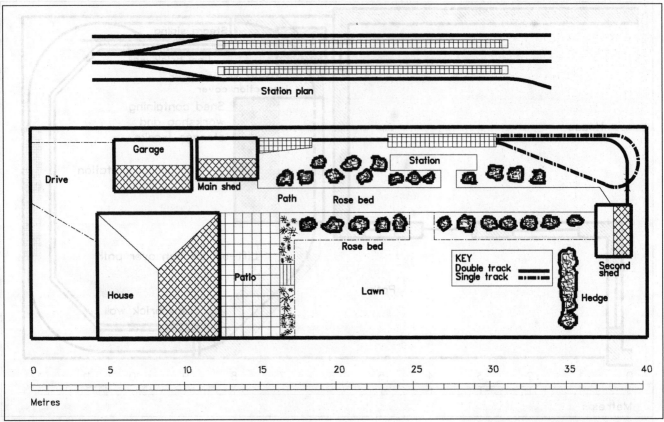

Station plan

Garage

Drive

Main shed

Path

Station

Rose bed

Rose bed

House

Patio

Lawn

KEY
Double track
Single track

Second shed

Hedge

0   5   10   15   20   25   30   35   40

Metres

Plan 4.4 *Terminus to terminus standard gauge raised baseboard scheme for a larger garden, with both termini in sheds.*

the owner can work single-handed if desired.

As the main terminus, nearer the house, will be the more elaborate of the two, the approach tracks and part of the pointwork are outside the shed, visible through an end window. This arrangement worked well at Bigston, allowing several reasonably long O gauge trains to be housed inside a moderate-sized shed. The major part of the garden is laid down as lawn – clearly as much of this can be devoted to flowers and shrubs as you care to maintain. There is space behind the second shed for a compost heap and a garden tool shed, otherwise the lawnmower and other tools will end up in the

railway sheds.

Although I have shown a conventional shed behind the garage, the possibility of erecting a double-length garage, or extending the existing one, should also be considered. Apart from the fact that this will give considerably more scope for the main station, a double garage is always a good selling point for any house.

Filling the garden

In Plan 5 I have taken the same house and garden and filled the entire plot with railway, producing a fairly elaborate system with interesting operating potential. Such a layout requires a pool of regular operators but unless it is sited in some out-of-the-way location far from human habitation, this is not usually a problem. The opinion of the rest of the family is another matter altogether, and I would suggest that it is only

feasible where both partners are deeply involved in the hobby and have absolutely no interest in serious gardening. However, many pre-war houses did have exceptionally long gardens, the idea being to devote the third nearest the house to lawn and flower beds and develop the rest as a kitchen garden, screened from the house by a substantial hedge, or climbing plants on trellis. Substitute railway for kitchen garden and you have the opportunity to create an interesting operating system.

On such a site in OO gauge it becomes feasible to copy the salient features of an actual stretch of prototype main line with reasonable fidelity. While exact copies of the prototype stations are probably out of the question – a thoroughgoing model of any large centre would occupy most, if not all, of the usual suburban plot

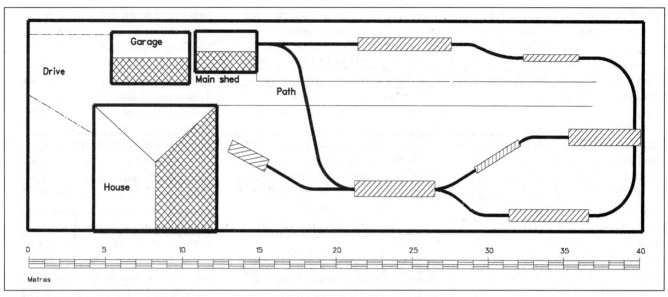

Plan 4.5 *An elaborate system layout on raised baseboards which occupies the bulk of the garden.*

– the major features can be reproduced and the bare bones of the prototype timetable followed.

On this theme, it is possible to consider modelling a secondary route in considerable detail. In one case I knew the owner took great pains to update his model to keep abreast of the latest developments. Unfortunately, he took this too far, for when the prototype fell under the Beeching axe, so did the model.

The sloping garden

So far we have assumed that the garden is either level, or has only a very gentle slope. This is not always the case; indeed, it has been our habit of selecting homes set on a hillside that has prevented my dabbling with outdoor systems.

Not all sloping gardens are ruled out of court: I know of cases where the owner has had parts of the layout 2 m (6½ ft) above ground level. Agreed, in one case this was only slightly over his own height, but for all that, it is not something one would suggest for general adoption. A slope

amounting to no more than 1–1½ m (3–5 ft) over the full length of a reasonable-sized plot can often be turned to advantage, as shown in

Plan 4.6 *A narrow gauge scheme for a sloping site, with storage in the shed and the majority of the layout at ground level.*

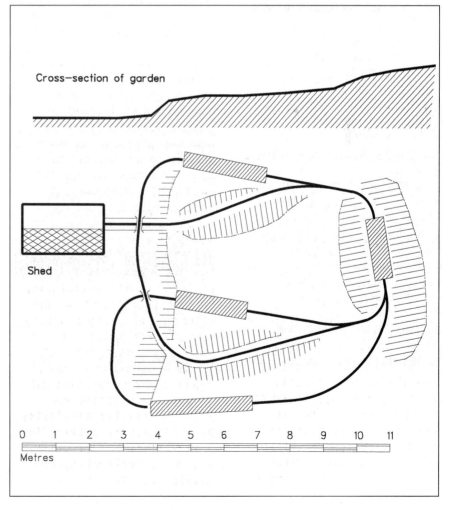

Plan 6. Taking full advantage of a project designer's inherent rights, I have postulated an extremely convenient profile, a fairly sharp slope followed by a gentle climb, culminating in a slightly steeper slope.

At the low level we have the storage shed. This is relatively small and is in practice no more than a fiddle yard where stock is run at the end of the day. From here the tracks are taken onto the 'plateau', where the main part of the railway is situated. A cutting is made in the steeper end slope (this needs to be very wide to avoid any risk of landslip). Unlike the prototype engineer, who must balance a prudent desire for a trouble-free future against the cost of land, we do not need to worry until we reach the boundary fence.

At this point we come to an intriguing possibility: extensive terracing and earthworks. This will involve a considerable amount of digging, and the provision of numerous retaining walls. If this can be faced, the ideal prototype is, if not exactly to hand, easily reached and well written up: the Swiss metre gauge. LGB offer a good selection of Rhätian models for 45 mm gauge. A slightly smaller 1 m system, using 22 mm gauge track and based mainly on Furka-Oberalp prototypes, has changed hands several times and, even in its native Switzerland, is not often seen in model shops. Agreed, most of the Swiss spirals are partly in tunnel, and creating an accessible spiral tunnel is not something I would recommend to anyone who wants a tolerably easy life. The Brusio spiral, which is completely in the open, is a much better proposition. The only point I would make is that if you intend to convert your garden into a tolerable replica of part of the Alps, it is best begun before your 40th birthday. It is going to take several years' hard work to hack out the basic foundations and at least another five for the landscaping to mature. But at the end, what a wonderful spectacle you will have to enjoy!

The quantities involved

At the outset I mentioned the question of overall cost. The sheer size of a garden railway means that you will need a large amount of track. It is not a case of buying a box of 25 lengths, be they in yards or metres. It is a case of needing around a dozen such boxes. And that is only the start. Even where the track is laid at ground level, you will need several 50 kg (110 lb) bags of ballast, not to mention similar quantities of builder's sand, aggregate and slightly smaller amounts of Portland cement. If you lift the track any distance off the ground, you will need even more sand and cement, plus bricks, building blocks or large stones for rockeries. Then there are the paths, which will consume more materials. Alternatively, with raised baseboards, you will need plenty of good quality timber and several sheets of outdoor quality plywood.

I have not mentioned plants and shrubs, but again these need to be kept at the back of your mind. Agreed, one can charge them up to the 'garden account', since presumably you would be planting something in the garden. This doesn't alter the fact that however you decide to cook the books, all expenditure comes out of the same basic income.

I shall be going into all these points in greater detail in later chapters, but it is important to consider this aspect of a garden railway when drawing up the preliminary plans. As I said earlier, there is always the risk of running out of funds before the line is complete. This is all the more likely since the ideal time to start a garden railway is the week after you move into the new house. Unfortunately, this is also the time when you are likely to be far too busy trying to work out how to afford the repairs and replacements and still meet a mortgage which has suddenly become far more onerous than it appeared in the offices of the building society. And the solicitor's account has yet to fall through the new letterbox.

Fortunately, paper and pencil are generally affordable, while a good way to forget your problems and/or work out your feeling of frustration is to take fork and spade and start digging the garden. There is nothing to stop you excavating the future trackbed, and if you can't begin tracklaying for some time, it will give the made ground ample time to settle.

Chapter 5

Preparing the Ground

Before we get down to the practicalities of garden railway construction, it is as well to consider some general aspects of garden construction and maintenance which apply to all work out of doors. The majority of these are dealt with in considerable detail in gardening and DIY books, though I feel that in many cases they either omit or gloss over the downside of their advice. So, without further ado, I must warn you that building a garden railway will involve you in some hard physical labour, particularly in the early stages. Nevertheless, with a little forethought and the selection of the right tools for the job, the effort can be reduced to no more than is involved in a good workout. We hear much of the virtues of aerobic exercise and jogging, yet little is said about the exercise a garden can provide. This is odd, since gardening has a delightful end product; you are hard put to it to do more than look back with relief at most other forms of exercise.

Landscaping and levelling

There are benefits to be gained from altering the lie of the land to provide a more attractive miniature landscape which will involve a fair amount of digging. This is generally regarded as tiring, back-breaking work. It certainly can be all that and more, as any GP will confirm. Yet, provided you treat it

as the skilled craft it is, remodelling a problem site need not do more than leave you pleasantly exhausted after a day's work in the open air.

As always, you need the right tools for the job. A good garden spade, with a long enough handle to avoid the need to stoop, is essential. A stout fork is also useful, particularly in heavy soil where forcing the spade into the ground can be too much effort. A respectable-sized wheelbarrow in good order will also be required to move the soil around the garden. An essential adjunct in anything but the lightest of sandy soils is the 'man', a small scraper made from a piece of wood. Its purpose is to clean the blade of your spade and the tines of your fork from time to time. It cannot be emphasized enough that unless your working surfaces are clean and bright, you are going to waste a lot of energy.

Most important of all, you need a plan of attack. For a start you will obviously want to remove any turf intact, for subsequent relaying. You need to allocate a free area for the turves meanwhile. Having cleared the turf, you now remove the topsoil. Don't worry if a little subsoil is included – in practice there isn't a clear-cut boundary, this only exists in book illustrations. Again you pile this in a convenient spot.

The real digging begins at this point. The amount of effort needed with medium and heavy soils will depend on the degree of moisture

present. A really sticky clay or marl is the worst – too much water and you have a gooey, gelatinous mess that sticks to everything; too little moisture and you begin to wonder if you haven't struck rock. For this class of soil, you may find the narrower border spade easier to work with.

The secret of comfortable excavation is a slow, steady rhythm. Do not overfill the wheelbarrow – not only does this make it less stable and a good deal harder to move, it negates the benefit you will get from a change of activity. Forget all you have read about the exploits of the legendary railway navvy, you are not making this your career. From time to time, stop digging and take a rest. Lean on your spade or the handles of your upturned wheelbarrow for a while and contemplate the results of your efforts.

The worst enemies of the amateur excavator are stones, but these are not altogether unwelcome. Indeed, if you have ground that is liberally scattered with large stones and small boulders, think of the money you are going to save when building your supporting walls. For the most part stones are fairly small, something between the size of a potato and a pea. These come in extremely useful as hardcore and, once again, we need to set them aside for future use.

If you are going to re-use turves it is advisable to do so within a week at the outside. This may not always be possible, so remember that they can also serve as a temporary retaining wall to hold back soil preparatory to terracing.

Paths

While paths are not absolutely essential for a garden railway, some areas of paving are needed for operating areas. The garden path falls into three categories: the major paths which get most of the usage, secondary paving which is used occasionally and light routes which are used only rarely. This last category is rarely considered in gardening books but is of considerable importance to the ground-level garden railway.

The major path is never less than 1 m (3 ft) wide and is usually provided by the builder. Its main manifestation is the path around the house. It is frequently made from concrete cast in situ, and has a substantial base underneath. The secondary path, the type we are most concerned with on a garden railway, follows much the same pattern but is normally only some 600 mm (2 ft) wide. In the old days, when almost every household used solid fuel, such a path was most readily produced by first laying down a layer of stones about 2–3 in (50–70mm) deep and then emptying the ash and clinkers onto this. Once the ash layer had reached 1¼–1½ in (30–40mm) in

depth and had been well trodden down, the result was a tolerably effective path. Today, with the spread of central heating, ash is a rare commodity, but the stone base can be covered with fine gravel and coarse sand instead.

This type of path can readily be upgraded in two ways. The most obvious is to add a further layer of concrete. To do this it is necessary to provide shuttering on either side to hold the concrete in place whilst drying.

Personally I prefer to use pre-cast paving slabs. Initially these can be laid directly onto the ground, though it is probably best to sink them flush with any grass – it makes mowing that much easier. With a little judicious packing to correct the inevitable irregularities, this is sufficient for light use. A proper foundation, covered with a bed of sand, will give better results, whilst bedding on the traditional five dabs of mortar is

Figure 5.1 Secondary and tertiary paths. The secondary path forms the main access to the railway and provides a firm, dry place to stand during operating sessions. The tertiary path is provided for occasional access to parts of the layout and is more commonly associated with the ground-level type of layout. It is formed from relatively small flat slabs placed a footstep apart through a flower bed or rockery.

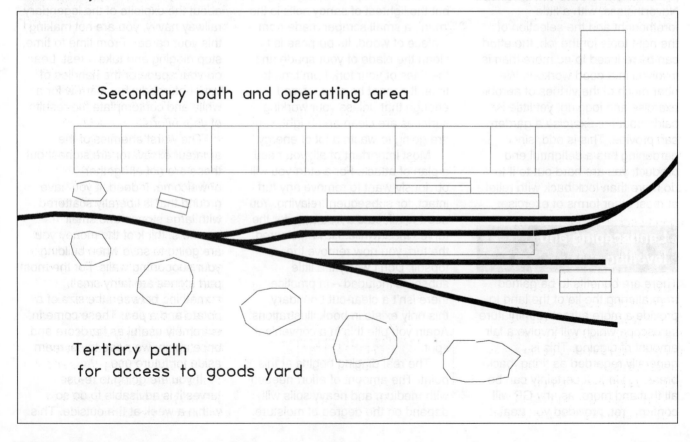

Secondary path and operating area

Tertiary path
for access to goods yard

Peter Denny's Trepolpen Valley Light Railway is provided with an extensive network of paths, allowing the operators to follow their trains around the system. As this illustration shows, the irregular path produced when broken segments are used adds to the charm of the scene. (Photo courtesy Peter Denny)

even better. This treatment is ultimately essential where a wide paved area is involved.

I say 'ultimately' since, where the paving is laid over made ground, some subsidence is only to be expected and it is best to leave the paving free for a year to ensure that when you do finally fix the stones in place, they are not going to settle any further.

Crazy paving is particularly successful where intricate curves

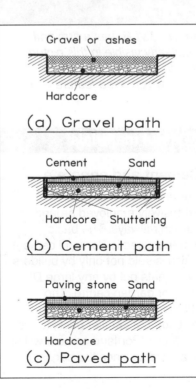

(a) Gravel path

Gravel or ashes

Hardcore

(b) Cement path

Cement   Sand

Hardcore   Shuttering

(c) Paved path

Paving stone   Sand

Hardcore

Figure 5.2 The three basic types of secondary path. The upper gravel path (a) is relatively simple to construct, being a shallow trough filled with stones and topped with ash or gravel. It can later be upgraded to a cement path (b) by enclosing it with shuttering, covering it with sand and then laying cement over the top. Although this appears simple, it does involve a lot of work and is extremely permanent. The lower path (c), made from paving stones, is in practice more flexible since the slabs can be lifted and relaid. The drawing shows a foundation of hardcore covered with sand, but initially the slabs can be laid directly onto the ground, providing it is level and free from large stones.

Lawnton, the principal station on Peter Denny's TVLR, has a firm path alongside for operators to stand on. Part is clearly visible in this picture, which shows the goods yard, station approach and one of the many braced girder bridges, built from piranha pine, which are a feature of this railway. (Photo courtesy Peter Denny)

are needed, but this does require a sound foundation and that the stones are fully bedded in mortar.

Tertiary paths need only be 300 mm (1 ft) wide, and can take the form of stepping stones at around 700–1000 mm (2–3 ft) spacing – in short, wherever it is convenient to step. Circular paving stones are made for this purpose; whilst gardening books generally show them laid across lawns, they are equally useful in an open flower bed or shrubbery where it is necessary to reach remote tracks.

Useful materials

Cement and concrete

Cement and concrete are extensively employed around garden railways. The basic material used is Portland cement, which is sold not only by builders' merchants but by any large DIY store or garden centre. The standard bag contains 50 kg (110 lb), but smaller packets are available. Portland cement will set in air and so once the bag is

opened it begins slowly to deteriorate. This is not merely a waste, it is not that easy to dispose of a chunk of concrete weighing some 20 kg (44 lb). Cement should be stored under cover for obvious reasons.

To produce concrete, Portland cement needs to be mixed with sand and aggregate. The latter is better known as gravel. Both of these materials can be delivered in bulk by suppliers, but you then have the stuff emptied on your front drive. Fortunately both sand and aggregate are also available in 50 kg bags.

A 50 kg bag is roughly the same as a hundredweight measure. It is used because it happens to be the heaviest unit a

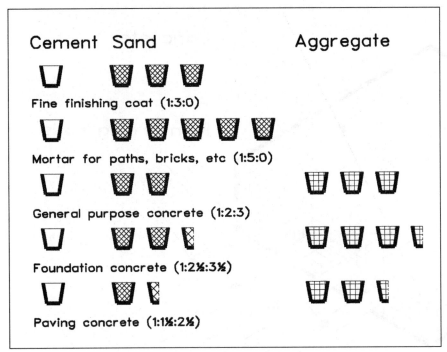

Cement Sand Aggregate

Fine finishing coat (1:3:0)

Mortar for paths, bricks, etc (1:5:0)

General purpose concrete (1:2:3)

Foundation concrete (1:2½:3½)

Paving concrete (1:1½:2½)

Figure 5.3 Although concrete is nothing more than a mixture of cement, sand and aggregate (small stones), varying mixes, some without aggregate, are best suited for specific tasks. This chart depicts the main forms; the quantities given are by volume.

fit man can conveniently carry about on his back. If you try to shift it in any other fashion you run the risk of injury. Garden centres and DIY stores generally have properly designed trolleys to move these heavy materials. It is just possible to heave a 50 kg bag off a trolley and into the boot of a car single-handed, but it is better to have a willing helper. At home, it really is a two-handed job to get the bag over the sill and onto a barrow.

For general purpose concrete you take 1 part by volume of Portland cement, 2 parts of sand and 3 parts of 20 mm aggregate. Foundations are made from 1 part cement, 2½ parts sand and 3½ parts aggregate. Paving requires a 1:1½:2½ mix. Bedding mortar for paving stones is made from 1 part cement and 5 parts sharp sand. The measures are made with any suitable container. A bucket is the usual measure but it is probably

better to use a 2-litre plastic paint can and double the quantities, i.e. 2 parts cement, 4 parts sand and 6 parts aggregate for general purpose concrete.

The mixture needs to be thoroughly mixed in a dry (or in the case of sand, damp) condition on a mixing board. This is a piece of chipboard or similar about 600mm–1m (2–3 ft) square. Using an old spade, turn the materials over in a neat heap until there is no distinction between sand and cement and the stones in the aggregate appear to be well coated.

Now open the centre of the heap to form a rough model of a volcano. Pour a small amount of water into the crater, using a watering can with the rose removed. Gently tip the top of the crater into the water, trying not to let the water escape. Make a fresh crater, pour in some more water

and begin shovelling the dry material around the edge onto the wet centre. Continue adding water, mixing all the while until you end up with a workable mix. This is a simple enough process, and in the relatively small quantities we will need is not particularly arduous work. Never attempt to mix up very large batches of concrete at a time, since it is advisable to get the concrete in place within two hours of mixing.

Paving slabs and other straightforward concrete fittings can be manufactured at home. Casting is best done on a rammed and levelled bed of fine sand, using a simple wooden mould. Once the concrete has begun to harden the mould can be removed and used again on a fresh section of the sand bed, but the parts should be left for at least 24 hours before being moved.

Reinforced concrete

While foundations, paths and track bases can be made with plain concrete, for the more elaborate parts of the garden railway, in particular bridges and viaducts, reinforced concrete is preferable. Concrete is strong in compression, but weak in tension. Fortunately, as steel and concrete have virtually the same coefficient of expansion, reinforcing with steel rods provides the strength in tension and minimizes the risk of breakage. Fortuitously, the wire used for the coathangers supplied by dry cleaners is of a suitable size for the relatively small sections we require. The twisted bit forming the hook needs to be cut away and the hanger opened out with pliers.

Reinforcing with steel rod is not quite as easy as it looks, since it is absolutely essential that the metal should be completely encased in the concrete and that there should

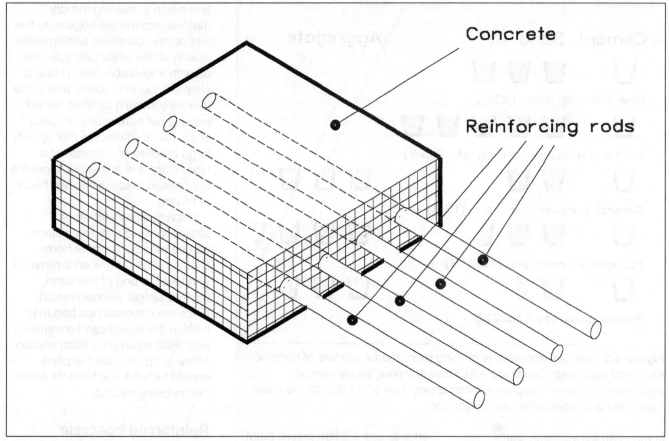

Figure 5.4 *Reinforced concrete is produced by casting steel rods inside the structure. So far as we are concerned, its main value lies in its use for bridges, etc.*

be no voids that allow rainwater to get to the steel. This will cause rusting which materially increases the size of the steel and will create sufficient pressure to crack the concrete and allow sections to slough off.

Timber for the garden

Garden railways require a fair amount of timber and other building materials. These are readily available from builders' merchants and DIY suppliers, but there is another source of supply well worth investigating. Many demolition firms set aside any parts of a demolished house they consider could have a second life. These include window frames, doors, joists and floorboards as

well as bricks, tiles and slates. A check through your local directory should provide a choice of sites within reasonably easy reach.

Second-hand timber and timber products have two inherent virtues: they are cheaper than new and they will be properly seasoned. At least, they will have done all the warping they are likely to do. A reputable demolition firm will, as a matter of course, burn any obviously defective timber on the site, but apart from that, they sell the products 'as seen' and without guarantee.

Cutting to size
One drawback with second-hand timber is that it is rarely the right size. To take a specific instance, floorboards are roughly 150 mm

(6 in) wide, and appear to be useful only for their original purpose, or for shelving. If you have access to a sawbench, however, they can easily be turned into side members for a raised baseboard.

A small circular sawbench is an invaluable tool for handling scrap timber. With it you can easily arrive at any section you require, within the capacity of the tool. A circular saw is a potentially dangerous tool and needs to be used with scrupulous care. Always allow the saw to work freely, and don't crowd the cut by pushing hard. In addition, use a push stick to complete the cut.

Wood preservatives
It is sound practice to treat all timber before use. Any well-stocked DIY store or timber merchant will have a selection of proprietary treatments in stock,

and the latter can also offer advice. The larger DIY outlets also offer advice, but in general their staff are salesmen first and technicians a very distant second, and are not necessarily expert in any field.

All preservative solutions, even the humble creosote, need to be handled with respect. The containers normally carry detailed instructions for use; if these are missing, don't buy the product. Read them carefully and follow them scrupulously. Remember, anything toxic enough to deal with fungal or insect infestation is not going to do good to any other living organism.

Work out of doors so that there can be no possibility of creating a pocket of toxic fumes. A wide drive is probably the best place. If you are worried about staining, spread a large plastic sheet over the area beforehand. This will be essential if your only spare space is the lawn, because grass will definitely not survive even a small amount of preservative.

Wear old clothes and watertight gloves. Inexpensive disposable plastic gloves which will only be used once are preferable to household types which may

acquire a few pinholes whilst handling the timber. Old clothes and footwear are *de rigueur*, and your arms must be completely covered. Protective goggles are not an excessive precaution, though ordinary glasses will protect your eyes from splashes. Should you get even the smallest spot on your skin, stop immediately and wash thoroughly in copious quantities of water.

Bricks

Bricks are a valuable building material, but here the demolition yard is not necessarily the best source. For a start, cleaning mortar from the bricks is a costly process, and secondly, a very real demand for weathered bricks among gardeners means that there is very little difference in cost between second-hand bricks and new common stocks. What is more, you can buy new bricks in bulk and have them delivered to your drive in a neat palletized block, whereas you will probably have to load the second-hand ones into the back of your car yourself. As there is a definite limit on the number you can put inside before you do serious damage to the rear suspension, you will have

to make at least two trips to equal the quantity you'll get in one delivery of new bricks. Once you've added in your time, the cost of petrol and oil plus the wear and tear on a vehicle which isn't properly adapted to the task, any price differential begins to disappear.

Piping

Plastic pipes are an essential adjunct of any garden railway project. There are three patterns readily available: the small-diameter type used mainly for overflows and, under stringent conditions, water pipes; the larger-sized pipe used for sink drains; and the very large downpipe which carries water from the guttering to the storm drain. These are stocked by DIY stores and builders' merchants and are often to be found in demolition yards and roadside skips. Another type is used as the foundation of rolls of carpet, but unless you opt to lay the carpet yourself, the fitters will usually take it back. Larger-diameter pipes are used extensively for gas and water mains, but are not so readily available to the amateur.

Chapter 6

Under Cover

Whilst a shed or similar outbuilding is not an absolute essential for the garden railway, it is certainly more than a luxury. Not only can it house the principal station and provide cover for the rolling stock, it can also contain the maintenance workbench and give shelter to operators during an unexpected shower. If all-the-year-round operation is planned, then the shed becomes a necessity. So, before we get down to the actual construction of the garden railway, it is essential to consider garden sheds in general.

Planning requirements

First of all, the planning aspects of a garden shed must be considered. The first hurdle is the restrictive covenant: some developers completely ban garden sheds, others stipulate that they must be of sound construction. I encountered this last condition in one house I owned. My solicitor said this probably meant that a shed from a reputable manufacturer was almost certainly acceptable, but that if it's legality was challenged, the lawyers would have a field day. However, restrictive covenants are notoriously difficult to enforce once the original developer has moved on.

A far more important consideration when erecting an outbuilding is the opinion of your immediate neighbours. It is as well to speak with them before carrying

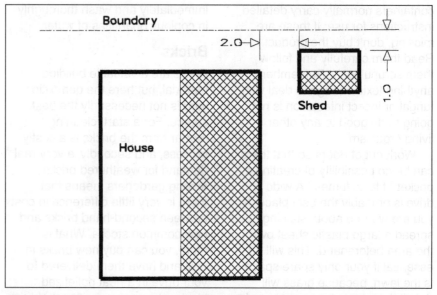

Figure 6.1 The recommended location of a wooden shed, with dimensions shown in metres. The 1 m (3 ft) clearance between shed and boundary is more than just a piece of bureaucratic interference with your rights, it is the minimum room you will need to maintain the back walls of the shed in any degree of comfort.

out any major work of this nature since, clearly, you might be interfering with their enjoyment of their property.

Bye-laws and building regulations are something else and must be followed. In general terms, as Figure 6.1 shows, a timber outbuilding must be 1 m (3 ft) from the boundary and 2 m (6½ ft) from the house. These are sensible stipulations, for the wide gap constitutes a fire break (and timber structures can catch fire), and the 1 m gap is just large enough to allow you to maintain the back wall. Any extension which increases the original overall size

of the house by more than 10 per cent must receive planning permission.

If you want to erect a large building it is as well to make an informal approach to your local authority before you get beyond the paper stage. While it is notoriously difficult to win an argument with a local government officer, the great majority are only too happy to co-operate if approached properly. It has been pointed out that the best way to deal with a bureaucracy is to find out which way the handle turns and push in that direction.

A timber outbuilding need not be an eyesore. Norman Eagle's very large railway room, which houses an extensive O gauge system, has been partially shielded with conifers.

The garage

Before we come to shed design and construction, we should deal with the most common type of outbuilding today, the garage. Where it is possible to make an opening in an end wall, and where the garage is wide enough to accommodate a set of storage roads along one side, it is an excellent site, particularly as it will hopefully have its own electricity supply. This also opens up the possibility of a substantial purpose-designed brick or concrete block building. This must have formal planning permission and is clearly in the luxury bracket, but it is so obviously ideal in every other way that it should be given more than casual consideration.

Figure 6.2 *A suggested design for a shed to house a high-level station.*

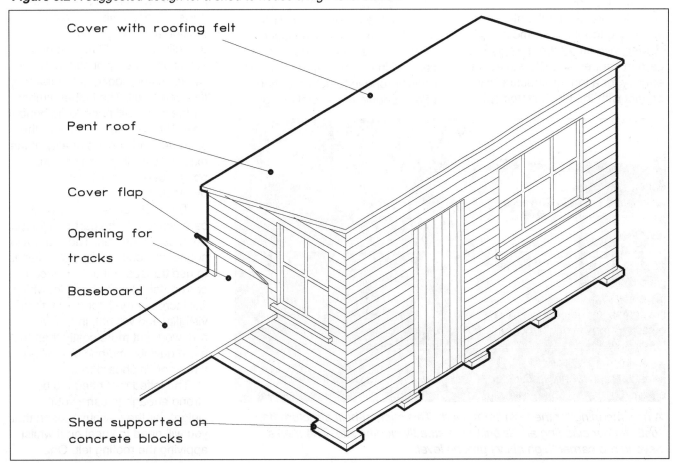

Timber sheds

For most of us, the timber building is the only affordable arrangement. Prefabricated section sheds are readily available from a number of manufacturers. The designs are something of a compromise, the door and windows are arranged in a manner that meets most requirements adequately, and the framing is set out to suit manufacturing convenience. One main object is to keep the whole thing watertight, which means that the designers do not take into account that someone is going to cut a large hole in the side to allow access for a railway, and few entertain the possibility that the owner might want to look out of the end. Indeed, many sheds only provide windows for light and ventilation.

A more significant consideration is that the standard sheds are too short for most garden layouts. At the majority of garden centres and DIY stores an enquiry for a longer structure will be met with the blank statement,

'They don't make 'em that long', which whilst true enough so far as it goes, overlooks the point that all you need do is butt two shorter sheds end to end, leaving out the internal walls. A specialist shed supplier will know this and be happy to quote for the necessary parts. Clearly, buying two sheds and throwing the ends away is not an economic proposition.

Building your own

A custom-built shed is rather more costly than one assembled from standard parts, though for anyone with a bent for carpentry, it is by no means difficult to make the whole thing from standard sections bought from the timber yard. In the 1930s, many books for the home handyman went into considerable detail on this subject, but as anyone capable of making a sound job of baseboard construction can work out the details of building a shed by making a close inspection of as many display models as he can find in nearby garden centres, I don't propose to do more than offer a couple of general designs.

The conventional shed, shown in Figure 6.2, has a pent roof rather than the more common apex pattern. This takes advantage of the fact that less headroom is needed over the railway, and makes construction easier. The door is in the side, and windows are provided at each end to give the operator a view of the line. The shed is supported on concrete blocks and ideally a strip of damp-proof material is placed between the concrete and the timber. A wooden shed should never rest directly on the ground: that is the best way to ensure that the base rots within ten years.

Doors and windows are the most difficult part of such a structure. The ambitious amateur craftsman can make them from scratch, but most of us will find it easier to follow modern building practice and use factory-made parts. A good timber yard can provide a full range, but a demolition yard will have a good selection not only of second-hand windows and doors, but of framing timber as well. The lapped timber for the sides will need to be bought new. The final appearance of the shed depends on the quality of the external cladding – an obvious point, but one frequently overlooked.

The roof needs a good deal of care, since it is the part that keeps out most of the rain. There are two sound approaches. The simplest is to use transparent or translucent corrugated plastic sheeting, which will increase the internal daytime visibility and will not, in the long run, work out more costly than the more obvious method of a felted timber or chipboard roof.

The felted roof needs to be strong enough to carry your weight, for the obvious reason that you will need to kneel on it whilst applying the roofing felt. One

A new meaning for the term 'tram shed'. This custom-built structure has rustic timber cladding and is built on a steeply sloping site. The tracks beyond are carried high above ground level.

The triangular junction immediately outside the stock storage shed on Peter Denny's Trepolpen Valley Light Railway. This section of the line is carried on raised baseboards. (Photo courtesy Peter Denny)

Finally, the shed needs to be provided with guttering and some arrangement for taking rainwater away. I haven't gone into detail on this, since the guttering itself is fairly obvious and is readily available at DIY stores. Although the rainwater can be led into a soakaway, or even discharged into the storm drain, the most favoured arrangement is to run the water into a plastic water butt, which can be a purpose-made device or any suitable plastic drum, such as a dustbin.

Ground-level shed

The normal shed implies a high-level baseboard; for ground-level railways the arrangement shown in Figure 6.3 is required. This is definitely a special purpose structure, since the shed is only half height, over an operating pit.

The pit is a major construction

Figure 6.3 Suggested design for a half-height shed erected over an operating pit on a ground-level system.

possibility is 12 mm chipboard, but the alternative of second-hand floorboards should not be overlooked. Only heavy grade roofing felt should be used, and, in addition to the conventional flat-headed clout nails, additional security should be provided by nailing laths along the slope of the roof and, equally important, under the eaves where the roofing felt is tucked over.

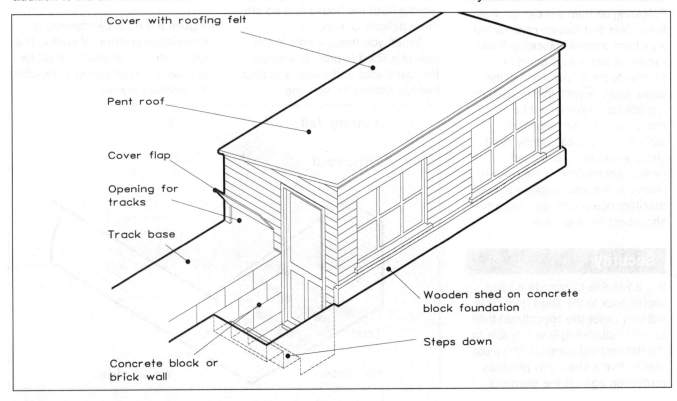

Cover with roofing felt

Pent roof

Cover flap

Opening for tracks

Track base

Wooden shed on concrete block foundation

Steps down

Concrete block or brick wall

in its own right. I have suggested concrete blocks, but clearly bricks are equally suitable. The timber upperworks need to be laid on a continuous damp-proof strip to prevent rot.

Equally important, though omitted from the drawing, is the matter of drainage. For a start, the open part of the pit needs to be appreciably lower than the shed floor so that in exceptionally heavy rainstorms there is no real risk of flooding inside the shed. Ideally, this pit should be connected to the storm drain, but this is definitely a job for an experienced craftsman. The alternative is a soakaway. This is nothing more elaborate than a deep hole filled with large stones, capable of absorbing a fair amount of water which will then percolate through the surrounding soil. A small sump covered by a grating is advisable as, in emergency, this will simplify the task of bailing out the water if the soakaway is overloaded.

Bricks and mortar

Following on from this design, it is fairly clear that, having constructed a pit from concrete blocks or bricks, the same techniques could be applied to the construction of the upper walls as well. In this instance the difference in cost will be marginal, but a full height brick outbuilding (one can hardly call it a shed) would be a costly and permanent addition to the garden. However, the advantages – of lower maintenance and greater security – should not be overlooked.

Security

It is advisable to provide a good secure lock to the shed door. This will only deter the opportunist thief, for any outbuilding is vulnerable to the determined criminal. You must realize that a shed only provides protection against the elements.

As our locomotives represent a considerable investment and are very easily stolen, it is advisable to keep them indoors overnight. This is particularly so with live steam locomotives, which are extremely valuable items. A brick-built outbuilding is marginally more secure than a wooden one, but the main risk arises because all outbuildings are of necessity remote from the house and so are more difficult to monitor.

When you make a hole in the side of a shed to provide access for your tracks and trains, you also provide access for rain and

Geoff Bigmore arranged a short extension to the main shed to cover the original approach pointwork at his main terminus, Bigston. A further extension into the garden was to follow. This photo shows the effect of this partial enlargement, a very straightforward matter where timber construction is involved.

***Figure 6.4** A simple method of covering over external tracks. The top cover is arranged to lift off for access, while an overlap of roofing felt covers the joint.*

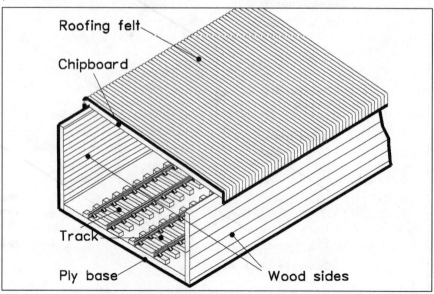

Roofing felt

Chipboard

Track

Ply base

Wood sides

One good reason for housing the principal stations inside a shed is brought out in this photograph of a corner of Geoff Bigmore's Bigston, where much of the scenic details on a primarily garden railway are made from card with brickpaper overlays. The weather is no problem where the models are housed in a weatherproof building.

animals. A protective flap is therefore advisable. A simple hinged board above the opening meets the bill, but two details need to be mentioned. The first is fairly obvious: you need to provide some form of hook and eye to hold it open during operation. The second is that you need to provide a bolt on the inside to prevent it being lifted by any animal in search of a snug berth.

Power supplies

An important function of the shed is to house the transformers and rectifiers needed for the low-voltage electricity supply to the layout. A mains voltage supply is therefore obligatory. I will have more to say about this in Chapter 15, but for the moment it is sufficient to say that this is not really a job for the amateur electrician. Apart from anything else, the relevant regulations are modified at regular intervals in light of experience and only a professional electrician is likely to be fully *au fait* with the best current practice. It doesn't pay to cut corners with mains electricity out of doors.

External cover

Even when the shed is 3 or 4 m (10 or 13 ft) long, it is still hardly long enough for a large O gauge station, and in Gauge 1 the situation is even worse. As most sheds are shorter, a straightforward solution is to have the approach pointwork outside the shed, visible from inside and easily controlled by point rodding from a mechanical frame. This pointwork can easily extend a good 2 m (6½ ft) beyond the shed proper. This section can have raised sides and a removable cover to keep the worst of the weather off the pointwork between operating sessions. As the sides are permanent, they can be embellished with stripwood piers and string courses and painted a dark brick colour to simulate a retaining wall.

This principle of covering external tracks can be carried to extreme limits. Figure 6.4 shows how the entire outside section can be housed in weatherproof troughs. While this is not a garden railway in the accepted sense, it is a very good way of extending an operating railway into the garden. This is mainly applicable to relatively small extensions to a garden shed, where one might wish to accommodate storage sidings. However, it has been carried to considerable lengths, where an extensive network of covered tracks and holding roads were employed to allow a station housed in a shed to be operated to a complex timetable. While this certainly is a railway in a garden, one would hesitate to call it a garden railway.

Maintenance

A well-built timber outbuilding will last for about ten years without attention, but with a little care it will have a working life of over half a century. In the main, it needs a regular coat of wood preservative. This is true even of the supposedly rot-free cedar cladding, and the more common softwood certainly benefits from an annual treatment. This is why the regulation keeping a shed 1 m from your boundary is to your advantage. The ground around the shed must be kept clear of weeds, and by the same token, do not plant shrubs close to the building. Above all, resist the temptation to have a climbing plant entwined over the walls. Pretty though this may look, it ensures that the wood will be permanently wet and, in many cases, the climber will thrust tendrils into the

timber. If you want colour around the shed, plant annuals and keep them well away from the sides.

Give the entire roof a careful inspection in the spring. (Roofing felt only has a limited life, and you should expect to have to replace it in due course.) If it appears defective, you then have the fine weather to work in before the rigours of winter return. This is not the sort of job you want to carry out during a bout of bad weather. Above all, do not wait for the first tear before thinking of replacing the roof; by then it may well be too late. It is a lot cheaper to replace roofing felt a year or so before it becomes absolutely necessary.

Chapter 7

High-Level Layouts

Although the current approach to garden railways favours the low- or ground-level layout, there is much to be said for the older practice of carrying the line at a height of around 1 m (3 ft) to bring the trains up to a convenient level for comfortable operation. This is particularly significant where serious timetable running is the rule, for much of the routine involved in working to a written schedule can only be readily carried out when both the controls for trains and points and the essential paperwork are set high enough to be reached without stooping.

Impact on the garden

It has to be admitted that the high-level layout is essentially intrusive. There is no way it can be held to enhance the appearance of the garden, though it is possible to minimize its impact. This need not be wholly negative: it does reduce the area of garden that requires intensive cultivation. At the same time, with careful design many of the maintenance problems created by the outdoor environment can be minimized, if not wholly eliminated.

The need to erect high-level baseboards adds appreciably to the cost of the layout, although, as we will see in the next chapter, the infrastructure of the ground-level layout is not necessarily dirt cheap. This is a side issue, however, for the high-level system is really an outdoor version of the indoor layout, the object being to

find room for an extensive system with plenty of main line. Clearly, the bigger the layout, the more the baseboard will cost. The real saving comes in not having to pay for walls and a roof, let alone increased taxes, whilst one is not involved in planning problems. Indeed, it would be impossible, in the normal suburban garden, to erect a railway room half the size of even a modest outdoor railway.

The delights of a garden railway can be enjoyed well past normal retiring age, but in order to do so, it is advisable to ensure that the layout will still be standing a quarter of a century after it was completed. Fortunately, we now have enough experience to be able to plot the principal pitfalls – or should I say layout falls?

Posts

It was widely accepted by the mid-1930s that the worst possible approach was to bracket the layout from the fence posts. As most homeowners are only too bitterly aware, fences are very vulnerable and the posts can easily rot or snap. The additional loading caused by the layout is sooner or later going to stress the post too far for its inherent strength. Remember, fence posts are only designed to hold up the fencing panels. The situation is different where a brick wall is involved, but today this is an extremely rare case.

High-level solid top baseboards on Geoff Bigmore's Bigston to Westbridge O gauge layout.

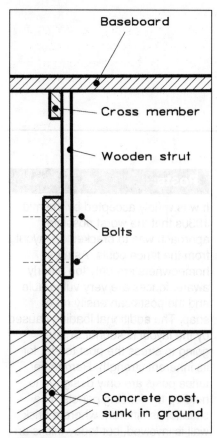

Figure 7.1 A vertical wooden strut bolted to a concrete spur buried in the ground makes an excellent support for a high-level garden baseboard.

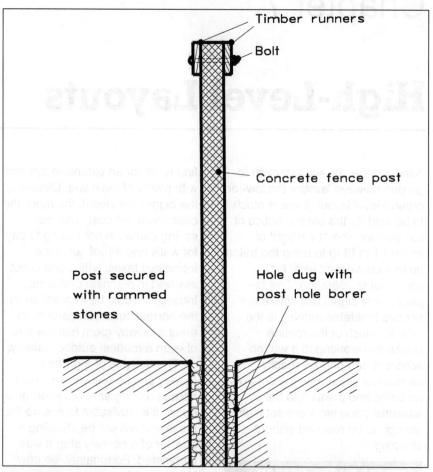

Figure 7.2 A full-height concrete post might be preferred. As these normally have holes cast in them for straining wires, the baseboard-supporting timbers can be bolted to the top. This drawing shows how the neat, straight, close-fitting hole produced by a post hole borer provides good support for the post with only a rammed stone filling.

Wooden posts

The original approach was to drive a wooden post into the ground. This worked well for a couple of years, after which one of two things happened: the posts either rotted, or they began to lean over. It became accepted that the timber needed to be buried at least 2 ft (600 mm) in the ground, which is easier said than done. This did not make any difference to its liability to rot and although careful preparation of selected hardwoods with powerful anti-rot solutions can be a partial solution, garden centres do not stock metal legs for the repair of rotten fence posts just because they look pretty – there is a regular demand for them. The

general consensus is that all-wood supports are best avoided.

Concrete posts

Fortunately a solution is to hand in any well-stocked garden centre: the concrete fence post. Although Ray Tustin dismisses this approach, he was clearly thinking of a custom-cast post, produced on site. On paper this is not a particularly difficult item to fabricate – one merely needs a suitable mould and ample reinforcing rods. In practice, the number of posts involved coupled with the slow rate of production even where several moulds are

available, makes it a formidable task. I suspect he dismissed the standard post because, although it does have holes cast in it, they do not appear to be in the 'right' place. A little lateral thinking is all that is needed.

Probably the most straightforward answer is provided by a method used by John Anning, where a wooden strut is bolted to a short concrete post sunk some 600 mm (2 ft) in the ground (see Figure 7.1). This is simple, straightforward and extremely effective, since the timber is carried well clear of the ground and the cross member carrying the

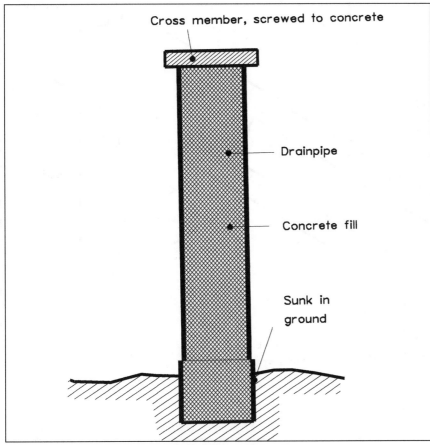

Cross member, screwed to concrete

Drainpipe

Concrete fill

Sunk in ground

Figure 7.3 An alternative support can be made by filling an earthenware drainpipe with concrete and sinking it a short way into the ground. The natural colour of the drainpipe is quite attractive, and will improve with weathering.

baseboard is screwed to the timber. If any problems should arise, it is not too difficult to support the baseboard on temporary struts whilst the permanent leg is completely replaced. Of course the concrete post will deteriorate in time, but with an expected lifespan of at least half a century, I don't think we need worry about that too much.

Digging the holes

What is essential is that the post is securely bedded into the ground. To do this you have to dig a neat hole some 600 mm (2 ft) deep. The normal garden spade is rather too wide for this purpose, the narrower border spade is better, but the

correct tool for the job is a deep scoop-shaped spade, rather like a greatly enlarged trowel. These are not too widely available but a good garden centre should be able to get one to order. As you are going to need to make a lot of post holes, it will be a sound investment. An alternative approach is to hire a post hole driller, which will produce a very small, neat hole to the required depth.

Having dug your post hole, you must then secure your post vertically in it. This is a job where a willing helper is a boon. In order to keep the post upright and at the correct level, it is a good idea to brace it with some temporary timber stays. Alignment is carried

out with a spirit level.

Although in theory the post can be secured by ramming earth back into the hole, in practice this usually means that the post begins to lean shortly after the first really heavy bout of rain. A collar of foundation concrete is the favoured approach, but where the hole is small and neat enough and an ample supply of stones is to hand, these can be firmly rammed around the post, as in Figure 7.2. A mixture of large stones and ready-mix concrete is an excellent, economical approach. Needless to say, the cement should be allowed to harden before any work is done on the layout proper.

There is no question that erecting the posts for a high-level layout is hard, back-breaking toil. There is a way round this. Your classified telephone directory should list several fencing specialists who will have the tools and expertise to do the job rapidly and efficiently.

Drainpipes and concrete blocks

It is clear that posts, whilst an obvious means of supporting baseboard sections, involve a good deal more work than their indoor equivalents, legs. There are other ways of supporting outdoor baseboards which are somewhat simpler to arrange and are less permanent.

One system involves the common earthenware drainpipe, which is filled with concrete (see Figure 7.3). At the most this will only need to be sunk a short distance into the ground. A timber top cross member can be secured to the concrete with standard woodscrews driven into wall plugs.

An even simpler support is a pile of concrete blocks, placed directly onto the ground (Figure 7.4). Apart from levelling the top of

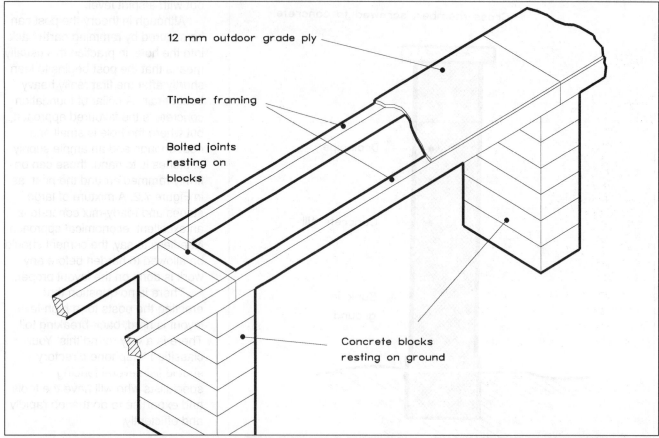

12 mm outdoor grade ply

Timber framing

Bolted joints
resting on
blocks

Concrete blocks
resting on ground

Figure 7.4 Outdoor railway baseboards can also be supported on dwarf piers made from concrete blocks lain flat, one on top of another. This method probably involves less effort than any other, since the individual blocks are not too heavy to move about with ease. At the usual baseboard height, no fixing is necessary: a dry pile is self-supporting.

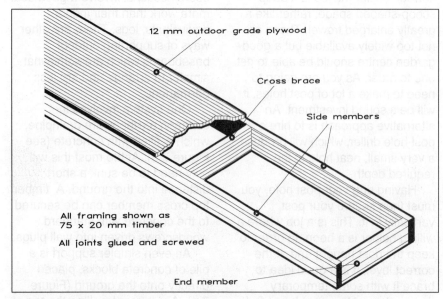

12 mm outdoor grade plywood

Cross brace

Side members

All framing shown as
75 x 20 mm timber

All joints glued and screwed

End member

Figure 7.5 Basic framing for a high-level outdoor baseboard.

the ground, no special preparation is required, nor is there any need to add mortar; the pier is secured by the weight of the blocks. A variant on this, which would require both a concrete foundation and the use of mortar, is a simple brick pier. Whilst this would be more attractive than a pile of concrete blocks, the common factor, the layout baseboards, would remain as obtrusive as ever.

Baseboards and track bases

The top part of an outdoor railway, the bit that carries the track, can take either of two basic forms. The most obvious arrangement is an external equivalent of the common indoor baseboard unit, a straightforward rectangular timber frame covered with a sheet of man-made board as shown in Figure 7.5. The main difference

The outdoor sections of John Anning's O gauge layout are supported on Dexion angle, covered with outdoor grade ply. Although this material is more expensive than timber, it allows very long straight stretches to span the space between supports.

On the open section of Geoff Bigmore's layout, the baseboard was made by spanning the space between the two side members with wooden battens. Although this arrangement looks a shade ungainly here, it is extremely effective and has the distinct advantage that it provides excellent drainage. Furthermore, when seen at the normal garden viewing distance, the effect is quite pleasing.

between the outdoor and indoor versions is that the top surface of the former must be weatherproof, so exterior grade plywood is the only practical material we can consider. Since the units will be at least 2 m (6½ ft) long, the side members need to be 75 x 20 mm timber, and all joints need to be made with waterproof glues and securely joined together. There is no real benefit to be gained from using brass screws for assembly; in most cases it is unlikely you will wish to dismantle the frames. Should you feel this might be the case, a liberal coating of grease on the steel screw usually allows it to be withdrawn without too much difficulty, provided the head has not rusted to the point where it breaks when the screwdriver is applied.

The baseboard should have an initial coat of wood preservative applied before erection; this will need repeating annually. As this will inevitably include the track, and since many preservatives have an unfortunate effect on the

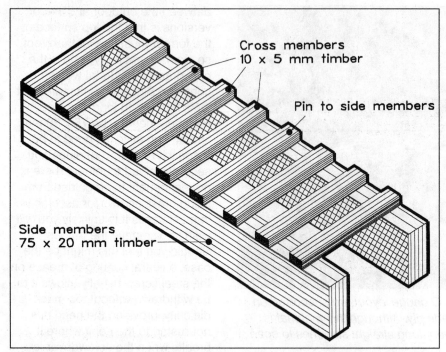

Figure 7.6 *An excellent baseboard can also be made from two parallel side members spanned by narrow cross members. This type of construction is extremely economical if a sawbench is available to produce the relatively small-section cross members from scrap timber of any convenient size, and it also provides ample drainage.*

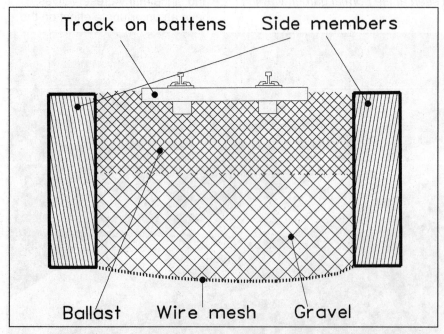

Figure 7.7 *Raised tracks can also be run on a trough of ballast bordered by two side members with a wire mesh base. Not only does this look exceptionally good, but the track is only held in place by the surrounding ballast, just as it is on the prototype.*

plastic bases of modern tracks, used sump oil can be substituted along this part. It seems to work remarkably well. A few drainage holes should be drilled in the top surface after tracklaying is complete. The sections are held together with steel bolts.

In pre-war days, before a truly weatherproof building board was readily available, several modellers covered the entire baseboard top with roofing felt, carrying the material down the sides and turning it under. The type with a generous coating of grit was preferred, for it gave the impression of ballast, and indeed it was often all the ballast an outdoor railway received.

This type of baseboard is normally used for stations and other places where several tracks together with their associated pointwork are close together. The outdoor equivalent of the open-top scenic indoor section is a relatively narrow unit carrying one or two tracks. While this can be a very narrow conventional baseboard, two alternative approaches have been used to great effect.

One is associated with home-built track. Here the two side members are linked by timber strips, which can be regarded as sleepers (see Figure 7.6). Rails can be laid directly onto these 'sleepers', or, if modern, ready-assembled, plastic-based track is used, the cross slats simply support the plastic sleepers. Whichever type of construction you favour, the advantages are first, the reduction in material used, and second, the provision of adequate drainage, an essential feature of all outdoor tracks.

Drainage is also the main aim of the second open-type baseboard, which is shown in Figure 7.7. Here the side members have a wire mesh bottom, covered

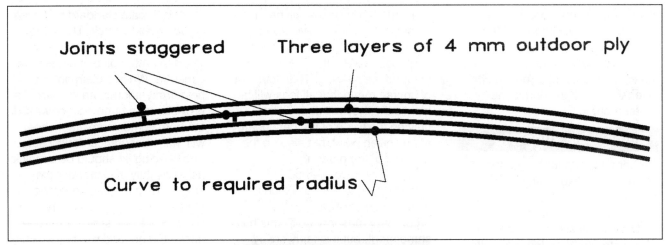

Joints staggered   Three layers of 4 mm outdoor ply

Curve to required radius

Figure 7.8 Laminated ply
construction for curved framing.

by a layer of coarse gravel and
topped with overscale ballast
which holds the battened track in
place. This system was developed
between the wars by a Mr
Courtice, who used perforated zinc
as the base, but this once
ubiquitous material has now
disappeared from the marketplace.

Curved sections

In both these systems, the side
members are bolted or screwed to
a central upright. It might seem
that this would only be possible
with straight track, since it is
difficult to curve timber of sufficient
thickness. The answer is to
produce a laminated girder, using
three or four relatively thin strips of
timber or outdoor grade ply of the
required depth (see Figure 7.8).
These are curved to the required
radius and held together with G
clamps until they can be
permanently bonded with glue and
screws. If a large number of
curved sections to a common
radius are required, it would be
worthwhile making a fixture for
bending them, using a second-
hand door as a base, since you
will want to make up lengths of
around 2 m or 6½ ft.

Transportable layouts

It is common practice to remove the
more vulnerable parts of an outdoor
railway when the weather begins to
deteriorate in late autumn, so that

they can be stored, refurbished and
replaced when spring returns the
following year. This process can be
taken one stage further by
dismantling the whole of a high-
level system, leaving the garden

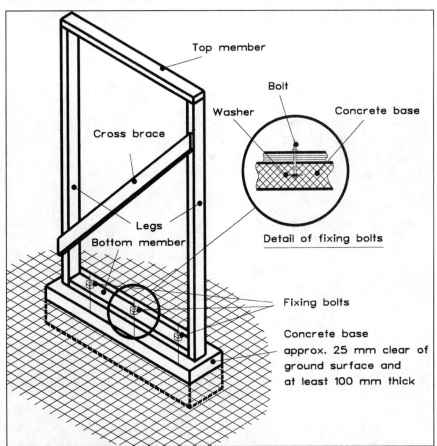

Figure 7.9 Timber supports can be bolted to concrete foundations, with
the result that the entire outdoor section can be dismantled for the winter
and parts of the layout taken to exhibitions.

clear for the winter months. This is, of course, a development of the common indoor transportable line and has the added advantage that the core sections of layout can be taken to exhibitions during the winter months.

Removable supports

Timber supports for an outdoor layout can be mounted on concrete foundations provided with fixing bolts. This is a common practice in full-sized construction, where structural girders are bolted to similar foundations, the most readily visible examples being the fixings for overhead catenary masts.

For outdoor railway use, the foundations need not be elaborate, but they do need to be at least 100 mm (4 in) thick and should protrude about 25 mm (1 in) above the surface. For the majority of

sites, the top surfaces will need to be set at a common level so that, when erected in a hall for exhibition purposes, it will not be necessary to introduce packing. This does not of course mean that all legs will be identical – they will depend not only on the width of the baseboard at any given point, but also on the gradient of the garden.

There are two methods of arranging fixing, one of which is to drill the concrete bases for a proprietary masonry bolt. This has some merit, but it is fairly costly, and depends on having a drill powerful enough to make the large holes required for such bolts. The

other is to cast standard bolts into the foundation block. This is done by suspending the bolts from a wooden batten placed across the concrete. While a plain bolt will hold firmly enough on its own, the provision of a large square washer, cut from some scrap steel sheet, will make assurance doubly sure. The spacing jig should be as thick as, or slightly thicker than, the timber you intend using for the base and, ideally, at least 10 mm (⅜ in) of the bolt should protrude above the nut and washer which is used to support it during the casting process. Clearly, you will need several such battens, which

This general view of Peter Denny's Lawnton station shows the arrangement of his high-level baseboard on an otherwise ground-level system. The raised section makes operation of the principal station much more comfortable, while a stone-paved operating area not only provides a good all-weather working space, but prevents undue wear to the lawn. (Photo courtesy Peter Denny)

ideally will have the holes drilled at standardized centres so that to a large extent, the supports will be interchangeable. Figure 7.9 shows the general principle, the support having a base batten and being provided with the usual diagonal brace. The base batten will, eventually, be subject to rot, but so long as the legs are dismantled every autumn, cleaned, inspected and thoroughly soaked in preservative, it should be decades before replacement becomes necessary. This will not involve replacing the entire support, only the base batten and the lower portion of the legs, which is a fairly straightforward piece of routine carpentry.

Removing bolts

Even if you do not intend to dismantle the entire layout during the winter months, it is still advisable to take into account the need to dismantle some part of the baseboard structure, either for maintenance or for modification. This means that you should consider the possibility that one day you will wish to remove the securing bolts. It will be too late to think about this several years after construction; this is something you need to consider at the outset.

I do not recommend brass bolts, they cost a great deal and are prone to their own form of corrosion. Agreed, my early experience in marine repair, where salt water plays havoc with every type of fitting, influences this view, but the fact remains that brass nuts can seize on their threads, with the result that the metal shears when you attempt to undo the fastening. As a well-rusted steel bolt will behave in the same way at lower cost, why bother with brass?

This brings me to the first point: always use hexagon-headed bolts rather than the common coach bolt. This enables you to apply a ring spanner to each end of a recalcitrant bolt and either force the nut to move or simply shear the bolt. Ring spanners are to be preferred to the open-ended pattern, which tend to slip off under extreme force.

However, an ounce of prevention is preferable to a ton of cure, so always grease your bolts liberally on assembly, making sure that there is a good coating over all the thread. Graphited grease is best for this job, but any stiff grease will last for at least three years. An annual inspection and re-greasing will reduce the risk of severe seizure to a minimum. If possible, use coated bolts, which are easily distinguished by their bright silver appearance and, much more to the point, appear to be the preferred offering at most DIY outlets nowadays. Finally, keep a spray can of releasing oil (such as WD40) on hand at all times. A preliminary squirt of this invaluable aid at least five minutes before you start undoing a bolt works wonders.

Annual maintenance

Raised timber baseboards will need regular maintenance. The most important part of this is an annual coating with a good wood preservative, ideally at the end of the operating season. This should be accompanied by a thorough inspection of all timbers.

Rot occurs when untreated timber is allowed to become extremely wet. It is most likely to happen in joints and, in particular, in timber in direct contact with the ground. Fortunately, a well-ventilated garden railway structure is unlikely to develop dry rot; the less severe wet variety is the most likely problem. Rot can set in at any time, so you should keep an eye out for any signs of severe problems throughout the year. If in doubt, jab with your trusty knife. Normally, the point should only just enter the surface, but should you encounter rot, the blade will sink into the timber for a considerable distance. If the rot is at all widespread, the timber will have a distinct concave surface, feel spongy to the touch and crumble away in the hand.

Today we have wood hardening fluids and fungicidal tablets, together with a two-part wood filler. These can arrest rot and restore the general appearance of the timber, but they are at best palliatives. Rotting timber should be replaced during the winter season or immediately before the line is re-opened in the spring.

Chapter 8

Ground-Level Layouts

It is ironic that although most railway modellers who worked out of doors in the 1930s began with a collection of Hornby track laid on the lawn, the idea of building a railway at that level was rejected in favour of something differing only in size and scope from an indoor layout. Yet the practicality of a ground-level scheme had been demonstrated at Bekonscot Model Village in the 1920s. Today the principle is well established and several tried and tested systems for building a railway at or near ground level have been developed.

Laying track on the ground

The simplest approach is to lay sectional track directly onto the ground. This worked with the old tin-plate tracks, though this was never regarded as anything more than a very temporary arrangement, since rusting was a serious problem. With today's greatly improved sectional tracks it is completely reliable; indeed, G gauge has from the outset allowed the modeller to lay down a temporary system on the lawn or,

as is more often the case, the patio.

This is fine for a temporary layout, but where permanence is the aim more is needed. In most gardens the topsoil will have been worked over for some years, making the top 100 mm (4 in) or so loose and unstable. Some trimming and packing will be inevitable, not merely at the beginning, but over a period of

This photo of part of Bekonscot shows ground-level track bordered on one side by a low wall and on the other by a rock edging.

Ballasted track in a pre-cast concrete trough on George Oakley's ¾in scale outdoor tramway layout.

Figure 8.1 *A method of laying track at or near ground level, using a shallow trench filled with gravel and ballast.*

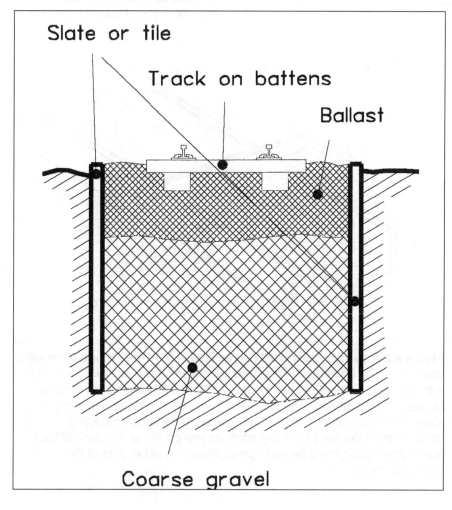

time as the trackbed moves with rain and frost.

A more satisfactory arrangement is to follow prototype practice, first by preparing a roadbed by judicious filling and ramming, then applying a ballast bed before laying the track. If the track is properly ballasted it should stay in position, but for added security we can adopt a very old technique and pin the track to longitudinal battens. As on the prototype, with this type of tracklaying it will be necessary to carry out regular checks on alignment, for quite apart from any earth movement, we have to contend with the action of the trains which, in most outdoor gauges, are quite heavy and impart a degree of side thrust on the rails. Whilst this is small in comparison to the forces experienced on the prototype, its effects are cumulative.

Working ballast

Unlike the indoor layout, where ballast is a decorative feature, in the garden it serves exactly the same function as it does on the prototype, holding the track in position whilst providing easy drainage. Scale-sized ballast is not going to perform this latter function, so what we need is a sharp grit, such as is used to resurface roads, or fine gravel. A good builder's merchant should be able to provide a suitable material.

Although the ballast can be laid onto the ground, it is inevitable that it will spread over the course of time and become mixed with the soil, reducing its value as a drain. Figure 8.1 shows an improved method of construction with a side edging. This can be slate, tile or even the corrugated strip sold for lawn edging. Where the line abuts grass it is important that the edging is firm and level so that you

Ground-level tracks bring the railway into intimate contact with the garden, but the two need to be kept separate for convenient maintenance. This is exemplified in this picture of part of the extensive garden railway at Bekonscot, where the lawn and plants are well away from the track, which runs along a wider-than-scale ballast bed.

service with only minimal maintenance. He advocated a base raised some 200–250 mm (8–10 in) above the general ground level, to reduce the amount of stooping involved.

Ray Tustin used breeze concrete, which consists of 1 part of Portland cement to 6 parts of finely crushed coke or cinders which have been passed through a 12 mm (½ in) sieve. When he was writing, all these materials were readily available; indeed, in most households disposing of cinders and ash was a daily chore for at least half the year. This difficulty apart, the idea is sound, for what he was making is a very spongy material which can be easily cut with a cold chisel and drilled with a masonry drill. It is also fairly easy to break up should you wish to alter the layout. However, there is

can trim right up to the ballast. You also need an 'overscale' clearance between the edging and the track so that the mower blades can be kept well clear of the rails. It should be possible to get a fair finish with the mower, but for the best effect a rotary nylon cord edge trimmer is needed.

Concrete base

In his book *Garden Railways* Ray Tustin recommends a concrete base. This provides a more rigid foundation for the tracks but there is always the possibility of the earth moving during severe frosts, which will lead to misalignment. Having said that, I have to admit that I know of several cases where concrete foundations have given sterling service for years. The most telling example was Ray Tustin's own layout. I had the pleasure of meeting him in the early 1980s, and learned that his line had given some 40 years'

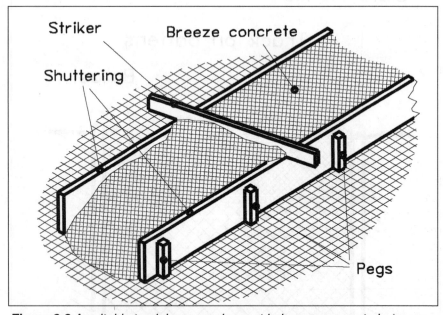

Figure 8.2 A suitable track base can be cast in breeze concrete between shuttering. The concrete is shovelled in between the boards and levelled with a striker – a length of timber about 50 per cent longer than the gap between the shuttering. This is moved from side to side as it is brought along the heap of concrete. A trowel comes in handy for collecting concrete from the front to fill any voids as you go along. For curved track, the shuttering is sprung between pegs placed on either side of the proposed curve.

no reason why you should not use a standard foundation concrete mix for such a base. Refer to Chapter 5 for the formula.

The concrete is cast between shuttering (see Figure 8.2). For straight sections this is most readily made from two or more second-hand floorboards, supported by a series of stakes. For curves I would suggest strips of hardboard which are pinned to the stakes. Once the foundations have set, the shuttering and stakes are removed for use further down the line. This means that the trackbed will slowly extend around the garden over a period of weeks, if not months. Although this means that the base will be cast in discrete sections, this is a distinct advantage since, should there be any settlement of the soil below the layout, it should be possible to lever up the section and pack gravel underneath. The matter of levelling was dealt with in Chapter 2, where the mechanics of setting out the layout on the ground were outlined.

To retain the ballast, Ray Tustin laid cement strips along either side of his breeze base. He therefore considered it essential to introduce drain holes at regular intervals. These consisted of lengths of 20 mm (¾ in) diameter plastic pipe set into the approximate centre of the foundations. This pipe is readily available from DIY stores; it is primarily used for overflows to header tanks. To prevent the pipes getting clogged with ballast, a wire mesh cover should be folded over the top before the cement is poured between the shuttering. However, Don Neal has suggested that drainage is not absolutely essential, claiming that rain rarely lay on his tracks for any appreciable length of time.

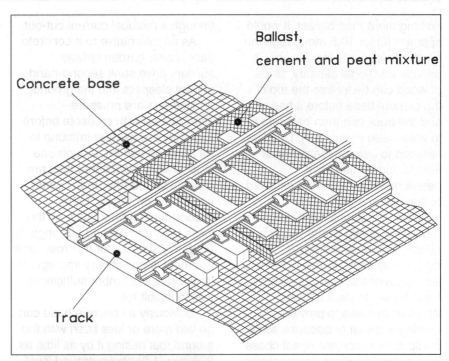

Securing the track

As an alternative to loose ballast, the track can be fixed in position with a cement-peat mixture, as in Figure 8.3. This mixture has virtually no strength at all, but it will stay in place and hold the track in position. It is not too difficult to

Figure 8.3 *Track can be laid on a concrete base using a weak cement-peat mixture as ballast.*

remove without damaging the track.

While experience has shown that 32 mm and 45 mm gauge tracks can be held in place with

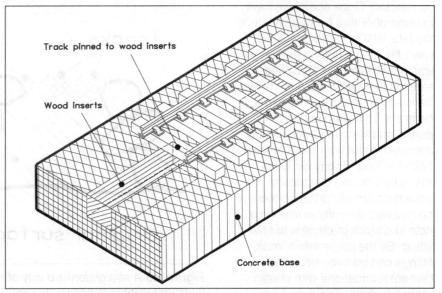

Figure 8.4 *Wood blocks can be pressed into the top surface of the concrete before it has set to provide a fixing for track. This is particularly advisable for 16.5 mm gauge track, which has relatively small sleepers and is therefore more difficult to secure with ballast alone.*

nothing more than ballast, it would appear that for 16.5 mm gauge the depth of sleeper is insufficient. To provide additional security, strips of wood can be let into the top of the cement base before it has set, and the track can then be pinned to these (see Figure 8.4). Don't be tempted to use the foam ballast sold for indoor use, as it deteriorates rapidly when exposed to sunlight and rain. Under optimum conditions it will only have a life of two years, which by garden railway standards is ridiculously short. It may not even last four months, since birds have been known to peck it away. Whether this was to provide nesting material or because some particularly succulent insect chose it as a dwelling place, I cannot say.

Fixings for signals

Ray Tustin suggested that blocks of wood should be inserted inside the shuttering to provide holes for signals. This is a good idea if you know in advance exactly where you intend to put them, as indeed you should. Once again, we have to remember that he was writing in the late 1940s, when the usual way of drilling a hole in masonry was the Rawltool, a hardened steel bit that fitted into a mild steel handle and was driven in with a hammer. This was hard and dangerous work, and you usually managed to hit your hand at least once per hole. Today we have masonry bits and electrically powered hammer drills, so there is no inherent difficulty in making a hole in a block of cement to take a fitting. By the same token, many fittings can be secured to the cement foundations with plastic masonry plugs. The important point to remember is that where mains equipment is used out of doors, it must be connected

through a residual current cut-out.

As an alternative to a concrete base, some garden railway builders have sunk second-hand railway sleepers into the ground. As sleepers are pressure-impregnated with creosote before use, they are as near immune to rot as wood can be, though one must always realize that they are only discarded after many years' use on the prototype. Other second-hand timber, such as the joists from demolished buildings, is not really suitable for this role, for it is almost impossible to impregnate large pieces of timber sufficiently well to inhibit rot.

Obviously a concrete base can be laid more or less flush with the ground, but raising it by as little as 300 mm (1 ft) above ground level materially reduces the amount of stooping involved and also lifts the railway above the level of small border plants. Whether soil is heaped along the side to form an embankment or not is a matter of personal choice.

Tracks on rockeries

The principle of raising track level above the original lie of the ground can be carried further by constructing a rockery. Unless the garden is liberally supplied with very large stones, or there is a source of these close to hand – a rocky seashore, for instance – a considerable outlay of money will be involved, as a cursory investigation at a garden centre will show. On top of this, the sheer weight of rocks needed for a long narrow rockery is a serious consideration; moving them into position is hard work. On the other hand, building a rockery does not call for overmuch skill.

The general principle is to lay out the base rocks directly onto the ground and then build up in the centre with earth, adding rocks as you go. Figure 8.5 shows a typical cross-section of a rockery complete with railway on the top level. This is shown laid in a deep bed of gravel, because the fact that

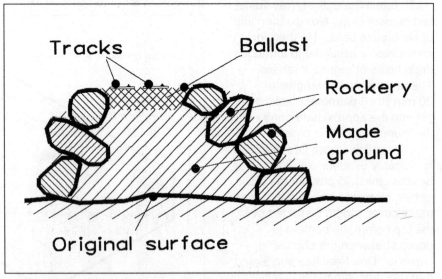

Figure 8.5 *A straightforward way of raising tracks to a more convenient working height is to build a rockery. The soil for the made ground is dug from another part of the garden. As rockeries can be quite extensive, this type of construction is more popular in districts where one encounters numerous large stones when tilling the soil.*

the centre of the rockery is made ground and as such is subject to settlement makes it inadvisable to lay a heavy concrete base on it.

Brick walls

As an alternative to a rockery, a pair of low brick walls can be built. This particular arrangement is more suited to a formal setting or in an older house with a walled back yard. Bricklaying is a skilled craft, but much of the expertise of the professional brickie is applied to speed of working, accuracy of finish and the ability to employ a suitable bond where strength is needed. For a low garden wall, a little irregularity is acceptable and unless the track is raised more than six courses there is no need to attempt anything more complicated than plain stretcher bond.

Brick walls should be laid on a decent foundation – at least 150 mm (6 in) is needed even for a low structure. This is made from foundation concrete mix. The bricks are laid in mortar, which is obtainable as a ready mix or can be made up acceptably from 1 part Portland cement to 6 parts of sand. The addition of lime to the mix improves the plasticity of the mortar.

As the techniques of bricklaying are adequately covered in many DIY manuals, I would recommend any reader who is interested to consult one of these. In addition, an hour or so spent watching a professional at work will provide more useful information than several pages of written instructions.

Weepholes

Where brick or concrete block walls more than 600 mm (2 ft) high support earth, it is usual to provide weepholes near the base so that any excess ground water can

Figure 8.6 Cross-section of an operating pit. Now you know where some of the soil for the raised sections of line has come from. Brick walls are shown here, but concrete blocks or even large stones found in the garden could be used instead. The soakaway is essential if you are not to have the pit filled with rainwater after a prolonged downpour.

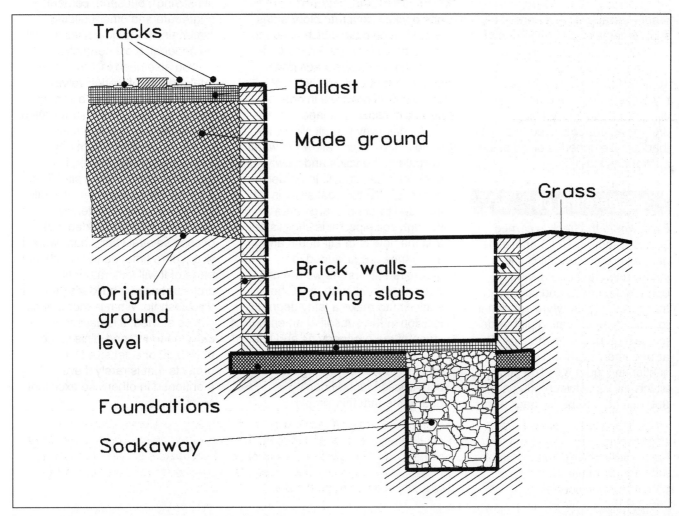

Harrowbarrow station on Peter Denny's first garden railway was provided with an operating pit. The sides were built up from local stone found in the garden, while the base was gravel.

readily escape. These consist of short lengths of pipe let into the brickwork. In one garden in rainy Devon I saw pipes used of only 10 mm (0.4 in) bore, whereas in my present home in a much drier climate, 40 mm (1½ in) bore drainpipes are employed. It seems that the size depends on what the builder has to hand.

The operating pit

Even where the track is carried 200–300 mm (8–12 in) above the general ground level, it is still inconvenient to bend down to operate the points and control the trains. A straightforward solution is to provide an operating pit beside all main ground-level stations. The arrangement is shown in cross section in Figure 8.6. The pit, which will be between 600 and 900 mm (2–3 ft) below track level,

has brick or concrete block sides and a paved base which needs to be at least 600 mm (2 ft) wide. A short flight of steps leads down into the pit at one end, while a soakaway is provided in one corner to assist drainage.

A soakaway is a pit filled with large stones which allow the water to settle in the voids and slowly soak into the subsoil. In gardening books, where the soakaway is intended to drain a large area through soil pipes, it is suggested that the hole is of fair depth and the stones are arranged In graduated layers. As we are only draining a small area, it will be sufficient to make a fairly deep incision in the subsoil at an early stage of the proceedings and use this as a dump for all the stones that are turned up during the construction work. I don't guarantee that this simple

arrangement will ensure a completely dry pit, since a torrential downpour will always create temporary pools in any depression, but it will take care of normal rainfall.

The work involved

A ground-level line invariably involves a good deal of digging and even more preliminary contemplation, since once you have begun casting concrete bases and erecting rockeries and retaining walls, you don't want to set about making major alterations. There is also the outlay for materials to consider: dirt may be cheap (though the current cost of building plots gives the lie to this old saying), but sand, cement, aggregate and other building materials, in the quantities we will be needing, most certainly are not.

You also need to consider the total amount of work involved. There is no doubt that a semi-formal sunken garden surrounded by a waist-level garden railway is an absolute delight from any angle, as, for that matter, is a neatly terraced sloping site. Even a modest rearrangement will take you a year, and an extensive remodelling of the garden can occupy several years' hard work in your spare time, during which time parts of it will look rather like a cross between a builder's yard and a rubbish tip. What is more, once you've started, it is necessary to carry on to the end. This is the downside of extensive DIY projects that is rarely if ever mentioned in otherwise excellent manuals.

Chapter 9

Civil Engineering

Perhaps the most fascinating feature of ground-level garden railway construction is that civil engineering is for real. This will have become apparent in the previous chapter, since the preparation of the roadbed involves earth-moving, laying foundations and erecting walls. It may well be felt that separating this from the provision of scaled-down railway features is drawing too fine a distinction; I do not propose to argue the point. I just happen to feel that the provision of cuttings, embankments, bridges and tunnels is best dealt with in a separate chapter.

Platforms

For a ground-level line, a concrete platform will resist the worst the weather has to offer and at the same time will support your weight should you need to stand on it.

It can be cast as a single slab between a pair of wooden formers (Figure 9.1). It is a good idea to scribe the edging stones before the cement has hardened; if you want to do all the paving, feel free. Casting a curved platform in this fashion is next to impossible, but one advantage of the garden site is that you can usually find room to have straight platform roads. Some reinforcing wires will help strengthen the structure and reduce the risk of cracking.

Alternatively, the platform sides can be precast in a simple mould and the centre filled with concrete

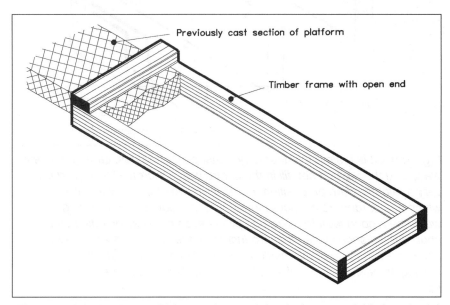

Previously cast section of platform

Timber frame with open end

Figure 9.1 *A simple mould for casting straight platforms, quickly knocked up from suitable-sized pieces of wood. As only a relatively short section can be cast at a time, the concrete is best made from ready-mix.*

A cast concrete platform at North Bekonscot.

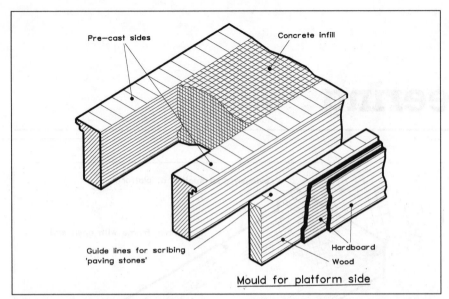

Figure 9.2 *It is a simple matter to pre-cast platform sides, cement these in place and then, when set, fill in the centre with concrete. The mould is a very straightforward proposition, made from two strips of wood, one of which has hardboard overlays pinned to it to produce the overhang. It would be a good idea to make up several such moulds, including some short curved sections, so that production of the cast sides can be speeded up. The top surface of the moulds can be marked with guide lines so that 'paving stones' can be scribed on the top surface before the concrete has set.*

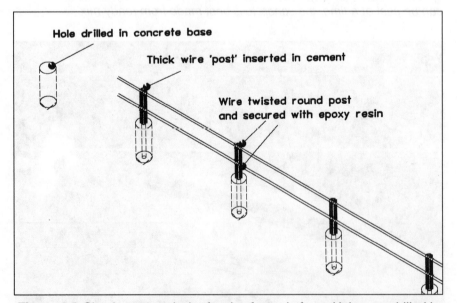

Figure 9.3 *Simple post and wire fencing for a platform. Holes are drilled in the concrete base for the posts, which can be made from round nails with the heads cut off. The wires are best secured with epoxy resin. The posts may be set in cement, as shown, or driven into plastic wall plugs and subsequently sealed with epoxy.*

(Figure 9.2). This not only allows for the edging to overhang, but makes it relatively easy to scribe 'paving stones' on the top of the concrete before it hardens. The sides should be carefully bedded in mortar and allowed to set before the centre fill is added.

Platform fencing

Platform fencing is best arranged by drilling holes in the hardened concrete for the fence posts. A traditional paling fence can be built up from stripwood, keeping all parts somewhat overscale since they will be subject to greater strain than on an indoor line. A post and tube fence (in practice, post and wire) is simpler to make and adequate for most purposes (see Figure 9.3).

Before we leave platforms, it is as well to mention that the greatest enemy of outdoor concrete is water. During most of the year it is not a significant hazard, but the moment the temperature drops below zero any water trapped in the pores of the cement will expand and crack the material. This can to a large extent be prevented by painting the cement with a proprietary sealant which, like so many materials for the garden railway, is stocked in DIY stores rather than model shops. Now that the encouraging increase of interest in this side of the hobby has led to the appearance of specialist retailers, this statement may well be technically inaccurate, but for the majority of readers the DIY store will be nearer, a significant consideration when you are dealing with bulk supplies weighing at least couple of kilograms apiece.

High concrete retaining walls are provided on this cutting at Bekonscot, not merely to keep the soil from sliding onto the tracks, but to maintain a wide space for access during maintenance.

Cuttings

The next items to be considered are cuttings and embankments. At first sight they seem simple enough, since all one does is dig a hole with sloping sides for a cutting and dump the spoil from this excavation to form an embankment. This would be fine in an arid climate, but rain will play havoc with this simplistic approach. Landslips are as likely on the garden railway as they are on the full-sized system. The slopes should be stabilized by planting so that the roots of the plants will bind the soil. Grass is the most obvious and prototypical cover to use, but it will need cutting with a strimmer for most of the operating season, and the cuttings will need brushing off the tracks. Low-growing plants are less trouble; heathers are ideal if the soil is not alkaline.

The major difficulty is drainage, for the slopes will direct all rainwater onto the track unless you take steps to prevent this. For the most part, the prototype solution, a drainage ditch along each side, will meet most requirements, but it will need to be made from concrete if it is to remain effective for any length of time. This will be fairly straightforward to arrange if you provide a concrete base for your track, since this will form one side of the drain (see Figure 9.4). For ballasted track, a length of plastic pipe with a series of 6 mm (¼ in) diameter holes drilled along its length, sunk in the approximate centre of the ballast bed, will greatly improve drainage, provided you can arrange some way of directing the lower end away from the track.

Embankments

Embankments are always made ground, using soil deposited from somewhere else. This means that some settlement will occur, particularly over the first winter. Where the track is laid directly onto the soil, it is a straightforward matter to add packing material to maintain the level of the line. There remains the possibility of landslip. Should this occur, you can console yourself that this also happens on the prototype. With a concrete base one merely casts a much deeper section and piles the earth alongside (see Figure 9.5).

While the embankment offers no appreciable tracklaying difficulties, the problem of drainage

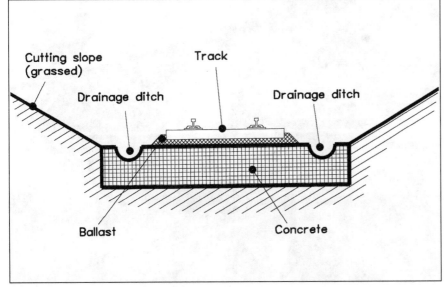

Figure 9.4 *A concrete base for use in a cutting incorporating drainage ditches. The gentle slopes make access easier and avoid the risk of slippage.*

This embankment on Bob Symes's Gauge 1 Onslow Railway is built up with small stones.

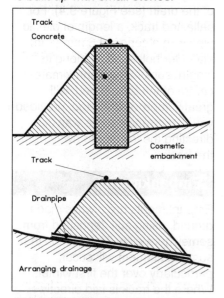

Figure 9.5 One way of constructing an embankment is to cast a very deep concrete base and then pile earth along the sides. Such an embankment is a cosmetic feature, but none the worse for that. It is a good idea to locate at least one drainage tube through the base of an embankment to prevent it acting as a dam, otherwise heavy rain may result in a 'lake' which drowns your plants and could threaten the stability of the embankment.

remains. Although water will not settle on the track, it will tend to accumulate along one side of the base of the embankment. In extreme cases, where the embankment runs across a dip in the ground, there is a distinct possibility that, in heavy rain, a large puddle will form. This is not going to do the foundations of the embankment a bit of good. It is sound practice to provide a culvert through the low point, using

nothing more than another length of plastic pipe.

Bridges

Bridges are an important part of the garden railway scene. In the 1930s, Meccano was a very popular base for girder bridges, either using the straightforward method of screwing 12½ in braced girders to a piece of plank or constructing an authentic trussed girder bridge from angle girders and flat strips. Needless to say, the finished bridge needed to receive regular coats of paint to inhibit rust. Today, Meccano is proportionately more expensive and, more to the point, spare parts are no longer widely available from good toy shops. On the other hand, we now have the extruded aluminium section which can be cut, drilled and bolted or riveted together to form a more realistic girder bridge which is resistant to the worst the English climate can offer.

Alternatively, a good model 'girder' bridge can be fabricated from stripwood. When painted and

The girder bridge in the foreground on Bert Grove's N gauge garden railway is made from plastic kits, while the timber trestle behind is scratchbuilt from stripwood.

This bowstring girder bridge at Bekonscot is made from metal angle and strip. The work involved is more than repaid by its virtual indestructibility.

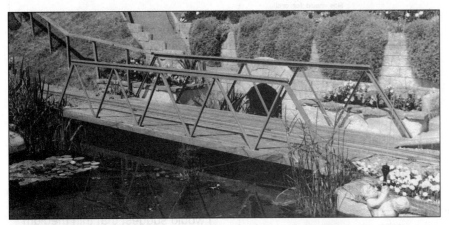

The braced girder bridge on the Beer Heights Light Railway, the 7¼ in gauge passenger-carrying line at Pecorama, is not, strictly speaking, a model, but rather a full-sized, properly engineered structure built from standard sections with welded joints.

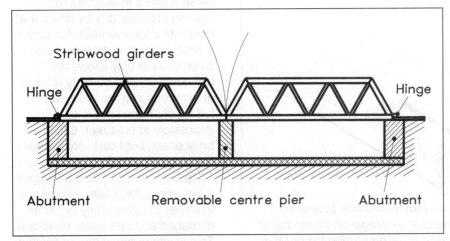

Figure 9.6 *Tracks can be carried across a path by means of a lifting bridge. This design, based on one of Peter Denny's outdoor systems, has a pair of wooden 'girders' supported on a removable central pier.*

viewed from a distance of some 2 m (6½ ft) (the usual outdoor viewing distance), the effect is quite acceptable. As long as the initial construction is sound and it is regularly repainted, a wooden girder bridge has a long life.

In all cases the normal practice is to provide much of the strength of the bridge by the base plank, which will be at least 12 mm (½ in) thick and preferably 20 mm (¾ in). A true-to-scale girder bridge with a prototypical deck is not impracticable, but unless correct bridge design principles are followed and the workmanship throughout is first class, it will possess neither the strength nor the durability to stand up to the rigours of garden railway use.

A simple braced girder bridge can be arranged to hinge upwards to provide a crossing over a path (see Figure 9.6). This is at its best when the track level is 200-400 mm (8-16 in) above the path, low enough to step over but not so low as to make it likely someone will trip. Where the bridge is around 1 m (3 ft) from the ground, it needs to be very substantial so that, should someone straighten up too soon when ducking under, the structure is not damaged.

Casting bridges in concrete

Masonry bridges and viaducts are normally made from 3:1 concrete, cast in moulds. The method used by Ray Tustin cast each arch in situ, using a complicated wooden mould such as the one shown in Figure 9.7. I have made one significant alteration to the original design, which had the low point of the track bed in the centre of the pier. This was done because a drainage pipe was cast in situ in the pier. Today, it is much easier to make a hole in the crown of the arch with a masonry drill.

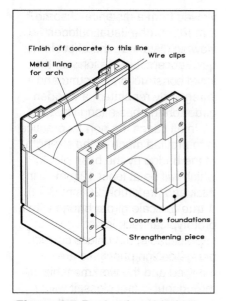

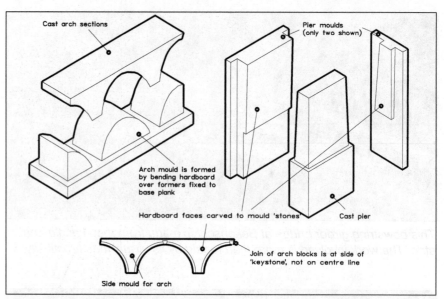

Figure 9.7 Design for a viaduct mould, based on that used by Ray Tustin. Each arch is individually cast on prepared concrete foundations, the mould being unscrewed when the concrete has set. The same mould can be used to cast a single arch underbridge.

Figure 9.8 Don Neal cast his viaduct in sections and assembled it on site. The arches are cast in pairs; each pier is an individual item. The viaduct sides are separate castings, permitting easy replacement to what, in practice, has been the most vulnerable part of the model. The arch sides and the pier moulds are lined with carved board to produce the stone effect.

Don Neal's method is more elaborate (see Figure 9.8), with separate piers supporting the arches, which are cast in longer sections. He faced the moulds with hardboard and carved the individual stones in reverse (see Figure 9.9), a process he stated took less time than he anticipated. I would suggest that thin medium density fibreboard (MDF) might be a better material to use for this. A small selection of woodcarving tools will be needed, which must be kept sharp throughout the carving process. It is fortunate that the most attractive finish for such a viaduct is roughly dressed stone, since this not only allows the individual units to be fairly large, it also means that the base can be left rough. I don't say it is impossible to create an effective brick effect, but I certainly wouldn't like to try.

In Don Neal's case the parapet walls were added later. He reports that over the years they became damaged and needed to be recast. This is where the separate casting of parts is an advantage, since it would be much more difficult to

Figure 9.9 The stone moulds are carved from man-made board. With CAD it is quite easy to achieve a very precise rectangle on an isometric sketch; it is less simple when using carving tools on hardboard or MDF, but an irregular finish is required if the effect of a stone viaduct is to be achieved.

A reinforced concrete bridge carrying a footpath over the Bekonscot garden railway.

replace the equally vulnerable parapets on Ray Tustin's pattern.

That all bridges will be alike is a good thing, since on most stretches of full-sized railway a standard design was employed for these structures. The moulds need to be well finished, not because the odd blemish is in itself significant, but because it will be repeated, in exactly the same place, on every unit of a viaduct and every bridge on the system. Before use, the mould needs to be thoroughly greased. Don Neal recommends heavy gear grease; Ray Tustin is silent on this point, nor does he mention that after use the moulds need to be scrubbed clean, using a soft wire brush.

Whichever system is followed, the 3:1 sand/cement mixture needs to be reasonably runny and must be put in a little at a time and rammed down in between to avoid creating voids. Reinforcing is essential. Don Neal advocates adding a little colorant to the mixture, and suggests lamp black. Each unit will take time to set: Ray Tustin suggests three days. The construction of a ten-arch viaduct is very definitely not a job for a long bank holiday weekend: it will need to be spread over an entire season. Winter should be avoided, for concrete laid during periods of frost will deteriorate rapidly, often within a matter of weeks. In view of the timescale, you might consider laying a track over a temporary timber viaduct made up of a series of stakes driven into the ground supporting a plank or planks, whilst the concrete viaduct is being built alongside (see Figure 9.10). This is in accordance with the spirit of prototype practice.

There is no reason why you should not cast a large single-arch bridge by the same methods. While the labour involved in making the mould will be proportionately higher, the time spent casting the model will be much lower than would be needed for a multiple-arch viaduct spanning the same gap.

Wooden bridges

There is something to be said for making bridges from wood. While it is theoretically a less durable material than concrete, with regular repainting it will last a very long time. If you are in doubt, consider how long wooden window frames and doors last. Apart from this, wooden bridges have their own attraction: the trestle viaducts of the far west of the USA and, nearer to home, Brunel's awe-inspiring West Country fans (see Figure 9.11) are widely admired. A garden setting not only provides

The GWR steam railcar and trailer passes over a reinforced concrete underbridge on Bekonscot. This was cast in a mould to provide the relief texture representing coursed stone.

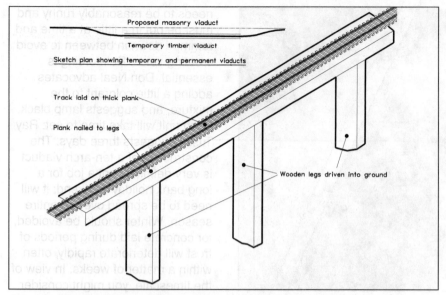

Proposed masonry viaduct

Temporary timber viaduct

Sketch plan showing temporary and permanent viaducts

Track laid on thick plank

Plank nailed to legs

Wooden legs driven into ground

Figure 9.10 A cast concrete viaduct of any length is not made in a day, or a month come to that. Therefore, it may be a good idea to construct a temporary timber viaduct alongside the future masonry structure. Utter simplicity is the watchword: all you need are a number of stakes driven into the ground and a plank nailed to the top. That the wood will rot in due course is an advantage, as it provides a good reason for getting on with the masonry structure.

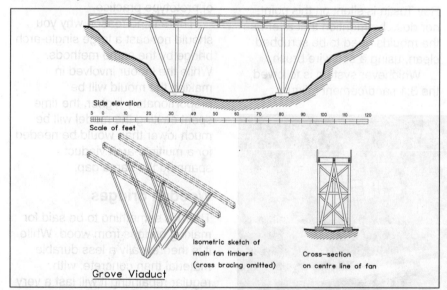

Side elevation

5 0   10   20   30   40   50   60   70   80   90   100   110   120

Scale of feet

Isometric sketch of main fan timbers (cross bracing omitted)

Cross-section on centre line of fan

Grove Viaduct

Figure 9.11 Brunel's timber viaducts were varied in design. The familiar fan type was used where wide, deep valleys had to be crossed. Smaller, shallower gaps were dealt with by a simpler raked structure, such as the very elegant one at Grove, shown in this drawing. The main legs were 12 in square cross-section, with the longitudinal beams built up from two such timbers bolted together, the joints being staggered. Most of these low viaducts only had the two raking spans, but Grove not only had a pair of central diagonal struts, but also boasted the elaborate timber girder handrail.

the length needed to do justice to these prototypes, it also allows one to stand back far enough to appreciate their beauty.

Tunnels

One of the sub-clauses of that section of Murphy's Law that applies to our hobby states categorically that the worst derailments always occur in tunnels. This is not a joke: the fact that both the track and train is completely out of sight means that any minor fault necessarily goes unnoticed. Get a handful of such faults together and you have trouble. This is bad enough indoors, but it can be even worse out of doors since here the tunnelled track is of necessity inaccessible under normal circumstances.

Or is it? A good deal depends on how the tunnel is designed, but before we look at this aspect, a more serious question is, why have a tunnel in the first place? There are two reasons: the first is purely scenic, and would apply mainly where one is modelling a railway where tunnels are part and parcel of the scene, but the main reason for introducing a tunnel must be to cross a main pathway, where the tunnel allows foot traffic to pass over without interfering with the railway.

Tunnels on a garden railway are usually made by constructing the tunnel walls and then covering this with soil; only occasionally will you need to dig a trench. This has particular significance for the path crossing: you should not lower the line to pass under a ground-level path, since this will ensure that the tunnel is filled with water whenever it rains. Of course, if you can tap into the surface water drains of the house you could get round this problem, but this will involve some

The Rockery Tunnel and approach bridge on Peter Denny's original Tamar Valley Light Railway.

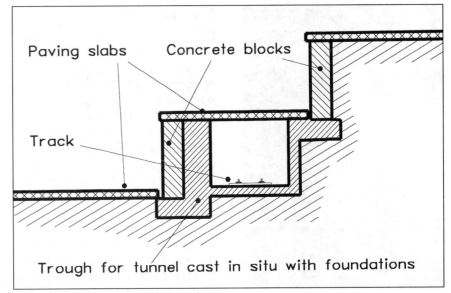

Figure 9.12 The most straightforward method of carrying tracks across a path is to raise the path and put the tracks in a shallow tunnel. This drawing shows the trough cast in situ with the foundations and covered with pre-cast paving slabs, thus providing access for maintenance.

extensive excavation and considerable expense. Raising the path is a simpler proposition (see Figure 9.12). A garden railway tunnel structure should include a slight fall for drainage purposes, leading to a point where water can run freely away from the line of the track.

Before we look at tunnel structures, we must appreciate that although this hole in the ground is a tunnel, to wild and domestic animals it is a ready-made lair. A secure cover will be needed at each end, though this cannot keep out insects. Spiders will be delighted to spin their webs inside, with the result that the first train of the day will emerge with a mesh of cobwebs across its front. One operator persuaded his cat to crawl through first, but gave no indication of how he persuaded it to oblige. Perhaps he owned a cat that liked crawling through drainpipes. A more reliable approach is to fix a block of foam plastic cut roughly to size to a long cane and flush out the tunnel with this. A wooden block about 10 mm

(½ in) smaller than the bore will also enable you to dislodge larger animals. Another possibility is to attach a foam plastic-faced clearance truck to the front of the first train.

Pipe tunnels

The simplest form of tunnel is made from a length of large-diameter plastic pipe, as shown in Figure 9.13. Provided it is not too long, the track can be slid in from one end, preferably after it has been fastened to a timber batten. As an alternative, conventional sleepered track could be replaced by metal angle section screwed to the batten. 12 mm extruded aluminium angle is ideal for this purpose, and will cost roughly the same as the track. Since this part of the model is completely out of sight, a grossly overscale but extremely robust length of track is needed. Obviously there would need to be a short section of sleepered scale track at each end. It is a good idea to drill some

drainage holes in the centre of the track batten, to ensure that the lower part of the pipe acts as the drain.

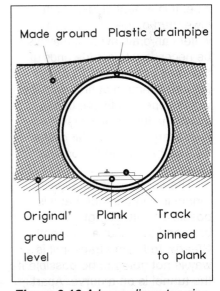

Figure 9.13 A large-diameter pipe can form a short tunnel. The track is laid on a length of wood which rests in the pipe. With this form of construction it is essential to have room at one end to allow the track and track base to be slid out.

At this point on Bekonscot, the single-track loop is carried under the footpath in a tunnel.

As the majority of tunnels are elliptical in section, rather than circular, a false front is needed. This needs to be securely fixed in place, and could be cast integrally with a concrete end support to the pipe. It is essential to clear the lower part of the pipe so that water can drain away; it may also be necessary to cut the ends of the track batten to fit inside the facade. Although at first sight this would appear to fix the batten inside the tunnel, it is only necessary to lift it a little over a third of the way up the bore to clear.

The success of the pipe tunnel lies in the fact that it is possible to lift a length of battened track out at one end. Clearly, removing track in this way is not going to be possible if the tunnel is on a curve. Apart from this, locating a suitable length of large-bore pipe is not quite as simple as it might at first seem: in many accounts of this type of construction I have encountered the ominous words 'I happened to have it by me'.

Cut and cover

On the prototype, where the bore is not far below the surface and there are no buildings above to complicate matters, tunnels are made on the cut and cover principle. A trench is dug out, the invert and side walls are built and finally the arch is added and covered with earth. In the garden a similar system can be followed, the main difference being that we usually dispense with the trench.

You can, if you wish, cast the trough as a single unit; the other approach is to lay a flat foundation and erect side walls. These can be cast, or you can use concrete blocks or house bricks set on mortar (see Figure 9.14). In either case there should be ample clearance between the walls and the track, not merely to make access easier, but to make it highly unlikely that derailed stock will come into contact with a rough wall. The top is provided by cast concrete slabs, either home-made or purchased; either way, they need to be sealed with mortar

Figure 9.14 A design for an O gauge tunnel by Ray Tustin. For larger sizes, concrete blocks can replace the house bricks.

since soil will find its way through any cracks.

The track is laid onto the concrete base before the top is sealed; indeed, it would be a good idea where practicable to defer covering for a full operating season to ensure that this section is not liable to derailments.

The concrete block would appear to make the tunnel excessively large, but this is a distinct advantage, for with this type of construction, you can make the tunnel large enough to allow easy access. On short tunnels, it is usually possible to reach in from either end and fish out any derailed stock, whilst one can carry out visual inspection with the aid of a torch and, possibly, a handbag mirror mounted on a stick.

Access hatches

Longer tunnels, particularly those on curves, would appear to be inaccessible and a potential source of trouble. The same situation applies to drains, which are equally likely to become blocked. The answer, in either case, is an inspection chamber, of which the main feature is a metal inspection hatch (see Figure 9.15). Combined with a large-section

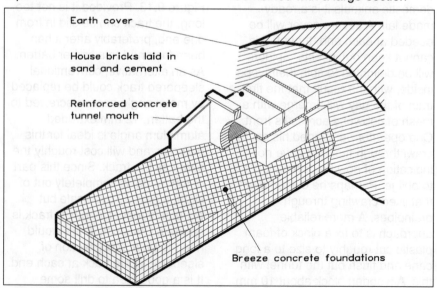

Earth cover

House bricks laid in sand and cement

Reinforced concrete tunnel mouth

Breeze concrete foundations

On Bert Groves's N gauge layout the end tunnel was constructed from heavy timber, well coated with creosote and capable of taking the full weight of an adult. This picture shows not only how access to the curved hidden tracks was provided by lifting off the step, but that a further handhole was permanently there for fishing out derailed stock.

'tunnel', a strategically located inspection pit will allow one to reach most of the hidden track without too much trouble. Although most access hatches are quite large, narrower patterns are used by telephone and cable TV companies. Some much smaller hatches are also used to cover stopcocks.

Whichever approach you choose, a tunnel is a major engineering project. It is not just that you need to build a substantial structure to carry the tracks underground, you will need to shift a very large amount of earth to create the model hill. You may very well need to go out and buy some. There may well be other problems involved in raising the level of a significant part of your plot

anything up to 1 m (3 ft) above its natural level: retaining walls to prevent the soil sliding onto your neighbour's garden, the relocation of the boundary fence to the new level and, above all, the drainage of the entire area.

Tunnels, which frequently involve a good deal of earth-moving to create an artificial hill, are major construction projects, but so are all significant alterations to the level of the garden. Inevitably they involve a certain amount of hard, back-breaking work. It is always possible to contract this work out to a landscape gardener, but not only does this cost money, it deprives you of two valuable benefits of rearranging the garden yourself. The first is that by moving the soil yourself, you have full control over the project, including the invaluable option of changing your mind as you go along. This is none too easy when you're employing experts who know their way is best.

The second is more subtle, the

deep sense of personal satisfaction one gets from a major project carried through to a successful conclusion. I speak from personal experience. In one of our homes – the one with the odd-shaped garden – I was initially confronted with several heaps of subsoil left by a generous builder. On fine weekends over the next 18 months I shovelled these into wheelbarrows, built steps from the discarded bricks I unearthed during my excavations, levelled the lawn areas, created banks which we planted with heathers, and slowly created a garden out of what had once been a stretch of meadow. Thereafter I could watch with a sense of pride as the shrubs we had chosen slowly established themselves. Then, when the time came to move, the first couple to view the house fell so in love with the garden that they not only bought the house on the spot, but were delighted to tell us, ten years later, that they hadn't changed a thing.

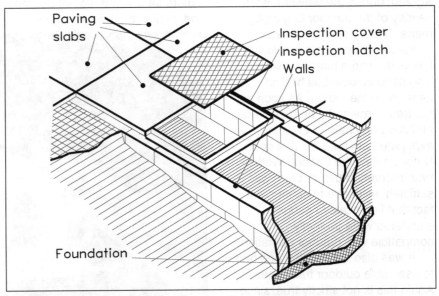

Figure 9.15 Where a large, long tunnel is required, access can be achieved through a standard inspection hatch. In this drawing the railway is carried under a patio. The 'bore' is large enough for an agile individual to reach inside whilst laying face down over the hole.

Chapter 10

The Permanent Way

In any model railway the track is the most prominent part of the model. This is true of an indoor railway and in the garden, where the length of main line is far greater and, for most of the time, is the only part permanently on display. Furthermore, since it has to stay outside through rain, snow, hail and sleet and withstand the passage of wild animals and pets, there is clearly no place for flimsy design or sloppy workmanship.

Coarse or fine scale?

There has always been an undercurrent of opinion that says that for outdoor use you must have an exceptionally robust track. Agreed, during the between-wars heyday of the outdoor O gauge railway, heavy-section rail and overscale fittings were employed, but as the same materials were also used indoors this had no bearing on the matter. As soon as the trade provided a near-scale rail and slide-on chair for O gauge, experimenters tried it out of doors. Unfortunately the Second World War intervened before there was sufficient evidence to confirm the fact that fine scale O gauge standards were perfectly compatible with outdoor operation.

It was also implied that one had to assemble outdoor track oneself. Again this is not strictly true, since several pre-war concerns offered ready-assembled 'Scale Permanent Way' in both 32 and 45 mm gauges. Of course it was considerably more expensive than the component parts, since it was hand-assembled. As an outdoor railway needed a lot of track, there was a strong incentive towards home assembly and it must be admitted that the old coarse scale track was quite easy to assemble.

Ready-assembled track

We will look at this aspect later, since today the accent is on ready-assembled track, both indoors and outdoors. Modern plastic-sleepered track usually costs less than the components for home assembly and frequently has very fine detail on its rail fastenings. The plastic base is now made from a material which does not degrade under sunlight, though it does appear that the application of preservatives, notably the old favourite, creosote, has a deleterious effect on the majority of plastic track bases.

The other component is the rail. Unlike full-sized rail, which is produced in a rolling mill from a white-hot steel billet, model rail is a specialized type of wire, produced by drawing a metal billet through a series of hardened dies, gradually reducing the cross section and imparting any profile required by the purchaser.

Common sense suggests that for outdoor use a rust-proof track is essential, hence brass or nickel silver is generally used. Stainless steel is now available for the larger scales; it is difficult to cut and file,

Peco Streamline O gauge track on the demonstration layout at Pecorama. Peco produce high-quality ready-assembled track and points for all current garden railway gauges.

The Peco track system also includes narrow gauge track. Here we see their SM32 track, 32 mm gauge, primarily for 16 mm scale, but equally applicable to any scale the user prefers.

since it has the annoying trait of hardening as it is worked. It is best cut with a fine abrasive disc secured on an arbour held in a low-voltage drill. This needs careful handling since a tool which will cut through hard steel will also cut through fingers. Should the disc break, pieces fly off in all directions, so safety spectacles are essential.

Rails have been drawn in mild steel from the earliest days of the hobby. It is after all the material used on the prototype and, within limits, can be used out of doors.

Still on the subject of rail, from time to time flatbottom rails have been offered in extruded aluminium. These are ideally suited for outdoor use, though soldering is, of course, extremely difficult. Aluminium doesn't actually corrode, but it does acquire a surface film when exposed to the weather. In its pure form it is easily attacked by sea water. Modern alloys are less prone to this

More Peco track, this time 45mm gauge track on the Bekonscot Gauge 1 system. The incomplete central crossover appears to be a part-finished cosmetic exercise, for although, on the ptototype, this station would have a crossover linking up and down roads, it is of dubious value on the model since it not only serves no useful purpose, it is completely invisible from the control panel.

trouble, but in any case, should anyone try to lay a model railway near the tideline, corrosion will be the least of his problems.

Sectional track

While modern tracklaying implies the use of flexible track sections, commercial sectional track in one form or another has been available for well over a century and not surprisingly has figured prominently in garden railway use. As I mentioned in the first chapter, many pre-war O gauge systems began life with tin-plate sectional track. While this was prone to rust, a thick application of paint inhibited corrosion for several years. This ruled out electric traction, but as clockwork was the preferred drive,

this was no problem.

Today outdoor sectional track is mainly confined to G gauge, but I see no reason why an experimental OO gauge ground-level garden line could not be laid with any of the current commercial sectional track systems. A trackbed of fine sand, well rammed down, would, I think, be advisable.

Self-assembled track

In the late 1930s, Bonds o' Euston Road placed advertisements in many boys' magazines extolling the virtues of their track system for model railways, with particular reference to its low cost. I can remember them in *Modern Boy*, *Magnet* and in particular *Hobbies Weekly*. The system involved solid drawn rail, in sheradized steel or brass, cast-metal chairs and hardwood sleepers. Rail was sold in yards, sleepers and chairs in hundreds. (Before I go any further it is as well to point out that although this type of track has of late been described as 'Bonds', it was supplied by Bassett-Lowke, Leeds and Milbro as well.)

The rail and chairs were actually closer to ⅜ in scale than 7 mm and are still used by Gauge 1 workers. The method of assembly was to thread the chairs onto the rail (taking pains to see that the cast keys were all on the same side) and then, after spacing them out, to pin them down onto sleepers (see Figure 10.1). There were also chairs with separate wooden keys, but these were mainly used indoors, since, just as on the prototype, the keys would work loose when exposed to rain and sun.

Threading the chairs

The correct procedure for threading chairs onto the rail is to start by filing a 'lead' on the rail

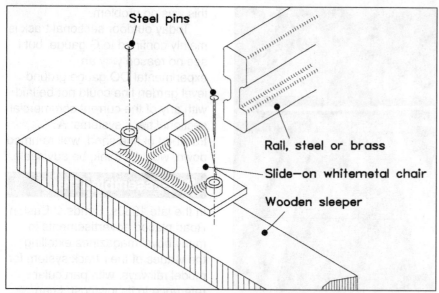

Steel pins

Rail, steel or brass

Slide—on whitemetal chair

Wooden sleeper

Figure 10.1 The component parts of traditional bullhead track. The cast whitemetal chairs have the keys cast integrally with the base, and have to be slid onto the rail and then spaced out according to the chosen pitch of the sleepers. The chairs are then pinned to wooden sleepers thoroughly soaked in a wood preservative, usually creosote. Steel pins are best, even for outdoor use, since brass pins are not only difficult to track down, more expensive and easily bent, they are also prone to work loose.

end, which makes it easier to ease the chair onto the rail. If all rough edges are removed, there is less chance of gashing one's thumbs whilst doing so. Some people make a simple fixture on the workbench to hold the chair so that it is only necessary to push the rail into it. Others claim this method is tedious, and prefer to slide the chairs directly onto the rail by hand. My own fairly limited experience suggests that whichever way you set about it, you really need three hands for the job.

As a yard length of rail is fairly long, it simplifies matters to slide half the chairs on one end and half on the other. This is how it is very easy to get the keys on both sides of the rail, which is extremely frustrating.

Bond's pre-war claim for low cost depended on a wide sleeper spacing, something approaching

3 in (76 mm). A 1½ in (38 mm) spacing was preferred because it looked better, questions of scale distances being rendered slightly academic by the overscale size of the components. Some workers aimed at 25 sleepers to the yard, which meant that 200 chairs and 100 sleepers would make 4 yd of track from eight yard lengths of rail.

In the heyday of the outdoor railway, bullhead rail was made in brass or sheradized steel. This consisted of a zinc coating applied to the rail before the final drawing, resulting in a smooth, silvery coat which was described as 'rust protection'. Indoors, on a reasonably dry site, rusting was virtually eliminated, but in very damp conditions the coating frequently broke down and the rail began to rust.

Despite this, treated steel rail is perfectly satisfactory for outdoor

use. It is, of course, essential to paint the track immediately it is laid. The top surface will be exposed, but regular use and occasional burnishing will keep rust at bay during the summer months. I have known cases where steel rail has been in use outdoors for over a quarter of a century without serious loss of material. It is clear that a regular coat of oil is essential to inhibit rust, used sump oil being highly recommended for this purpose, not for any special qualities, merely because this is the easiest way of disposing of it legally. Failing that, any bulk supply of oil will do nicely. It is applied with a cheap flat brush and dispensed from an empty fruit tin. Some users add a little paraffin to dilute the oil and make it easier to apply. Only a very thin film is needed, and live steam workers need not bother; their locomotives will oil the track as they go along.

Flatbottom rail

In pre-war days, flatbottom rail was rarely used. This was not merely because no 'proper' (i.e. British) railway used the section (in point of fact, they did), but because not only was it not widely available, it was fairly expensive. Neither objection applies today.

Another consideration was that the usual advice was to secure the rail to the sleeper with brass round-head screws. Quite apart from the cost, the mere thought of inserting all those tiny screws into the sleepers was enough to put one off the process. This advice was definitely a belt-and-braces approach, a way of getting round the fact that proper spikes were not available. Screw fixing is advisable for large-scale passenger-carrying tracks of 5 in gauge and upward, but for 32 and 45 mm gauges flat-headed brads

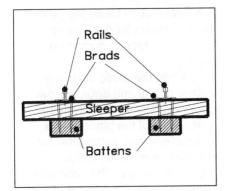

Figure 10.2 *Cross-section of flatbottomed track on battens. The rails are held down with broad-headed (gimp) pins which pass through the sleeper into the longitudinal battens. On high-level baseboards with a solid ply top, the pins will pass into the ply. Not only can you use materials which are on sale in any good DIY outlet, you save on fixings as well.*

are perfectly adequate (see Figure 10.2). The majority of readily available brads are ½ in (12½ mm) long, which means they will protrude through the normal sleeper.

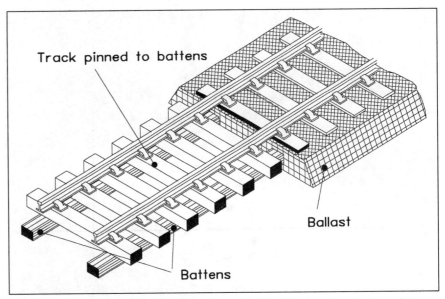

Figure 10.3 *Plastic-sleepered track can be fixed to wooden battens for outdoor use in ballast. These not only preserve the alignment of the track, they also provide additional grip in the ballast.*

Battened track

This makes it all the more advisable to lay home-built track onto battens (Figure 10.3). These are nothing more than lengths of stripwood running longitudinally under the tracks to provide additional rigidity. Battened track forms a fixed unit that can be lifted and relaid with ease; it also gives additional security when the track is laid in loose ballast. Indeed, I would advise the addition of battens to flexible and sectional tracks when these are to be laid in ballast.

Pointwork

It will be obvious that there is no difference between points constructed for outdoor use and those intended for an indoor railway. Space does not permit a detailed description of constructional methods here; for this I would refer the reader to my recent book *Model Railway Manual* (Patrick Stephens, 1994).

Making sleepers

Sleepers and battens can be purchased, but if you have a small sawbench it is a fairly straightforward business to make your own from selected offcuts about 1 m (3 ft) or so long of

Scratchbuilt bullhead O gauge track on Geoff Bigmore's outdoor layout. This section is carried on an outdoor grade ply sheet so the sleepers are pinned directly to the top surface before being ballasted.

This level crossing marks the division between the 'solid' and open baseboard sections on Geoff Bigmore's layout.

straight-grained timber. The prototype sleepers have a 12 in x 9 in cross section, which is 10 mm x 7.5 mm for Gauge 1 and 7 mm x 5 mm for O gauge. Yes, for O gauge it should be 5.25 mm thick, but even the best sawbenches

O gauge battened bullhead track laid on the open baseboard section of Geoff Bigmore's Bigston to Westbridge layout.

aren't that accurate and if you can work to the nearest millimetre you're doing well. Narrow gauge workers can calculate the size for their chosen scale; here we are mainly concerned with the principles involved.

The first thing to remember when using a sawbench is that it is a very dangerous instrument which needs to be used with extreme care. In particular, keep your fingers well away from the blade and use a push stick to apply gentle pressure to the end of the timber being sawn. Don't push too hard, it places excessive load on

the motor, and should the push stick slip you stand a very good chance of cutting yourself on the blade.

Setting the guide is largely a matter of trial and error. My own method is to measure from the inner tooth of the blade with a carpenter's rule, setting the cut to a full measurement, erring as much as ½ mm on the wide side. A preliminary cut on a piece of scrap wood will enable me to make an accurate assessment of the actual size being cut, then a gentle tap with a light hammer will move the guide closer to or further from the blade. Alternatively the guide can be set by placing a strip of the required thickness between the blade and the guide. You can allow an error of ¼ mm either way, but it is best to cut up rather more sleeper strip than you think you are going to need for the next session of intensive track construction.

It is a trifle tricky, even with a good mitre guide, to cut the thin stripwood to sleeper length on the sawbench. A standard mitre block provided with a fixed stop makes a good cutting jig though in view of the large quantities involved, a special-purpose fixture to do the same job is well worth considering (see Figure 10.4).

Rot-proofing sleepers

Once you have a quantity of sleepers cut, you can move on to the second stage, saturating the timber with preservative. The basic principle is simple and straightforward: the wood is placed in a suitable container and either wedged tightly in place or held down with some weighted wire mesh. For our purpose, chicken wire is about right. The container is then filled with a preservative liquid and left to settle. After at least a day, the level is checked and the

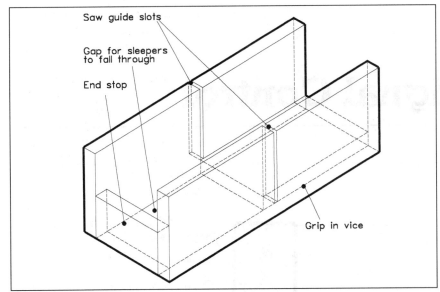

Saw guide slots

Gap for sleepers to fall through

End stop

Grip in vice

Figure 10.4 A straightforward jig for cutting stripwood into sleeper lengths. With the jig held in the vice, the stripwood is held in one hand and the tenon saw in the other; when parted, the sleepers fall through the hole. For a de luxe version, attach a canvas bag underneath with the help of some small hooks (the wrapping around Dry Sack sherry makes an excellent holder). To speed production, form half a dozen strips into a block, secured with several sticky tape wrappings. In this way each cut provides six sleepers.

fluid topped up. This continues for at least a week, until there is no appreciable drop in the level, indicating that the wood is now thoroughly saturated. The preservative is then drained off and the treated timber spread out to dry.

Standard sleepers are easily dealt with: a large open-topped can will hold several hundred. The longer crossing timbers and battens require a long flat receptacle. Unless you happen to stumble across something at least half a metre long, it will be necessary to make a suitable container. A serviceable trough could be made by moulding fibreglass over a smooth, slightly tapered baulk of softwood.

Widely available car repair kits have many uses around a garden railway, so a word or two about their use is advisable. Once again we are dealing with a material which is not only toxic in itself, but produces toxic fumes into the bargain. The only bonus is that the resin is not prone to splash, but even so, protective gloves are again essential. Because of the fumes, it is best to work in the open, or at the very least, at the front of the garage with the door wide open.

The kits come with detailed instructions which omit one point which, in the context of car repair, is irrelevant: the resin sticks to virtually anything. Accordingly, when you are producing a form on a mould, it should first be coated with a parting agent. This is a specially formulated gell which prevents the resin coming into contact with the mould. A cheaper alternative for this particular job is a couple of layers of newspaper. The fact that you will then have newsprint inside your trough is of no importance whatsoever, but if you are bothered you can soak it thoroughly and scrub it out with some wire wool. One beauty of a fibreglass trough is that, should it spring a leak, it can be sealed by the application of a fibreglass patch, which then forms an integral part of the repaired unit.

Chapter 11

Point and Signal Control

If there is one facet of the garden railway where the rigours of outdoor operation give rise to difficulties, it is in remote point and signal control. Indeed, on many lines the difficulties are side-stepped by the simple process of fitting manual levers to the points and letting the operator set the route by hand.

With local manual control, the niceties of scale realism are ignored, so the favoured approach falls into the 'crude but effective' category. Point levers are made over scale and no attempt is made to simulate a prototype design.

Manual point lever

Figure 11.1 depicts a well-tried point lever design which only requires a modicum of workshop equipment. It is made from brass strip, brass rod and brass or copper tube. I have not given any sizes since the basic requirement is a suitable bore tube and a close-fitting rod. For 32 and 45 mm gauge anything from 6 mm (¼ in) to 10 mm (⅜ in) bore tube is suitable.

The base strip is made long enough to fit across the point timbers on either side of the tiebar, which are extended to provide a mounting. The tube, which has a diagonal slot cut in it, is soldered to the base, with a good fillet of solder to ensure a firm joint. The diagonal slot is angled so that a 180° turn is more than sufficient to throw the point blades. The rod

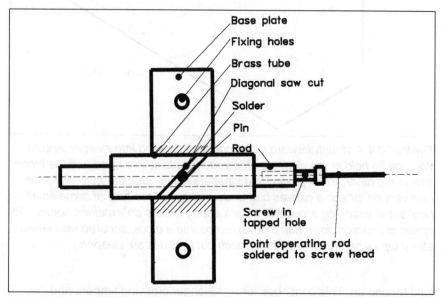

Figure 11.1 *A simple, robust point lever for manual control. No sizes are given, as these depend on the scale of the layout and the tube and rod most readily to hand. Although this calls for some advanced metalwork, this does not extend beyond simple drilling and tapping. A lathe is definitely not needed.*

has one hole tapped to take the operating lever. A tapped hole in the end takes a brass cheese-head screw which has a length of wire secured to it with solder. Both the rod and the screw must be well lubricated with thin grease to prevent their seizing through the action of weather. While brass does not rust, it can and usually does get a dark coating of oxides and sulphides when left in the open without regular polishing. The operating lever is a length of rod about 30–40 mm (1–1½ in) long; this is the one part of the mechanism that could at a pinch be made from steel.

Electric point motors

Conventional electric point motors have been used in the garden, for although electrical equipment and water do not mix, a simple watertight cover can be provided which fits over the point motor so that it is not completely sealed and gives ample protection. The best material for these covers is fibreglass, moulded around a wooden former to produce an integral, seamless unit. (As I mentioned in the last chapter, fibreglass and resin are obtainable from any car accessory supplier in the form of a body repair kit.)

You can't go far wrong by following the prototype! The small hut which supposedly contains the ground frame for working Beer Sidings on the Pecorama outdoor layout actually houses an electric point motor.

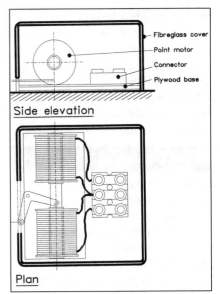

Side elevation

Plan

— Fibreglass cover
— Point motor
— Connector
— Plywood base

Figure 11.2 An electric point mechanism can be housed in a watertight cover, say fibreglass. It should have an open bottom, to help keep condensation to a minimum, while the fact that the casing can be lifted clear allows you to wipe the equipment dry from time to time. The point motor is screwed to a plywood base complete with screw pattern connectors so that the entire unit can be readily removed and taken to the workshop for maintenance. It would be well worthwhile standardizing the base so that unit replacement is quick and easy should there be trouble during the operating season.

The cover will keep out most moisture, but it will still be necessary to remove the point motor for overhaul from time to time, possibly during the winter months as well. Therefore not only should the mechanism be secured with brass screws to a wooden base, but the electrical connections should be made through a short length of screw-connecting strip. Standard commercial twin solenoid or motorized point motors can be used in this fashion. Figure 11.2 shows a suggested arrangement.

In view of the relatively small number of motors required on many garden railways, it might be felt preferable to build a motorized pattern in the railway's own workshops. This would, I suggest, be dependent on finding a source of small motors and gears at bargain prices. This is clearly a true model engineering project, but the work involved is balanced by

The electric mechanism for operating this point on the Bekonscot railway is contained in the lineside hut, with the cranks covered by a tin-plate casing. This is showing some signs of superficial rusting despite the regular maintenance given to all parts of this system.

the fact that this type of mechanism is, by its very nature, much easier to strip down and repair than a commercial product. To put it another way, any equipment manufactured in the company's shops can always be sent back to the maker.

Rod control

However, if you are prepared to make the equipment yourself, a much better system of remote control for points on a garden railway is a beefed-up version of the prototype point rodding, worked from a central lever frame using round rodding and bell cranks.

Figure 11.3 gives details for simple point rodding components. The rod is 2 mm diameter coated steel wire, as supplied by all good dry cleaners in the form of those hangers that seem almost to breed in most wardrobes. Opened out and carefully straightened, one coathanger will give a useful length of rodding. This can be

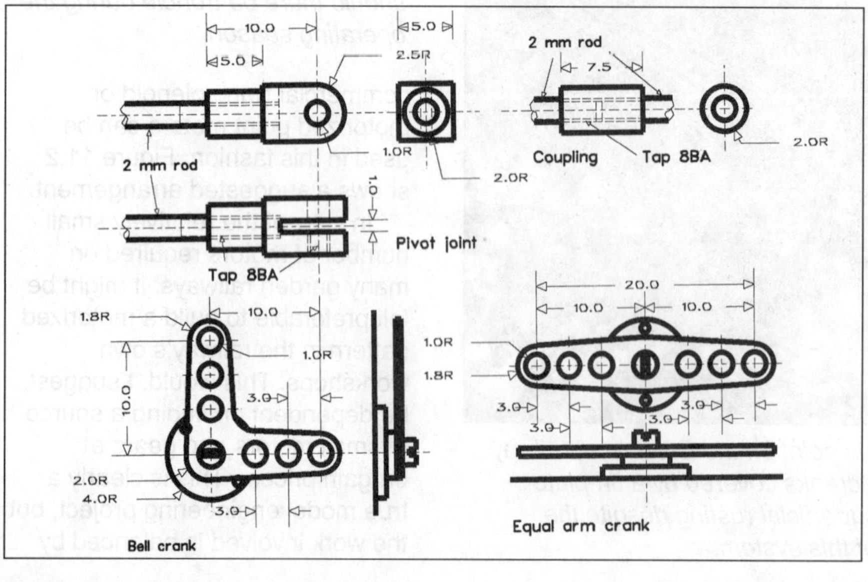

Figure 11.3 *Components for a high-class rodding system for point operation. Several of the components require the use of a lathe.*

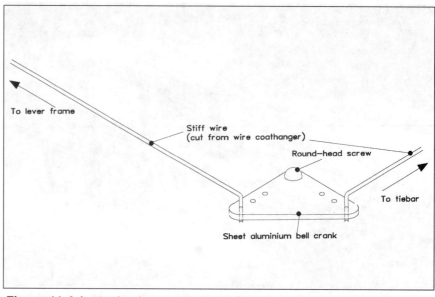

Figure 11.4 *A very basic arrangement of point rodding, using simple triangular bell cranks and coathanger wire, bent at the ends to fit into the holes. As with the more elaborate fittings shown in Figure 11.3, the success of this system depends on the care and craftsmanship put into the manufacture and assembly of the parts. Indeed, if anything this requires more care, since unless everything is in correct alignment, the rods will pop out of the holes in the cranks.*

threaded 8 BA or 2 mm metric, which opens up several intriguing possibilities.

The most useful is the joining collar, a piece of 4 mm dia rod drilled and tapped to suit the rod. This is held in place with two nuts and a spot of paint or other

sealant. It is possible to drill the hole in the vice, though one would need to be very skilled to get it dead true every time. Should the railway's workshop include a lathe, then the job is much more straightforward. Although brass might seem to be necessary, steel is perfectly suitable, as the coat of paint needed to seal the nuts in place will protect the metal. In practice, the rod will rust through before the collar.

Where a lathe is available, it is possible to make neat fork ends to link up with the bell cranks and other fittings. These are detailed in Figure 11.4. However, a simple bent end is quite good enough. The bell cranks can be cut from suitable sheet metal, brass, steel or aluminium, depending on what happens to be available. Two possible sources of supply are steel dividers from filing cabinets that have been converted to

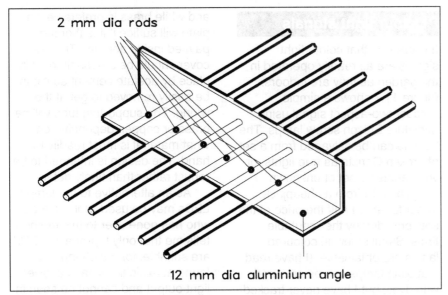

2 mm dia rods

12 mm dia aluminium angle

Figure 11.5 *Outdoor point rodding requires supports, readily made from a length of extruded aluminium angle drilled to take the rods.*

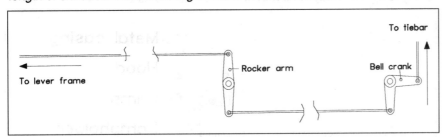

To tiebar

To lever frame

Rocker arm

Bell crank

Figure 11.6 *On long rodding runs, the expansion of the metal in full summer sun, which can reach temperatures approaching 45°C, can affect the throw of the points. A simple rocker arm halfway along equalizes the expansion. The prototype uses a more compact arrangement of two angled cranks, but this simpler system is more suited to model railway usage. However, there is nothing (apart from the extra work involved) to prevent anyone copying the full-sized expansion crank.*

suspended filing, and redundant aluminium baking trays.

The rod or rods are carried in angle brackets, drilled 2.1 mm dia to provide a small clearance (see Figure 11.5). On ground-level layouts the angles can be screwed

to sleeper ends or fixed to the sub-base with masonry plugs. The rods will need regular greasing, as is the case on the prototype. In theory this was the job of the lengthmen, but I don't think my Uncle Tom was the only signalman to do his own oiling in between their regular visits.

Figure 11.6 shows an expansion joint. This is used in the centre of a long run of rodding so that changes in length due to temperature variations are equalized. It would only be needed on very long stretches.

Lever frames

There are now some very good commercial lever frames on the market. The Gem version, whilst ostensibly for small scale indoor lines, is adequate for the job, though you may need to use unequal arm cranks to increase the throw. The pattern produced by Model Signal Engineering

The manual lever frame at Westbridge on Geoff Bigmore's layout. This box operated all the original main line points and signals at that end of the layout. Small 'ground frames' on the bottom left controlled later additions. Part of the electrical control panel can be seen. Good use has been made of ex-RAF meters and switches of Second World War vintage.

produces a more satisfying type of frame based on full-sized practice. The manufacture of a mechanical lever frame, with or without its locking table, is well within the capacity of a small, well-equipped home workshop, but it is by any standards a major proposition and will occupy at least one whole winter's modelling session if it is to give sound reliable operation for a number of years.

Hydraulic control

In his book *Model Railways* Henry Greenly provided drawings of a pneumatic system of point control where a close-fitting piston in a tube was actuated by air pressure created by a similar ram attached to the lever frame. When I first saw this in 1938 I was both fascinated and slightly puzzled, since it seemed to me that not only would the yards of copper tube needed to link the two rams work be very costly, but the efficiency of the piston was, to say the least, doubtful even with the relieving grooves. By the time I had completed my apprenticeship, I was certain it was one of those bright ideas that couldn't perform as promised.

However, if we substitute neoprene tube and replace the air with hydraulic brake fluid, we have a totally different situation. As for the pistons and cylinders, a visit to a car breaker's yard should provide the basis for an experimental set-up, though in the long run I feel that it would be preferable to manufacture these in the railway's own shops. This is clearly a model engineering project, but I do know that hydraulic point operation has been successfully applied on garden railways. Its advantage is that, unlike all other methods, it is as near weatherproof as it is possible to get.

Colour light signals

It is obvious that colour light signals are as readily operated in the garden as they are indoors. Figure 11.7 shows a simple outdoor two-aspect signal using miniature Edison screw lamps. The holders can be salvaged from a set of broken Christmas tree lights, or you can use a set of unknown origin bought from a cheapjack trader for about half the price of the sets provided by the reputable firms. Small screw-in coloured lamps are obtainable. (I have read that plain lamps can be coloured with dyes, but I have never tracked down the dyes, let alone tried this for myself.) The body is all-metal, and while brass is preferable, tin-plate will suffice if it is thoroughly painted inside and out. The rear cover should be a push fit, held in place by acetate cement so it can be easily removed to get at the wiring. The supporting tube will be brass or copper, depending on what material is most readily to hand. The design is intended to be robust rather than finely detailed.

As an alternative to the lamps, LEDs may be used. Bob Ledger, who has gone over to this method, tells me that only top-quality LEDs are suitable, for the cheap ones found at exhibitions have a lower light output and cannot be seen in bright daylight, let alone under direct sunlight.

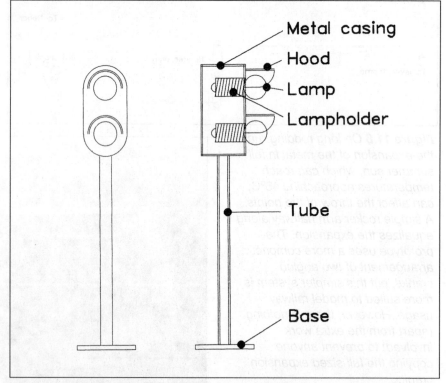

Figure 11.7 Colour light signals are very simple devices, which in the larger scales can be readily built up in any well-equipped modelmaker's workshop. For outdoor use there is very little to go wrong, so long as the lamps screw into holders and can be easily replaced without partially dismantling the signal. The drawing shows a basic two-aspect signal; the same principles can be applied to three- and four-aspect heads. There is of course no reason why accurate models of prototype signals should not be made, whilst the use of LEDs in place of lamps is worth consideration.

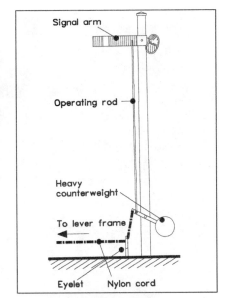

This two-aspect colour light signal on John Anning's layout is easily dismantled. The connection to the control panel is through a 5 DIN plug and socket. This photo shows the third rail fitted to this Southern Electric layout for authenticity. Power supply to locomotives and EMUs is by stud contact.

This junction signal at Bekonscot has its actuating solenoids sunk into the ground. The operating rod passes through a long brass sleeve to minimize the entry of water.

Figure 11.8 The outdoor semaphore signal can be operated in much the same way as its prototype, with a nylon fishing line replacing the full-sized wire. In this case, the counterweight on the operating arm should be overscale so that it performs its prototype function. On high-level sections, a sub-baseboard weight can be substituted; this can be any piece of moderately heavy scrap, such as a large nut. In place of the prototype pulleys, small brass eyelets which can be screwed into the sleepers or baseboard are used.

Semaphore signals

For many years semaphore signals intended for garden use were fairly crude, but experience has shown that for 7 and 10 mm scales this is not necessary. Scale-sized hardwood posts will stand up to a good deal of wear and tear, but if it is felt that they are in a particularly vulnerable location,

This signal on the Bekonscot railway is actuated by a solenoid contained in the tin-plate 'chest' alongside the post.

brass or even steel is a suitable substitute. Signal arms can be true to scale and provided with working lights. For further information on signals, I would refer you to my book *Model Railway Signalling* (Patrick Stephens, 1991).

It is not too difficult to provide 7 mm scale semaphores with prototypical operating gear, at least as far as the balance arm at the bottom of the post. That leaves us with the business of remote control.

In the early days, the favoured method was to use fishing line run

An impressive signal gantry on John Anning's 7 mm scale Southern Railway layout. The signals are mounted on a simple plywood structure which slides under the baseboard and are actuated by standard double solenoid point motors. A multi-pin plug and socket provides connection to the control panel.

through eyelets. As this thread, while very strong, tended to stretch with variations of humidity and, even more, with age, a simple adjuster was provided. The system was a close copy of the prototype wire operation, but fell into disfavour because of the unreliability of the thread. Of course, this was before nylon and other plastics replaced the linen or flax thread of the bad old days. Modern fishing line is perfectly suited to the remote control of outdoor signals, and is shown in use in Figure 11.8.

Electrical operation by solenoid is another possibility. In such cases I would suggest that the solenoid coils are sealed with epoxy resin to minimize trouble and that the mechanism is regularly lubricated to minimize rust. It is also possible to use a double-action point motor, in which case the precautions given above should be followed.

Signals are one feature of the outdoor layout that are almost invariably brought inside during the winter. Even if an overhaul is not needed, a thorough check and lubrication is necessary before they are replaced in the spring.

Chapter 12

Buildings Out of Doors

Perhaps the most imposing of all the structures at Swissminatur is this magnificent model of the Swiss Parliament buildings at Bern. The setting is prototypical, with the steep slope down to the River Aare.

There are two distinct approaches to buildings for a garden railway. The most popular is to keep them to the irreducible minimum – station buildings, signal cabins, goods sheds and locomotive sheds, in roughly that order of priority. Anything else is not so much expendable as totally invisible. The other approach is to turn as much of the garden as possible into a miniature town served by a railway system. The oldest and best-known example of this is the Bekonscot Miniature Village in Beaconsfield, Beds, a project that has been copied extensively throughout the world. One notable example of this is Swissminatur at Melide, near Lugano, Tichino, Switzerland, where you are promised a trip around Switzerland in an hour. This is blatant misrepresentation: to do bare justice to this magnificent collection of models based on prototypes throughout the Confederation you need at least twice that amount of time so, should you be in a position to visit it, allow at least a full afternoon.

The importance of maintenance

Clearly, model buildings out of doors have, like their prototypes, to stand up to the effects of

Another fine building at Swissminatur is this superb model of the Stockalper Palace at Brig. Here the setting is imaginary – the prototype is surrounded by other buildings rather than flower beds. In the distance one gets a glimpse of the concrete Alps.

weather. At first sight, this might seem to require very durable materials, but the only common modelling medium that has not, to my knowledge, been used successfully out of doors is cardboard. However, before we look at materials and methods, one important general observation needs to be made. As with any full-size building, our miniature replicas require regular maintenance. Therefore, unless the building is too large for easy removal, it should not be built into the ground but secured in place by fitting it over a fixed block.

While we are primarily concerned in this chapter with buildings, the foregoing remarks also apply to other features such as level crossing gates, footbridges and even quite large bridges, which also benefit from ease of removal. Leaving aside the question of maintenance, which usually involves no more than repainting, there are clear

advantages in being able to put everything possible into store during the closed winter season.

Lest it be thought that a model building will suffer if left outside, let me say that so long as the model is well built and receives regular attention, it will last a long time. In the case of the pioneer village of Bekonscot, we are talking about more than 70 years. Agreed, a programme of continuous maintenance and renewal has gone into this, but it goes to show that there is no reason why an outdoor layout, particularly one at or near ground level, should not include a small town. At least there is usually ample room, and since model buildings have an even wider appeal than model railways, any effort put into this aspect of the model will be amply repaid.

Plastic buildings

Despite initial qualms, it has been established that plastic building kits do stand up to outdoor use for

a good many years. While this might seem to restrict this useful material to the smaller scales, a good selection of kits for the larger gauges is now available, with particular emphasis on G gauge. The accent is towards European mainland and US prototypes, but the kits have proved amenable to being Anglicized.

Sheet metal

Before I turn to what is undoubtedly the most favoured material, wood, a brief mention should be made of sheet metal. Occasional use has been made of aluminium: it is reasonably priced, not too difficult to obtain, rust-proof and relatively easy to cut. The main problem is making unobtrusive joints. The most suitable way would be to cement the parts together with epoxy resin, but from observation it appears that the ubiquitous pop rivet is commonly regarded as the best fastening. In the largest scales this is not too obtrusive.

Wooden buildings

Wood has always been the favoured material for outdoor building construction. It is easy and pleasant to work with, needs only simple, low cost hand tools and is readily available at a not too exorbitant price. Provided the finished structure is given the traditional three-coat finish of primer, undercoat and top coat externally and a sealing coat internally before being exposed to sun and rain, and is then repainted regularly, it will last for years. The main difficulty in the past, the tendency for large sheets of wood to crack along the grain, has been solved by the advent of truly water resistant glues for plywood.

Construction methods are the same as those employed for

Lawnton, on Peter Denny's current narrow gauge garden railway. The main station buildings are basically those that were built for his '50s layout, but they have been carefully maintained ever since. The elegant footbridge has a wooden base, with the spidery girders soldered up from OO gauge bullhead rail. (Photo courtesy Peter Denny)

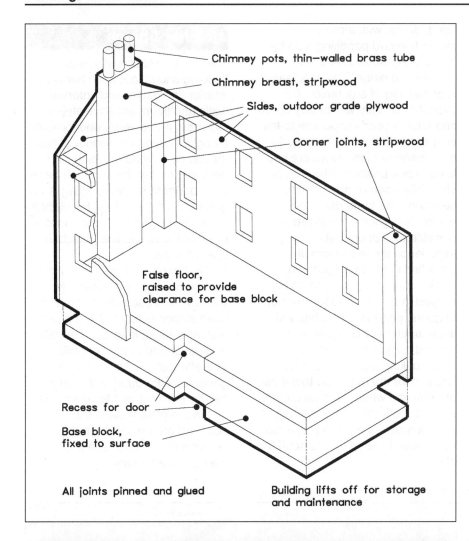

Chimney pots, thin—walled brass tube

Chimney breast, stripwood

Sides, outdoor grade plywood

Corner joints, stripwood

False floor, raised to provide clearance for base block

Recess for door

Base block, fixed to surface

All joints pinned and glued

Building lifts off for storage and maintenance

Figure 12.1 Construction of a basic timber-based building for a garden railway. The outdoor grade ply sides are secured at the corners with stripwood reinforcement and all joints are glued and pinned. There is some merit in making the roof a separate structure which is either a close fit on the building or secured by a couple of strategically located brass screws under the eaves. This makes it possible to get at the interior for maintenance. An exterior building with a loose roof can be used as a store for small tools, oil and other useful items. Another possibility is to house the first-aid box in it, in which case a model cottage hospital or health centre would be very appropriate.

internal models (a basic example is shown in Figure 12.1). Each wall is cut out individually, with the necessary openings for windows and doors pierced. A fretsaw is the traditional tool for this task. Internal holes are cut by drilling a hole close to the cutting line, on the waste side, inserting the blade, tightening the saw and then carefully sawing to the line. With small units the normal procedure is to cut round each side in order, turning the workpiece at each end. Where the wall is at all large, you may find the depth of the saw inadequate to do this, but then you can work from one corner. A power jigsaw, fitted with a very fine blade, does not have this limitation and requires less effort when dealing with thicker boards.

Although the side walls can be simply butted together, the joint is stronger when backed by a length of stripwood. Although modern glues do provide a tenacious bond and, when properly used, are stronger than the timber itself, pinning is advisable, not merely to

For some unaccountable reason, pubs are a popular subject for modellers. The Earl of Bekonscot is an excellent example of the genre.

provide strength, but to hold the parts together whilst the glue is hardening. Although we normally accept that a pin or nail can be driven through timber with little difficulty, it is much better, where fine pins are concerned, to drill a pilot hole in the upper layer. This not only reduces the distance you need to drive the pin through, it also provides a firm support at the same time.

Windows and doors

Windows and doors can be made in much the same manner as for indoor structures (see Figures 12.2 and 12.3). In the larger scales it is possible to make glazing bars from small wood sections, but although it is by no means impossible to make 16 mm scale models of actual window frames, complete with individual glazing secured with mastic, I fancy anyone with the necessary skill and inclination for this class of work would far rather apply his or her expertise to modelling coaches. On the other

hand, doors, with more straightforward panelling, can be modelled to scale and even arranged to hinge. This last feature is something of a gimmick, for even though they will initially open and shut, a year's exposure to the elements will put paid to that. As in the smaller scales, doors are best fixed in one position. This can be shut, fully open or any point in between. The large doors on engine and goods sheds are a possible exception, but in my experience these are usually modelled in the open position.

For the most part, glazing is applied internally, and for use out of doors, glass is advisable, with sheet acetate or perspex as a second choice. It is well worth while making a proper rebated housing for the glass, so that it can be removed when the time comes to paint the frames. Alternatively, judicious use of masking tape will be needed to keep the paint off the glass.

Interior fittings

There is no reason why an outdoor building should not have basic interior fittings. Indeed, internal walls and floors act as useful stiffeners and prevent one looking straight through the windows. How far you go beyond this is a personal matter, for although there is no doubt that interior fitting is great fun, how much of it is visible when the building is a good metre or more below the line of sight is questionable.

On the other hand, low-voltage lighting on a garden layout can be worthwhile, especially where the main station is located in a shed, making it feasible to operate trains well beyond the onset of twilight. The effect of tiny lights against the general background of the railway can be entrancing. Miniature screw lamps are preferable to the soldered pattern, and robust construction should take priority over scale accuracy.

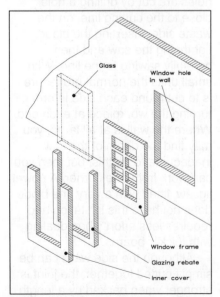

Figure 12.2 Construction of a straightforward exterior window frame.

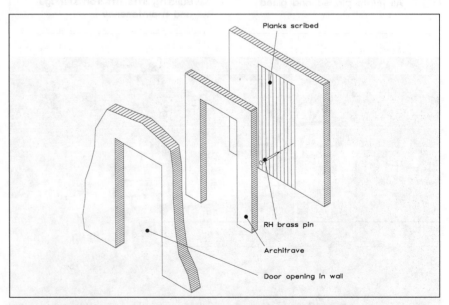

Figure 12.3 A basic door for outdoor use. It pays to keep things as simple as possible, since apart from any other consideration, outdoor buildings rarely get close inspection from visitors. It rather defeats the object if you need to point out the special parts of your model.

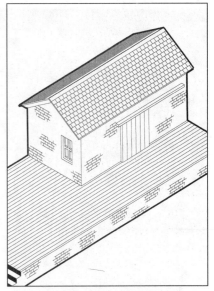

Another Bekonscot pub is the Barley Mow, complete with thatched roof and small-scale fence.

Brick finishes

One problem with buildings out of doors is the difficulty of representing brick or stone finish on a sheet of plywood. The methods employed for an indoor layout, such as the application of

The railway side of Bekonscot's Barley Mow, with the GWR steam railcar in the middle ground.

card 'bricks' or the use of a paper or embossed card overlay, are clearly ruled out. There are several possible approaches. The second most tedious would be to scribe horizontal brick courses over the sides whilst in the flat; the most tedious would, of course, be to add the vertical courses as well. While such scribing has been done on plastic sheet and card for indoor layouts, these materials do not have a grain. On plywood the main difficulty would undoubtedly be keeping each scribed line straight and parallel with the rest. However, I know of two very

Figure 12.4 *A simple lock-up goods shed, with the brickwork shown in patches. This is a shorthand method of indicating what the material is supposed to be, and is surprisingly effective.*

effective methods that are relatively simple and remarkably effective.

The first, which I saw in use in Weston-super-Mare in 1940 and have shown in Figure 12.4, is to paint the building brick red, then to add random patches of coursed brick with white paint. This is an application of a technique employed by illustrators and architectural draughtsmen to indicate a large area of brick, and despite its apparent crudity it is extremely effective. Although it doesn't photograph well, it satisfies all but the most critical of viewers. I suspect this has a lot to do with the fact that one has already accepted a 1:43 or thereabouts scale building as a representation of a full-sized structure and so the conventional representation of brick is sufficient to allow the suspension of disbelief.

An alternative arrangement, devised by Peter Denny, is to cover the entire building with

Bekonscot's solicitors, Argue and Twist, occupy this fine half-timbered building.

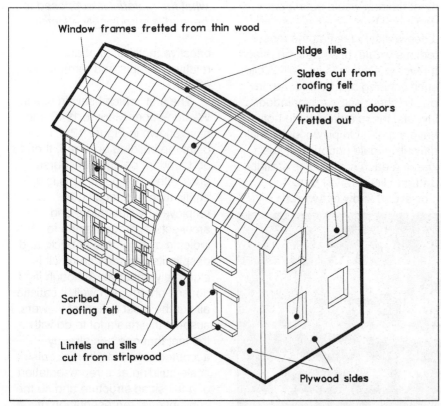

Window frames fretted from thin wood

Ridge tiles

Slates cut from roofing felt

Windows and doors fretted out

Scribed roofing felt

Lintels and sills cut from stripwood

Plywood sides

Figure 12.5 *A wooden carcass can be completely covered with smooth-finish roofing felt, which can then be scribed to represent brick or stone. The courses can easily be picked out in paint. Incidentally, undercoat, which has a flat finish to begin with, gives a good, if slightly short-lived, protective surface. Unfortunately, the selection of colours is very basic.*

bituminous roofing felt, which is then scribed to represent stone (see Figure 12.5). He used Cow gum, the rubber-based adhesive used by illustrators and layout artists, though this was before contact adhesives were readily available. The buildings have stood up to some 40 years of exposure to Cornish weather and remain waterproof to this day. For once the cheaper product is best – the 'better' grades of roofing felt have an additional coating of fine stones and are clearly unsuitable.

While concrete structures can be represented by painting wood with external wall paint, this is only economic if the paint is being used on the house, since it is only obtainable in large quantities. However, concrete buildings are not that common and for the more usual applications of this material, the real thing should be used.

Roofs

As on the prototype, the roof on a model building must be weatherproof. To a large extent, modelling the roof out of a single sheet of outdoor grade ply meets this requirement, but something more substantial is called for. Fortunately, common roofing felt comes to our aid.

It can of course be used directly over a wooden foundation. This is how it is normally used and it will be completely satisfactory in this role. However, the felt can be easily cut with a heavy duty Stanley pattern knife, so it is not too difficult to create 'slates' from roofing felt using exactly the same technique that is used to make a detailed roof for an indoor model (Figure 12.6). The main difference, apart from the size of the tiling, is that the successive layers of roofing felt slates are secured with flat-headed clout nails.

Many of the buildings at Bekonscot have their roofs covered with 'tiles' cut from strips of roofing felt. The damage to several of the 'tiles' seen in this picture is due to visitors rather than the ravages of weather. Note the 'ridge tiles' made from a folded strip of roofing felt.

The ridge tile will however need to be produced by folding a long narrow strip of roofing felt gently to form an inverted 'V' section which can then be stuck over the top rows of felt 'tiles'. This will ensure that the vulnerable ridge is well protected.

Modelling timber prototypes

Speaking of the real thing, it should be remembered that until comparatively recently, many railway structures were wholly or in part timber buildings. At first sight, this appears to be the ideal way of arriving at a prototype finish, but a little caution should be exercised. There are no inherent problems involved in making a detailed model of a timber structure with the full interior framing and individual planking reproduced

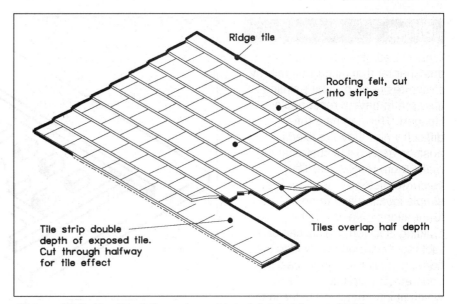

Figure 12.6 Roofing felt can be cut into 'slate' strips and laid over a wooden roof base.

exactly to scale, providing a drawing of the prototype exists and can be copied. Whether such a structure would stand up to the effects of the weather over a period of years without disintegrating is another matter, and I for one would be chary of exposing such a model in this way. The simpler – and faster – method of scribing planks on the outer skin of a wooden building is perfectly adequate for all but the most detailed of model railways and, in view of the normal approach to garden detail, this course is to be preferred.

The station buildings at Hanton on the Bekonscot garden railway are an excellent example of a 1:32 scale model of a timber prototype. The footbridge, an excellent example of metalwork, is perhaps the most sophisticated of all the railway structures on the system.

Bases

I mentioned at the beginning of this chapter that all garden railway structures need regular painting if they are to have a reasonable lifespan. This can be a trifle difficult when they are fixed in position and so it is customary to make them removable. The favoured method is to provide a simple locating fixture on the foundations onto which the building is lowered. This can be a rectangle of wood screwed to the base, a similar rectangle cast in concrete or a couple of dowels which fit into matching holes in the bottom of the building. This means that garden railway buildings are rarely bedded into the ground.

The base block is usually made from a piece of outdoor grade ply, 9 mm or 12 mm thick, screwed down to the base. Should, over the course of time, this block become unserviceable, usually because of rot, the screws can be drilled out and a new block substituted, with fresh fixings in a different place.

Obviously, on high-level baseboards the base already exists. On ground-level lines, a concrete base needs to be prepared, the obvious exceptions occurring where the base already exists, i.e. at platforms, or around tracks laid on a concrete base. Tempting as it might be, it is not a good idea to bed a timber building into the soil. On the other hand, a concrete structure can be provided with scaled-down foundations and become a permanent part of the model scene.

Concrete buildings

External buildings may be cast in concrete, using simple moulds. The arrangement shown in Figure 12.7 comprises four stripwood sides and a quantity of window- and door-opening moulds. These are screwed down to a blockboard base after being carefully positioned according to the master plan. In all probability the most straightforward way of doing this is to make a full-sized drawing and lightly stick this to the blockboard. Locating the various parts is then just a matter of putting them in place and checking that they are all square and correctly aligned.

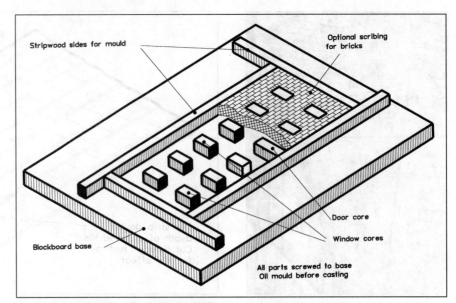

Figure 12.7 A simple mould for casting flat sides for buildings in concrete.

After use, they can be stored for future buildings. Since the openings will be standardized, it is not unduly difficult to set up templates and jigs for the windows and doors.

Ready-mix is poured into the mould and levelled off. It is then possible to scribe 'bricks' on the setting concrete, using simple squares and straight edges. While this takes a good deal more time than it did to get my computer to set out the bricks on the drawing, it is one way of keeping the project going whilst each side hardens. This is not a quick method, but it does produce an extremely durable building shell.

Chapter 13

Garden Railway Horticulture

If you want an in-depth treatise on gardening, you must look elsewhere; there are plenty of books on the subject. Not that I propose recommending any, for without exception they are intended for the keen gardener and assume that the reader requires perfection and is prepared to spare no efforts towards this desirable end. The requirements of the railway gardener are somewhat different. Indeed, a plot with poor sandy soil, scattered with large stones and small boulders, is ideal for our purposes, though the serious gardener would condemn it as next door to useless. Of course, when you set out to grow plants, you need to understand the basic principles of cultivation, but unless you are a glutton for hard work, the finer points can be set aside. Building and maintaining the railway will always come first; the garden itself should take second place. The only exception to this rule is where your partner is delighted to take over the actual cultivation and tackle the hard work involved.

Fortunately, the right plants will grow of their own accord. If a plot of land is left to lie fallow, before long vegetation will begin to emerge and the land will revert to its original condition. This may take little more than a decade. A lot of the early growth will be classified as weeds, which are better described as 'plants growing in the wrong place'; rhododendrons on the Festiniog

This aerial view of part of the O gauge garden railway at Pecorama shows how a high-level system can be enhanced by the provision of shrubs and small bushy plants. A privet 'landscape' is shown at the bottom of the picture.

Railway are a very pertinent example of this principle. This also emphasizes another important point: once you discover the species that thrive on your soil, you are well on the way to a trouble-free garden.

High-level baseboards

Clearly, a special approach is needed for high-level baseboards. One school of thought maintains that it is best to cover the immediate area with fine gravel and soak this with weedkiller to keep everything tidy. Where the railway is out of sight of the house, this simple course has much to commend it.

Assiduously trimmed privet forms the landscaping on this corner of the O gauge garden layout at Pecorama.

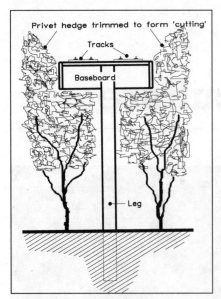

Figure 13.1 *The appearance of a high-level baseboard can be improved by planting a hedge underneath. Choose a small-leafed evergreen such as privet, and trim the top to simulate a section of landscape.*

Before the war, Victor B. Harrison planted privet under his Gauge 1 outdoor baseboards and then trimmed the growth to form a 'landscape'. Unfortunately, privet needs very frequent trimming and drains all nourishment from the soil over a wide area, so it has fallen out of favour. Box, slow growing and with a denser, more attractive leaf, is a better choice. Either way, the wood framing will be buried in evergreen foliage and therefore will be more liable to rot (Figure 13.1).

The hedging can be trimmed to produce cuttings and even allowed to carry over the tracks to form a tunnel (see Figure 13.2). This last idea is best used where a hedge, at right angles to the track, forms a screen. This is a very effective way of dividing an unadorned high-level main station section from the more attractive ground-level main line.

Another approach was adopted by my old friend Geoff Bigmore –

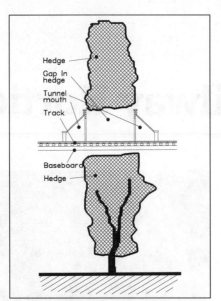

Figure 13.2 *A tall hedge can form a scenic break between a high-level section and the more scenic ground-level part of the line. The line passes through a gap in the hedge and the effect of a tunnel is simulated by a pair of tunnel mouths. These need to be easily removable so that foliage inside the 'tunnel' can be clipped short.*

roses. These too are fast-growing plants, but trimming is largely carried out by the annual pruning. It is therefore a simple matter to do this in late autumn, so that the legs and framing are clear of foliage and can receive their annual maintenance. The cut-back roses should be covered with plastic carrier bags to protect them from the preservative.

I would also suggest that the roses under the baseboards should be regarded as a source of cut flowers for the house. This is as pleasant a way of trimming a hedge as any I know. A screening hedge of taller roses can be left to flower unrestricted, while occasional deadheading will ensure a succession of colourful blooms from mid-June to October. Apart from that and the annual pruning, roses thrive on near

neglect and only need an occasional spray with a combined fertilizer and fungicide.

Pruning

As for pruning, despite all that has been said on the subject, this is largely a matter of cutting the plant back at the end of the growing season in order to encourage new growth. I suspect that much of the mystique surrounding this process arises because rose-lovers consider this one of the more pleasurable parts of rose cultivation, when at the end of a flowering season you look ahead to the following year and apply your craft to shaping the bush as you want it to grow.

There are two schools of thought about pruning: according to one, you do it to encourage stronger growth, according to the other, to shape the plant the way you want it to grow. The first is largely a matter of hacking back and removing dead wood, the second need be no more than cutting off branches which are going the wrong way from your point of view. My wife favours the former, while I prefer the latter, and the garden thrives whichever way it's handled.

Grass

Most garden railways include large areas of grass. Advice on lawn cultivation is readily available; the recommended procedure calls for a good deal of hard work, digging, raking, rolling and seeding the ground. Alternatively you can lay down turf. I've tried both methods – they both work well.

There is a simpler approach. You level the area by scraping the soil from the high points and raking it into the hollows, removing as much of the large stones and other rubbish as your patience will stand. You then leave the levelled ground to its own devices. By late spring you will have a fine crop of weeds, which you behead with a mower (this is why you removed the stones). The weeds will return, you mow them again. After a while, most of the weeds become discouraged and you are left with rough meadow grass and the flat-leaved weeds that afflict all lawns. If these annoy you, apply a lawn weedkiller. If, at the end of the first year, there are any obvious bare patches, scarify with a rake and apply lawn seed liberally. If you carry on mowing for a couple of years, and give the area an occasional application of a combined lawn fertilizer/weedkiller, you end up with a respectable patch of hard-wearing grass.

If anyone has doubts that regular mowing and a little attention can transform an area of rough grass, a visit to Bekonscot will dispel them. There, a large expanse of rough meadow has been turned into a stretch of fine sward. Although this is the end-product of 70 years' work, the majority of the improvement took place over the first five years.

Low-level planting

Whereas with high-level baseboards, any plants are basically below the level of the tracks, ground-level systems have a more intimate association with the flowers and shrubs. Common sense suggests that one should seek out miniature plants to preserve some semblance to scale, but in practice, the mixture of a small scale railway and full-sized shrubs is, on the whole, a happy one.

Before we think about the plants, we should consider the soil in which they are to grow. This is particularly important where the

railway is to run on a raised bed, since here it is on 'made ground'. While in civil engineering parlance this is merely soil excavated elsewhere and dumped in the required location, we have the opportunity to enhance the soil as we fill the raised section.

Improving the soil

For a start, all soil put into a raised bed should be carefully graded to remove not only the stones, but more significantly, roots of persistent weeds such as ground elder and bindweed. The lower part of the bed can be a general mixture of subsoil and topsoil, but the top can be greatly improved by mixing at least 50 per cent organic material into the soil. This can be peat, though concern for wetlands has led to a feeling against this material which, 30 years ago, was highly regarded by the 'back to nature' enthusiasts. There are several substitutes based on bark and fibre, while home-produced compost is an excellent source of humus. A particular favourite of mine is the sawdust and wood chippings produced by my sawbench and power planer. Although this initially lacks the rich brown colour of the commercial product, it rots down over winter and lightens the soil. A slow-acting fertilizer such as bone meal should also be added before planting begins.

It is often suggested that you can alter the acidity of the soil in this fashion. Whilst this is initially possible, within a few years the relatively small 'non-standard' soil leaches out and you are back where you started. There are chemical compounds on the market that can be applied to counteract this, but in general, if you live on a limey or chalky soil, you can't grow heathers or other

acid-loving plants with any degree of success without taking inordinate pains over the process. This of course does not apply to container-grown plants, where the soil is separated from the base ground; but we aren't, in general, building garden railways on plant pots.

Tunnel covers

There is one exception: where a plant pot is placed over a tunnel inspection cover. You need to consider carefully the type of plant you grow in this situation. While a spreading shrub may be fine on a drain cover, where hopefully we will never need to move it, we will be lifting the tunnel cover at least twice a year, at the start and end of the running session. A cheap and colourful annual is a better proposition. A current favourite for this task is impatiens, better known as 'Busy Lizzie', but a good alternative is the nasturtium, which is so easy to grow it could almost be classed as a weed.

Tunnels bring us to another subject, roots. In the main one leaves this to the plant concerned. Provided you start with a suitable soil cover and then give them sufficient water and an occasional dressing of fertilizer, roots look after themselves. Indeed, they have remarkable powers of penetration, and will find their way through minute cracks in concrete or masonry. Therefore, it is advisable not to plant anything with a deep root system over or near a tunnel.

Planting techniques

Although modern nursery techniques provide plants with a proper root system in a small block of compost, making their initial planting much more reliable, it is still necessary to follow a few

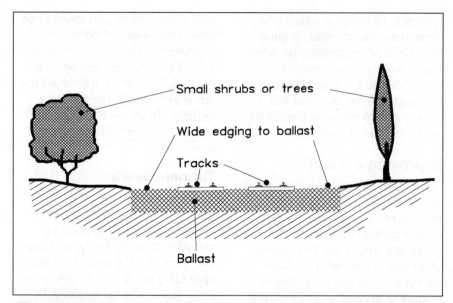

Figure 13.3 *Where tracks are laid at ground level on ballast, it is advisable to have an overscale width of ballast so that the application of weedkiller to the trackbed does not in any way affect the nearby plants. These need to be established far enough from the track so that their eventual growth does not impinge on the loading gauge. This is particularly important where miniature shrubs and trees are concerned, since their beauty lies in their natural shape and would be spoilt were it necessary to carry out lopsided pruning to provide room for the trains.*

simple rules. One is to dig a large enough hole and fill this with water. In dry weather, pouring a bucketful of water onto a quarter square metre before doing more than contemplating planting out is a good idea. An application of liquid fertilizer is also advisable.

The plants should be firmed in with a little compost, and then given more water. Then, for at least a week, the plants should have a good watering every evening, just before dusk or when they are in the shade. If dry weather persists, examine all plants daily and water regularly. A little leaf curl is not cause for alarm, in general all the plant needs is between a quarter and a half litre of water. Regular watering is essential on raised beds because they are more subject to drying out than the base ground.

A question of size

The most important consideration is maintaining a sensible clearance between the trains and any nearby plants (see Figure 13.3). It is important to check the spread of the plant and allow a little margin for error. Today, many suppliers provide neat printed plastic tabs that not only give you some idea of what the plant will look like, but give its approximate height and spread as well. As a general rule, never plant anything closer than 75–100 mm (3–4 in) to the edge of the trackbed, regardless of what the label says.

There are two common groups of garden plants that are well suited to lineside location, heathers and alpines. The former require an acid soil, the latter are much more adaptable and, once established, seem immune to

neglect. Furthermore, unlike heathers, which tend to spread, alpines usually form clumps. An exception is the sedum genus, which spreads almost indefinitely, but provides excellent ground cover.

The smaller-leaved border annuals can be worth looking at, they offer a quick, colourful finish and are generally quite inexpensive. While they can be grown from seed, for the reluctant gardener this is a very hit-and-miss system. Now that plants come in plastic trays with a good root system in a compost block, one can more or less guarantee results.

Alyssum and lobelia are particularly suited for this purpose, providing they can be planted at least 150 mm (6 in) from the trackbed. Another border plant, ideally suited as a finish to a low wall, is aubretia. It is a rampant spreader but, once established, can be savagely hacked back when it threatens to put leaves on the line.

Shrubs and trees

So far I've discussed common plants that are easily found in any part of the country. There are several slow-growing shrubs and trees with small leaves which are natural 'scale models'. Some 40 years ago a specialist horticultural supplier contacted *Railway Modeller* with details of their miniature trees. Although our experiments at indoor cultivation did not bear fruit, I was interested enough to follow this through by purchasing a book on the design and cultivation of sink gardens, *Miniature Gardens*, by Anne Ashberry (C. Arthur Pearson, 1951). It is now out of print and if a successor has been published, I've not chanced across it.

I don't propose to quote the

Shrubs and small trees form an attractive backdrop to Peter Denny's TVLR. The viaduct is a recent replacement of the 40-year-old original. (Photo courtesy Peter Denny)

Miniature trees close to North Bekonscot station.

extensive lists from the book, since many of the plants were extremely small, extremely costly and more suited to the relatively small canvass of a 1 m (3 ft) long sink than the larger expanse of a garden railway. For example, the 'larger' trees were stated to be 18–24 in (400-600 mm) high and dismissed as no more than a short-term fill-in. A 600 mm high tree is not out of proportion on a 7 mm scale system and the three 'large' miniature trees recommended were:

Chamaecyparis Lawsonia Ellwoodii, a slender spire of feathery glaucus foliage. Stated to reach a height of around 16–20 in (400–500 mm) in six to eight years.

Juniperus squamata Meyeri, a beautiful tree of spreading, irregular habit with a grey-green foliage.

Picea albertina conica, a lovely pyramid of pale green, which will in a few years form an excellent conifer.

There are also several grafted varieties which provide a reasonably fast-growing version of a very small tree. A popular genus is the Acers (maple), which unlike the three listed above are deciduous.

Some miniature villages have a small nursery attached, where they propagate miniature plants. They can advise on suitable varieties and in some cases sell you their surplus stock. Specialist nurseries generally provide catalogues, though these will not necessarily be illustrated. A letter to a leading gardening magazine will usually tell you of a supplier in your immediate vicinity. While it is helpful to collect the plants yourself, don't be misled by a small tree in a tiny pot. Even the rapid-growing *Cupressus Lawsonii*, which will quickly top the 10 m (33 ft) mark if not taken in hand, is quite small when you first plant it.

Bonsai techniques have miniaturized this tree at Bekonscot. By planting it in a small pocket of soil, the root system is restricted. If anything, this plant is under scale.

Bonsai

Before we leave miniature trees, we need to consider *Bonsai,* since these are the high-profile miniature tree and one will naturally wonder if the process is of any value to the railway gardener. What I have read on the subject leads me to believe that the process is intended for

More bonsai at Bekonscot. To the bottom left we see the downside of the technique – the tree has died.

indoor use, since part of it involves a deliberate restriction on root growth. This is easy to arrange in a container, but less practical out of doors.

However, Bonsai techniques are applied with considerable success at Bekonscot to produce miniature trees. Only a few of these are as small as the conventional Bonsai tree, since these would be far too small for the setting. What is clear is that these

results are the product of rigorous pruning by experienced gardeners and that the miniaturization has been at the expense of the natural shape of the tree. I would however admit that I am at one with Ms Ashberry, who said she found something repugnant about the whole process.

Advanced techniques

Although I have suggested that you should try to create a trouble-free garden, this does not necessarily rule out some advanced horticulture. You may well consider the possibility of propagating your own plants. Unlike many gardening techniques, propagation is a matter of encouraging a natural process, the only real difficulty being that it does require a controllable environment, a greenhouse or, at the very least, a cold frame and, by its very nature, it will be months before you find out if you are doing it right or wrong. But should you need large quantities of plants, for example, enough miniature conifers to create the effect of an Alpine forest, it is a process that makes sound practical sense.

Just how far you develop the horticultural side of your garden railway must be a personal decision. There is a good deal of work involved, though if the railway toolbox contains a pair of gardening gloves, a pair of secateurs, and a set of border tools – fork, trowel and scarifier – a good deal of the garden maintenance can be combined with work on the permanent way. As I said earlier, where one's partner wants to attend to the business of pruning, weeding and general tidying up, a ground-level garden railway running through an attractive garden not only combines two excellent hobbies, it strengthens a personal relationship as well.

Chapter 14

Ponds and Waterways

For the ground-level garden railway, water is an essential ingredient, since without it the various plants that embellish the scene would wither and die. It is also the main ingredient of the weedkilling spray that is needed to keep the ballast free from intrusive weeds. Another significant contribution is undoubtedly the ornamental pond and all its ramifications.

Ponds

Ponds are a very popular garden feature, so much so that a small industry has grown up to provide the essential equipment, while there are several excellent textbooks providing a mass of information and advice, much of

An elegant bowstring bridge spans part of the extensive lake at Bekonscot.

which is largely irrelevant to the special case where one is using water as part of a scenic model. Furthermore, the excellent commercial fibreglass ponds and plastic pond-liners available are not ideal as scenic accessories to a realistic garden railway. So long as you are content with a small model lake which lies alongside the railway, the fibreglass pond has its points: it is simple, reliable and fairly trouble-free. It would even be possible to carry a viaduct across the water, since the piers can be anchored to the semi-rigid base with a little fibreglass or epoxy resin. The results of these can be quite pleasing, but if you wish to add a model waterway to the garden scene, you need to be prepared for a considerable amount of work.

Clearly, you can't go out and buy one ready-made, but then half

the fun lies in creating the system. As you have already discovered, soil is extremely porous. You can dig a hole, pour in a bucketful of water, go to fetch another and come back to find that the first one has soaked away. Your model waterway requires an impermeable bed.

While plastic liners and fibreglass mouldings make excellent bases for ponds, the only practical base for a purpose-built waterway is cheap and versatile concrete. It can be slightly porous and it may crack if the ground moves, but various sealants are available to deal with these difficulties. Probably the most useful are bituminous paints, which are simply brushed onto the surface to form a thick barrier.

Any risk of cracking can be minimized by applying the concrete over a bed of sand (see Figure 14.1). This must be laid damp so that it will stay put on the sides; the amount of water needed will depend on the type of sand used. The right consistency is reached when it is possible to squeeze a small quantity of sand in the hand and leave the impression of the folds of skin in the sand. Strictly speaking, you need moulding sand to do this properly, but we are not in the business of casting iron or brass.

The skin of concrete needs to be reasonably thick, not less than 30 mm (1¼ in). It will be applied with a pointing trowel, which can also be used to form the interior

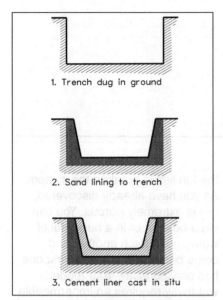

Figure 14.1 The stages in making a concrete waterway. Initially, a trench is dug a good 200 mm (8 in) wider than the proposed channel or lake. This is lined with damp sand, about 50 mm (2 in) thick, and finally the cement channel is cast in situ, the concrete being trowelled into position and smoothed with the trowel and wooden blocks shaped to produce smooth corners.

shape. It is a good idea to introduce reinforcing rods into the concrete. Home-made wooden forming tools will come in handy to form the banks and other features of your waterway.

Providing the flow

A waterway implies a flow. You will need to arrange the system to provide a fall, and you will also need some system for replenishing the headwater. There are plenty of pumps on the market, but, as always, it's not as simple as that. I would suggest that the most suitable approach to providing flowing water is to begin with the pump and its associated equipment. Once you've determined, by trial and error, just how high your pump will deliver

and how fast the flow will be, then, and only then, can you start to plan your watercourse.

Perhaps the most surprising thing is that a comparatively small pump is perfectly adequate for our purposes. It is only where you want to have a very high waterfall that you need to think in terms of a high flow rate; where you are feeding a simple river system you will only need to lift the water a relatively short distance, so the smaller fountain pumps are just about right for the job. The normal garden pump is intended to produce a fountain in a pond. The majority are self-contained units, working on a low voltage fed from a separate transformer. This is advisable, since it is not a good

idea to get mains voltages near water.

Don't be tempted to use the pump from a scrapped washing machine, for not only is it a powerful device, but by the time a modern washing machine reaches the end of its working life, the pump is in pretty poor condition. If you want to experiment with second-hand equipment, take a good look at the little 12v self-contained pumps used in car windscreen washers – they have a very respectable output for a simple waterway.

A further factor to consider is the length and diameter of piping involved. The longer the pipe, the higher the resistance, so good practice keeps all piping as short

It does look as if the members of the Bekonscot Canoe Club enjoy living dangerously, for this scene is just above the highest part of the cascade. There is a very strong flow on this large system, far more than would be needed in the normal garden.

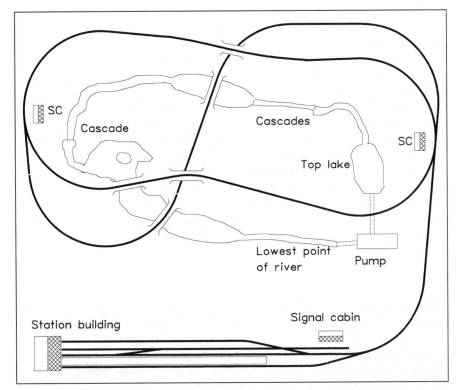

Figure 14.2 A ground-level layout incorporating an extensive waterway. This forms a near-complete circle so that the pipework associated with the pump is kept as short as possible.

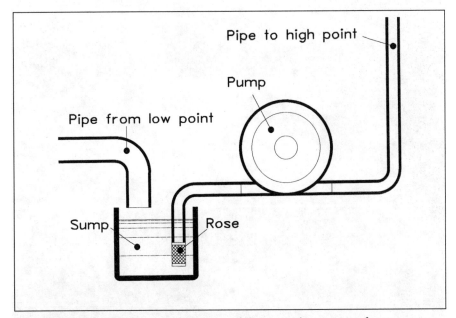

Figure 14.3 Schematic arrangement of the pumping system for a miniature waterway. A large-diameter pipe from the low point of the system discharges water into a large sump. The pump draws water from here through a suction rose and discharges it through a pipe to the summit pond. It may be advisable to provide an overflow to the sump, though this does depend on whether the storm drain is handy.

as possible. This would appear to make it very difficult to arrange a respectable-sized watercourse, since the high point will need to be at least 3 m (10 ft) from the low, and this may well stretch to 10 m (33 ft) in a large garden. In practice the only time this will prove a problem is where the railway is built on a sloping site, since there are two very simple ways of shortening the pump piping.

The best is to lay the model river to a U-shaped plan, like the one shown in Figure 14.2. This immediately doubles the length of the watercourse while reducing the distance the water needs to be moved by the pump. Unfortunately, this isn't always possible, so we place the pump near the high point and take the water from the low point to a sump at the other end through a large-diameter pipe (see

A working watermill is an attractive feature that is not too difficult to arrange on a large-scale model. This overshot wheel at Bekonscot is the most straightforward approach; the undershot pattern requires a very fast flow and would probably fall foul of the scale effect.

Figure 14.3). Again this is a U-shaped system, but up to half of it is in a pipe. While the pump has to lift the water around half a metre, it can do so with the minimum amount of piping. Sink drainpipe is more than adequate for most schemes. As a wide range of sockets and fittings are available for the standard plastic pipe, there is no need to worry if you need to introduce bends in the piping.

The sump

The sump should have a large reserve capacity to take care of any sudden influx of water. It is the place where the majority of debris that falls into the water system finishes up, so we need not only to prevent debris getting into the pump, where it will do no good whatsoever, we also need to be able, from time to time, to scoop out most of the muck.

The standard method of preventing muck getting into a pump is to fit a suction rose. This is usually an enlarged cylindrical chamber drilled with a pattern of small holes, but it can be a tube of fine wire mesh, fitting onto the pipe at one end and provided with a cap at the other.

The sump may be the low-level lake, but it is best where it is a completely separate, utilitarian container close to the pump. Any large plastic container will do, provided the top is open so that you can introduce the necessary pipes and still have room to clean out the bottom. A standard bucket does the job admirably. The suction rose should be lifted at least 20 mm (1 in) from the bottom so that it remains clear of any debris.

At the end of the waterway we need to provide a pipe to take the water to the sump. It is a good idea to place a wire mesh guard in front of this outlet so that the larger

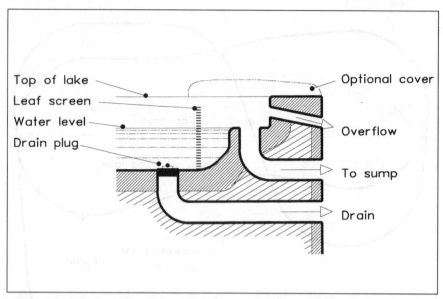

Figure 14.4 At the low end of the system the outlet to the sump should be protected by a wire mesh leaf screen, to keep the larger flotsam from clogging the outlet. To drain the system, a common sink drain socket with its associated rubber plug is simple to arrange and extremely effective. The overflow is not essential, and is only really necessary if the outlet is connected directly to the pump, otherwise the sump acts as an overflow.

A view up part of the cascade at Bekonscot. This only shows part of the total fall, which is spread over a space larger than many complete garden railway systems. You can do a great deal when you have a meadow at your disposal!

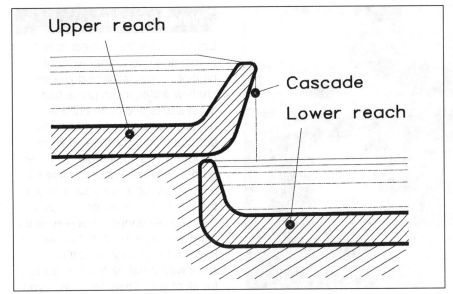

Figure 14.5 Cascades and weirs can be arranged along the waterway to ensure that the entire system does not drain dry when the pump is switched off. They are created by casting the concrete river bed in discrete sections.

bits of flotsam – dead leaves, twigs, etc – do not get into the pipes, let alone into the sump (see Figure 14.4).

Draining the system

It is also advisable to provide some means of draining the system. Probably the most effective is a standard sink drain unit, complete with close-fitting plug, leading to a length of sink drainpipe. You can use the garden hose to refill the system, but topping up during the dry summer months is more conveniently done with a bucket.

Weirs and cascades

A model river with a gentle slope from high to low would appear to be the ideal arrangement. In practice it may prove unsatisfactory since shortly after the pump is switched off, the whole of the water in the system will have drained into the bottom pool. It will probably overflow onto the garden unless the pool has

been made large enough to take the extra water. Far better have the river broken into level sections linked by weirs or cascades, for not only will this mean that the system remains wet at all times, it will also allow it to be divided into discrete units which simplifies the job of casting the river bed (see Figure 14.5).

Bridges

While it is more in accordance with prototype practice for the railway to run alongside the river, it is much more fun to have the railway cross the river at least twice, providing a valid reason for some interesting bridges. Modeller's licence is a wonderful thing. We take it a stage further by planning the railway first and then organizing the river to create the best scenic effect.

Where the waterway crosses a path, or needs to pass across a station, it will usually be best to arrange a culvert – in other words, a length of plastic pipe bedded in cement. It could be possible to

drive a pipe under an existing concrete path, though as this will need to be done at a fairly low level, not only will you need to do a good deal of excavation, but you will probably also find it best to make an inverted siphon by putting a pair of right-angle corner joints at each end of the pipe.

Incorporating boats

One good reason for incorporating water into a garden railway is that it provides an excuse to include rail-served quays and even piers. This in turn brings us to model shipping. Here a note of caution needs to be sounded: ships are very large. A small pleasure steamer in 7 mm scale will be over a metre long, a coastal freighter will be slightly longer, while even the relatively small canal narrowboat is just short of half a metre. As for bulk carriers, forget them.

Unless, of course, you are prepared to fiddle the scales. This would be essential should you wish to provide moving craft on your lake, because even on a large pond there is not room to manoeuvre large-scale craft. Anything above 1:96 scale (⅛ in to the ft) is going to be much too big. Granted this, a moving ring of craft is just about feasible.

The standard practice is to connect the boats to a continuous chain which runs around a series of sprockets fitted at the bottom of the lake. At one corner of the lake a smaller chain links this system to a vertical shaft driven, through reduction gearing, by an electric motor. This is housed in a lakeside building. The main chain is carried on a series of sprockets running in plain bearings on stub axles mounted in the cement base of the lake. It would appear that the readily available bicycle chain and sprockets are perfectly suited for this purpose.

At Swissminatur, the main lake is large enough to allow large models of Swiss lake craft to move around on an endless chain. The model shown is of the Lake Geneva paddleboat, La Suisse.

Water hazards

Before I leave the subject of water, I must add one further word of caution. If you fall face down into shallow water, it can prove fatal. Most adults and older children usually manage to lift themselves out, but a young child – anyone under six – is vulnerable. A water garden is wholly inappropriate for as long as there are youngsters in the family. Much better wait until they are old enough, not only to be experienced enough to handle the hazard, but to help build the waterway. It will be much more fun for all of you. Then, later on, if you have grandchildren to stay, drain the system. It is simply not worth taking the risk.

Chapter 15

Electricity Outdoors

It is very appropriate to follow a chapter on water in the garden with a consideration of electricity supply to a garden railway since the two subjects are linked. It is not true, as some people suggest, that electricity and water do not mix. Regrettably, they do this all too often, with disastrous results. For this reason I must begin by establishing the safe way to provide power to the garden.

Safety in the garden

The most serious situation occurs when high voltages are present in damp, let alone wet, conditions. Although water is an indifferent conductor of electricity and has been used as the main element of some early heavy duty resistances, it is a far better conductor than flesh, leather, cloth and plastic and acts as a very effective bond between any object and earth. We are all familiar with the long-standing British regulations that not only prohibit absolutely a mains-powered socket in a bathroom, but outlaw anything but a cord-operated pull switch in this location. The same conditions of damp and water vapour can also be present out of doors.

The mains supply is capable of pushing out a lot of amps. Normally the current is kept to reasonable limits by the impedance of the load, and an overall limit is set by the fuses. This might appear to be sufficient protection, but unfortunately a fuse

takes an infinitesimal amount of time to heat up to the point where it ruptures. While this appears to happen almost instantaneously, the surge will last long enough to kill you if you happen to be in contact with the live wire and are well earthed, as you will be if you are also in contact with a damp surface.

To a degree, a good pair of shoes with thick rubber or plastic soles will insulate you sufficiently to reduce the shock to your system, provided the uppers are watertight. Wellington boots and dry leather gloves will further increase your personal insulation, which is why road workers handling electrically powered tools normally wear both. Certainly it would make good sense to follow this practice when using power drills and saws on earth, and to postpone such work when the garden is damp after rain. It should be obvious that you do not use mains-powered equipment out of doors when it is raining. Should the extension socket lead look damp, play safe and unplug the lead first.

Residual current devices

Fortunately there is now a reliable, safe and affordable way of minimizing the risk when working with mains equipment out of doors, the residual current device (RCD). This is an extremely sensitive trip that disconnects the circuit should there be a sudden surge and works fast enough to limit the

potential shock to a near negligible degree. It comes in two forms: a plug-in device which is placed in the mains socket before the extension lead or appliance is connected, or a special 13 amp switched socket which incorporates the RCD cutout. Both devices have a test and reset button.

Even with an RCD you should not use faulty or worn equipment, and leads should have their outer casing in good order and the connections to plugs and sockets properly made. Furthermore, all mains-powered devices used in the garden should be of the double insulated pattern. This can be taken for granted with modern DIY power tools, but check for the double square symbol on the equipment rather than taking the presence of a twin-core lead as a guide.

Mains electricity in an outbuilding

The garden shed, garage or outhouse is, as mentioned briefly in Chapter 6, a very suitable place for providing an electrical supply to the garden railway. This is rightly governed by very strict regulations and the following remarks are only a paraphrase intended to indicate what is needed.

For a start, it has long been the practice to have a separate consumer unit (fuse box) in an outbuilding. All outlets in the shed must be taken from this, whilst the supply to the outbuilding has to be from a separate fuse on the main consumer unit. You will need at least two outlets, one rated 5 amp for lighting and one at 15 amp for a twin power socket. This will require a fuse and lead rated at 30 amp. Alternatively, the power supply could form a small ring main, in which case the outlet would be rated at 30 amps and the supply from the house would need to be upgraded to 45 amps. In either case, the shed consumer unit should have a spare outlet.

Taking the supply to the shed

The supply to the outbuilding must either be carried above ground on a straining wire, as shown in Figure 15.1, or taken through a durable conduit. The straining wire is marginally cheaper, but except for a very short span at the side of the house, very unsightly. Where it passes over a path a clearance of over 2 m (6½ ft) is advisable so that there is only a minimal risk of accidental contact.

A low-level conduit need not be taken underground but as it is both stupid and against regulations to fasten it to a fence (which can easily be blown down), it is usual to bury the feed. This immediately introduces the possibility of the conduit coming into accidental contact with a spade whilst someone is digging the garden. A simple solution is to bury the conduit under the path leading to the shed *and to make a note of the approximate route for the benefit of the next householder.* While feeding a cable through a conduit is a straightforward process, this is again a job best left to the experienced professional who will have all the necessary tools needed to handle the pipes. I would once again stress that these

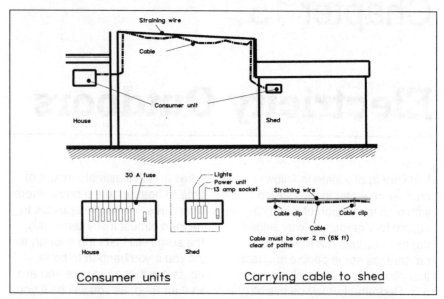

Figure 15.1 The provision of a mains voltage supply to an outbuilding such as a garden shed is governed by strict, but common sense, rules. Where the supply is taken above ground, adequate clearance must be maintained across paths and the cable must be supported on a steel straining wire. This is not a task for any but an experienced electrician.

notes should not be regarded as anything more than a basic specification: the work should be left to an experienced electrician.

Connecting a shed to the mains by means of an extension lead plugged into a convenient socket (via an RCD) is technically possible, provided the lead is not permanently fixed in any fashion. It is then classed as a temporary connection, and bends the regulations to their limit.

Lighting the layout

The provision of proper illumination will allow late evening operating sessions to be carried on through much of the year, weather permitting. There are kits for garden lighting on the market, some of which use low-voltage lamps to eliminate any risks. A wall-mounted mains voltage floodlight is a convenient way of illuminating the nearer operating areas.

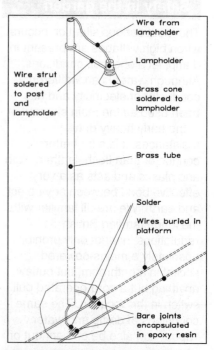

Figure 15.2 A platform lamp based on Ray Tustin's system. The design is strictly utilitarian rather than a scale model. He buried the wires in the concrete platforms and sealed the soldered joints with pitch. Today epoxy resin is a far superior sealant.

Low-voltage layout lighting can be very effective at dusk and after dark. Train lighting is, in the larger scales, most readily arranged through battery power, using yellow LEDs rather than small lamps, since the LED takes less power and only needs a 3v supply. For fixed layout lights it is probably best to operate the standard 12/16v lamps from their own transformer, separate from the main layout supply. While there are good reasons to run the bulbs indoors at a lower voltage to give longer life, for outdoor use I think it will be better to supply them with the full 16v. It is advisable to use screw-in lamps so that there is no difficulty with replacement.

Low-voltage supply

It is something of a relief to turn to the more innocuous, but so far as we are concerned, much more important, matter of low-voltage supply. Model railway low-voltage supplies are provided by double wound transformers coupled to bridge rectifiers where appropriate. A modern transformer is a very robust unit, but like most electrical equipment, does not take kindly to being doused with water. Therefore the transformers must be housed inside a weatherproof building, which is why most electrically operated garden railways have their base in a shed or garage.

Outdoor low-voltage wiring

Even where the main station is also housed in the shed, it will be necessary to take a 12v dc or 16v ac supply out into the garden, often for some considerable distance. We immediately encounter the problem of voltage drop. On a garden railway, where

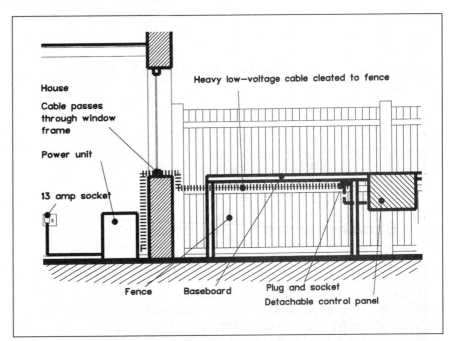

Figure 15.3 Low-voltage supply to the layout does not need to follow the stringent rules that apply to mains voltage wiring. The most important point to observe is that the transformers should be in a weatherproof outbuilding or, as shown here, inside the house. The power leads to the layout have to be of large cross-section to minimize voltage drop, while all but the simplest of external control panels should be removable and connected to the layout wiring through multi-pin plugs and sockets.

The control cables on John Anning's layout can be seen looped below the Dexion angle supporting the trackbase. The multi-pin plugs and sockets connecting the signals are also visible.

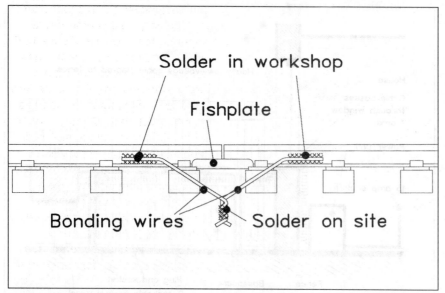

Figure 15.4 *It is not possible to rely on the fishplates or rail joiners to provide electrical continuity out of doors and all rail joints must be bonded. These bonds also form a convenient place to attach feed wires, since the job is well within the capacity of a low-powered rechargeable electric soldering iron, which is a much more convenient tool for outdoor use as there is no long trailing lead involved.*

a feed point can be well over 15 m (49 ft) from the power supply, the resistance of the wire needs to be taken into account. Remember, we are only starting with 12v, and many locomotives begin to falter at anything below 6v, so we don't have a great deal to play with.

There is a straightforward solution – use heavier wire. The most useful comes in the form of the heavy duty single wires used in mains voltage conduit wiring. These wires are not normally available from DIY sources, but can be ordered through electrical retailers and are available in three colours, red, black and green/yellow. It is of course equally possible to use standard two-core+earth mains cable, but I do not like the thought of using what is, to most people, mains supply cable for low-voltage supplies. It is all too easy to get the two mixed up, with lethal consequences. However, the external sheathing is

readily removed by holding one end of the bare earth wire in a substantial pair of pliers, grasping the other leads in the spare hand and pulling. You get a length of red and blue cable and a good supply of bare copper wire, which has many uses around a garden railway.

Bonding the track

Voltage drop over long outdoor tracks is another problem, for the rail joiners will rapidly acquire an inner oxide film that does no good to electrical continuity. The solution is to bond every rail joint at the outset, in the manner shown in Figure 15.4. Normally this involves soldering a length of wire across the joint. For outdoor use it is better to solder a short length of bare copper wire at each end of a length of track before laying. The two ends are then twisted together on site and this smaller joint is

more readily soldered under outdoor conditions.

Ground-level wiring

With high-level baseboards the wiring is carried underneath the boards in much the same way as on indoor lines. With ground-level systems, something else is needed. A popular method is to carry the wires through buried plastic tubes. It has been suggested that these could be buried under the concrete foundations for the track, but since we are unlikely to be using a large fork or spade close to the layout proper, it is safe to bury them alongside the track. There are two points to note here. First of all, there needs to be plenty of spare room inside the tube so that an extra wire can be inserted. Equally important, the tube needs to be laid on a slight slope so that water will not accumulate inside.

In Figure 15.5 I show an alternative system I saw some 45 years ago at Bekonscot, which is

Track supplies at Bekonscot are now carried through buried conduit – in other words, plastic pipes. Very heavy wires are used because of the size of the system.

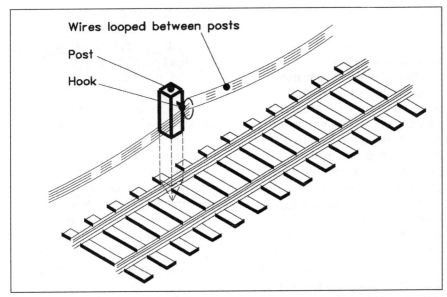

Figure 15.5 *On a ground-level layout, low-voltage wires can be carried alongside the tracks on small posts.*

in turn a close copy of the method employed on the prototype. Hardwood posts about 10 mm (0.4 in) square are driven into the ground beside the railway to stand some 50–75 mm (2–3 in) proud of the ground. One, two or three small hooks are screwed into the post, and the wires are then draped along the hooks. They need tying together as cables, for which use the proprietary plastic garden tie, which is easy to fit, very neat and should last as long as the insulation on the cables, and so is probably worth the extra expense.

Outdoor control panels

When the main station is under cover the control panel is likewise free from the ravages of the weather. Exposed stations will likewise have exposed control panels. Unfortunately their mainstay, the panel mounting miniature toggle switch, is not designed for such arduous duty. The toggle, whilst a close fit in its sleeve, is not by any stretch of the

imagination watertight, and any leakage into the contact chamber will inevitably create all sorts of problems. This will be even more marked with the sub-miniature toggle switch which is so popular today.

The only commercial switch that I can positively state will be suited for continuous exposure is the miniature tumbler pattern switch, often called the 'doll's house switch', since its main function today is for lighting circuits in dolls' houses. At one time it was the easiest of low-voltage switches to find, since it formed a staple feature of Woolworth's electrical counters in the good old days when their goods were sold unpackaged from open-topped counters. With this type of switch one gains access to the contacts by unscrewing the cover, allowing any oxide film to be removed by a gentle scrubbing with an emery board. Today it is a very specialized product and not only takes some tracking down, but is correspondingly more costly than the few pence charged some 30 years ago. I would imagine that semi-rotary wafer switches, with their wiping action, would also stand up to exposure out of doors,

but have never put this to the test.

The very basic home-made wiper switch shown in Figure 15.6, which requires a couple of brass round-head screws, a length of brass strip and possibly some form of knob if you want to be posh, is probably the best all-round pattern, all-weather low-voltage switch. It isn't exactly elegant, but it works.

A simpler solution is to connect the control panel to the layout through one or more multi-pin plugs and sockets. Unfortunately the current favourites, the D pattern plugs and sockets produced primarily for computers and similar electronic devices, are not truly weatherproof. Computers don't like having liquids spilt on them and so no-one bothers to make anything watertight. The DIN-type plugs and sockets, closely associated with audio equipment, are more robust and should give a good life out of

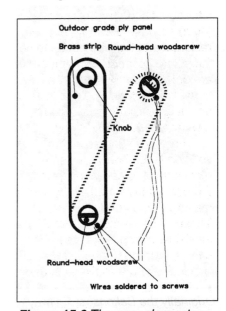

Figure 15.6 *The very elementary switch shown here is one of the few types which can be left permanently out of doors. Although the scraping action tends to keep everything clean, an occasional rub with abrasive paper will maintain good contact.*

doors, but are limited to a maximum of 9 pins. Another possible unit is the SCART plug used for connecting video recorders to TV sets or monitors.

The best arrangement for outdoor control is the hand-held controller, which can be plugged into a 5-DIN socket. While this system is associated with electronic controllers, there is no reason why the old resistance control should not be used in this way if a non-standard voltage is chosen.

Motive power

We now arrive belatedly at the reason for all this equipment, the locomotives themselves. Most standard gauge 7 mm scale models today are powered by electric motors, whether the prototype is moved by steam, electricity or diesel. A high

Originally the Bekonscot Railway was electrified with centre third, the standard arrangement when the line was first conceived. Now converted to two-rail, remnants of the third rail can be seen passing through a pipe tunnel. These remain because of the difficulties of removing track from such a site.

proportion of Gauge 1 models are similarly powered and many narrow gauge workers also find electric traction the most convenient method available.

It has been established for some 40 years that satisfactory pickup can be obtained on an outdoor line at the standard 12v input and that the most serious problems centre around the old problem of voltage drop over long sections, which was covered earlier in this chapter. It goes without saying that both track and wheels need to be kept clean at all times if pickup is to be reliable, but this is an equally big problem with large indoor layouts.

Raising track voltage

One way of minimizing the effects of voltage drop and pickup problems is to use a higher line voltage with standard 12v motors. This depends on intelligent use of the controllers, which are rarely, if ever, set to full power. The object is to adjust the setting so that the locomotive receives something between 8v and 12v after the various losses through the track and, in particular, the pickups. If we take a case where the pickup accounts for 6v, then by absorbing another 8v in the controller, the locomotive is working at around 10v. If a further 2v are lost on a long section, the controller is turned up slightly to compensate. This technique is, in energy terms, grossly inefficient since it assumes that over half the power output is dissipated in resistances in one way or another.

With a high line voltage, resistance control is normally used. Clearly standard electronic controls cannot be used, but purpose-built thyristor units are feasible since these can be readily obtained for use on higher voltages. On the electronic side, it

should be possible to fit an electronic voltage limiter into the locomotive so that no matter what the input might be from the pickups, the motor cannot get more than 12v.

The use of 24v motors is another possibility. At one time suitable motors were readily available on the surplus market, but although such items occasionally surface at exhibitions, the supply is erratic. Where diesel or electric locomotives are used, the motor bogies can be wired in series to allow a 24v line supply to power two identical 12v motors.

The virtues of stud contact

Today, two-rail traction is almost universal for OO gauge, the only exception being the HO gauge Märklin stud contact system. Most new construction in O gauge is also two-rail, but in Gauge 1 the Märklin models are stud contact. The immediate advantage of stud contact was that it allowed three-rail locomotives to be readily converted and, in the case of commercial O gauge models, continue to pick up from a centre third rail. This was also the case where centre rails were used on 16.5 mm gauge, hence it was adopted by Märklin to keep a continuity with their pre-war and immediate post-war production. Their system uses very closely spaced studs.

Several of my friends not only use stud contact on their garden railways, they consider it to be superior to two-rail. For a start, as all locomotive wheels make the return connection to the tracks, and the skate tends to rub the top of the studs clean, the system has much greater inherent reliability. Even more to the point, should you wish to operate live steam locomotives, stud contact allows you to avoid two inherent hazards.

The first arises because model steam locomotives spew oil all over themselves and anything else in the near vicinity. A lot of this oil ends up on the rails and rapidly produces gunge, the biggest enemy of two-rail operation. Stud contact is less vulnerable to this hazard.

The second problem lies in the steam locomotive itself. Every method of insulating wheels currently in use will break down if raised to a high temperature and, in the process, ruin the wheels. While the normal operating temperature does not approach the danger point, there is the ever-present risk of fire due to spilt fuel. This is bad enough with any steam locomotive, as the locomotive will almost certainly require a repaint. If the insulation of the wheels is also damaged, a complete reconstruction will be called for. So, with live steam, two-rail is a risky business.

The principle of stud contact is simple, and is demonstrated in Figures 15.7-15.9. The locomotive is equipped with a long skate, carried from a central insulating block by a pair of links, which form a parallelogram and so allow the skate to move up and down whilst remaining virtually level. The current is picked up from a series of studs set along the centre line of the track, connected by a wire under the sleepers. At pointwork, the studs rise by small increments to carry the skate clear over the rails. At least one worker recommends that wherever possible two skates should be fitted.

Initially, the connecting wire was soldered to the studs, but it was soon realized that if a thick-headed stud was driven down onto a wire looped around its shank, the

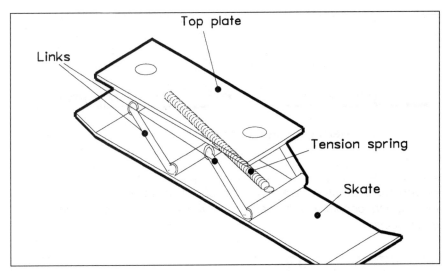

Figure 15.7 *An isometric view of a typical parallelogram stud contact shoe. The skate, made from heavy brass strip, is kept in contact with the studs partly by its own weight but mainly by a tension spring. The unit is fixed to an insulated cross member on the chassis and, except on close inspection, is out of sight.*

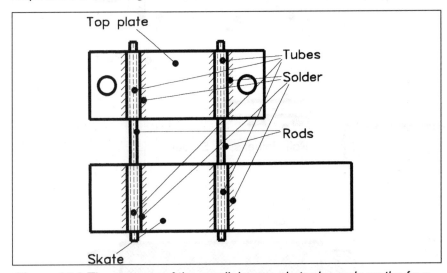

Figure 15.8 *The success of the parallelogram skate depends on the four tubes being accurately aligned. A straightforward approach is to align top and bottom parts with lengths of straight rod when soldering.*

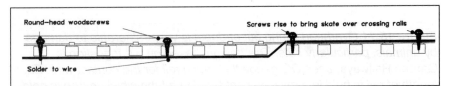

Figure 15.9 *Conventional stud contact supply is through a series of contacts fixed along the centre line of the track. Small round-headed woodscrews are commonly used, connected by a length of bare copper wire which is soldered to each screw. The studs rise at points and crossings to carry the skate clear of the rails.*

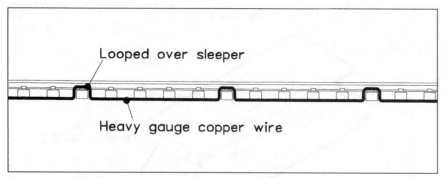

Figure 15.10 On plain track, stud contact pickup is very easily arranged by looping bare copper wire over and under the sleepers, as shown in this cross-section.

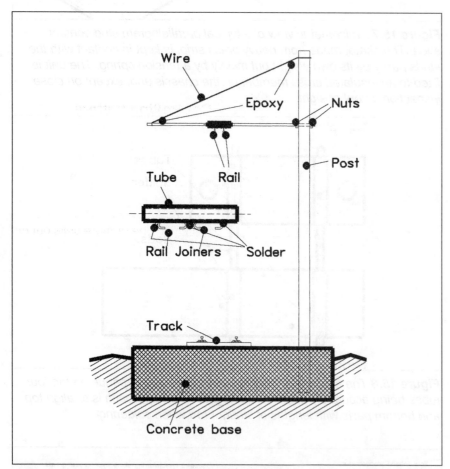

Figure 15.11 Overhead wiring out of doors is very vulnerable to damage by animals, particularly cats. This design, based on a suggestion in Garden Railways, *uses OO gauge flatbottom rail for the contact wire. Each length of rail is held in a rail joiner soldered to a tube which in turn is held on the support rod with epoxy resin. The rod passes through a hole drilled in the upright rod and secured by a pair of nuts. The tension wire is secured to the support rod and post with more epoxy resin. The idea is that when a cat jumps on the overhead, the rail is only pulled out of the rail joiners and can be readily replaced.*

connection was quite satisfactory. In another arrangement, shown in Figure 15.10, a heavy gauge bare copper wire is threaded over and under the sleepers. This system would be particularly suitable for ready-to-lay plastic-sleepered track. A suitable wire can be ripped out of twin+earth flat mains cable. This will leave a pair of heavy duty red and black insulated wires for track feeds and returns.

Overhead electrification

Overhead electrification has been used out of doors with some success. Indeed, where the layout is 100 per cent electric traction one can use the catenary for its proper purpose. Mixing overhead and two-rail wiring can get very complicated, and reverse loops or triangles are ruled out of court. Since one virtue of the garden layout is that you have ample room for these useful track formations, this is a serious consideration. Of course, overhead traction used in conjunction with a stud contact system imposes no such restrictions.

One serious difficulty with outdoor overhead is that you need a large amount of bare brass or bronze wire. Outdoor overhead needs to be robust rather than true to scale, because it faces numerous hazards. Leaving aside the risk of damage from overscale feet (one should be more careful), and ignoring the fact that it will be the perfect perch for garden birds (they weigh very little), there is the ever-present fact of the neighbour's cat, which is only too likely to launch itself off the fence onto your main line. Figure 15.11 suggests one way of dealing with the problem.

Battery-powered traction

Another option for outdoor electrification, which eliminates

These tiny battery-powered diesel locomotives on James Slater's SM32 garden railway began life as toys. British 32 mm gauge practice still harks back to its low-cost origins. (Photo courtesy Railway Modeller*)*

steps.

However, where self-contained power supplies are involved, there is no need to use the standard 12v. Several firms at the larger model railway exhibitions can be found offering pattern motors for 6v and less. These are almost always cheaper than similar 12v motors sold by the same concern because of their non-standard nature. The larger types are powerful enough for large-scale locomotives. Indeed, the very small 1.5v and 3v motors usually regarded as only fit for toys have a very considerable potential when applied to small railcars and such fun items as working permanent way tractors.

Controlling battery-powered locomotives

Speed control of a battery locomotive has to be mounted on the locomotive. The simplest arrangement is to fit a small rotary switch to reduce the line voltage by cutting one or more cells out of the circuit. While this will usually

many of the problems mentioned in this chapter, is battery power. The wide availability of rechargeable ni-cad cells has made it possible to fit most locomotives with their own power supply. There could be some difficulty with OO gauge locomotives, for although there are now some very small ni-cad batteries on the market, their power output is also small. A battery-filled bogie van semi-permanently coupled to the locomotive seems the most satisfactory solution. O gauge and upwards presents few problems since in addition to the standard batteries there are several types of high-output batteries intended for model boats and similar installations.

A ni-cad cell delivers 1.3v as against the disposable unit's 1.5v. Eight cells in series will only develop 10.4v, so you will need nine cells to get anything like the full output. However, most 12v locomotives run at around 10v anyway, and as the lower output of

the ni-cad is rarely mentioned, many enthusiasts have been perfectly happy with an eight-cell battery. Speed control is generally arranged by means of a small rotary switch which allows the motor voltage to be varied by 1.3v

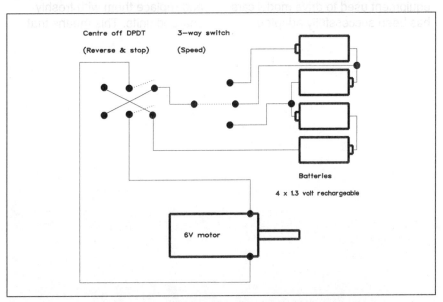

Figure 15.12 Schematic wiring diagram of a 6v battery-powered locomotive. Crude but highly effective speed control is achieved by switching out individual cells in the battery, while forward, reverse and stop control is through a centre off DPDT switch.

only provide three or four speed settings, it is in practice sufficient for most purposes. A sub-miniature centre-off DPDT switch provides stop-start and reversing control (see Figure 15.12).

Much more to the point, battery locomotives are best geared down so that, even at full voltage, the actual speed is low. Provided the operator can easily outpace the train, it is quite easy to reach into the cab and adjust the controls. I have had experience of this on Peter Denny's Trepolpen Valley Light Railway and can vouch for its convenience.

Of course, it is possible to arrange microswitches under the locomotive which are actuated by lineside ramps which can be lifted or lowered. This is the direct descendant of the old clockwork trip switch and is much more reliable than its mechanical predecessor, but it cannot be more than a means for bringing a train to a halt and restarting it.

Radio control is the ultimate in battery power control. The standard equipment used to drive model cars has been successfully adapted for this purpose, the steering mechanism being employed to actuate the reversing switch. This arrangement is growing in popularity, the more so because it is operationally compatible with radio-controlled steam.

Recharging batteries

Battery locomotives are the modern equivalent of clockwork drive. They share the same tremendous advantage for the outdoor worker, that there is no need to burnish the railhead before each operating session. The main disadvantage is the need to recharge batteries at regular intervals. There are two approaches to this. One is to recharge the locomotive whilst it stands on a special length of track or, alternatively, by plugging a lead from the charger into a biased socket on the locomotive. A 3.5 mm jack and plug is the most suitable fitting for this purpose.

The other is to arrange the battery compartment so that it is easy to remove the individual cells and replace them with freshly charged units. This means that you will need at least two complete spare sets of batteries, but it does obviate the chance of an operating session coming to an abrupt stop because all the batteries have been exhausted.

It is a good idea to run ni-cad batteries down completely before recharging. It is claimed there is a 'memory' effect, so that if a battery is given a half charge, it will only accept this charge thereafter. With a large number of cells, it would make good sense not only to number each cell, but to keep a record of charging and use in a small notebook. I would suggest that the individual cells have an alphabetical marker for the group, and that each cell in the group has a number, i.e. cell A1, A2 ... A7, A8. This will enable you to keep track of several dozen near-identical units. At the very least, you must establish a charging routine to ensure that you can operate as and when you wish.

After all this, I get a nostalgic feeling for good old reliable clockwork. It is a great pity it is no longer readily available.

Chapter 16

Steam Power

One of the great attractions of the garden railway is its suitability for steam power. This is not to say that small-scale live steam is incompatible with indoor operation, but it does require a large, well-ventilated room if the fumes are not to become oppressive. The Gauge 1 Association's evening sessions at the MRC's clubrooms at Keen House were not known as 'fumigation night' without reason. In the garden, the balmiest of breezes soon disperses the products of combustion, whilst any risk of fire is greatly diminished.

It is only possible to cover the main points of live steam in a single chapter. Several books have been written on the subject and many pages in *Model Engineer* and *GardenRail* are devoted to the design, construction and operation of miniature live steam locomotives.

The Mamod steam locomotive was an influential force in the revival of small-scale live steam in Britain. Although low-powered and of limited capacity, it was an affordable entry-level machine, though like all direct drive oscillators, it had two speeds, flat out and stop. Unlike earlier locomotives of this type, it was well engineered, while the use of solid fuel tablets which burned out before the boiler was more than half emptied made it far safer than its older counterparts.

Safety first

While live steam operation is great fun, it should not be treated lightly. There are two very real areas of high risk. The first we have already mentioned, fire. Apart from in the very rare coal-burning locomotive, the fuels employed are not merely highly flammable but, being either a liquid (methylated spirit) or a gas (butane), are subject to spillage. Common sense precautions, such as never refuelling a locomotive with its burner lit, and keeping the fuel containers in a metal box which, in case of fire, can be

readily smothered, greatly reduce the risk. Simple fire-fighting equipment such as a bucket of water and a fire-resistant smothering blanket is normally more than adequate; indeed, proprietary extinguishers which, whilst extremely effective, have a limited shelf life, can prove an illusory safeguard since in practice a serious fire is extremely rare. The water bucket has a separate use, since the best cure for a minor burn is to plunge the affected part into cold water as quickly as possible.

A first-aid kit and some instruction on the treatment of burns is advisable, as is adequate insurance cover. Most personal injury policies have exclusion clauses and it is as well, both when taking one out or when renewing an existing policy, to point out, in writing, that you operate live steam models. Where the line is open to visitors, third party cover is essential.

Although fire is a common hazard, one experienced live steam operator has said, in print, that the loss of eyebrows is only to

The Roundhouse 0-4-0 saddle tank Billy, *available for both 32 and 45 mm gauge. Based on typical 2 ft gauge industrial practice, with internal gas firing, modified Walschaerts gear and optional radio control, it is a good beginner's machine. (Roundhouse)*

be expected! The major danger comes from a boiler explosion. Mercifully these are extremely rare, but this is due to the fact that, at present, live steam is largely confined to enthusiasts with a leaning towards model engineering who tend to work in association with older, more experienced modellers. The current promotion of live steam carries the risk that less cautious individuals will come to own and operate them.

I do not wish to appear

The Roundhouse live steam model of the original Lynton & Barnstaple 2-6-2 tanks, available for both 32 and 45 mm gauges, though it is only true to scale for the former gauge. (Roundhouse)

alarmist, but anyone with wide knowledge of live steam modelling practice knows of examples where someone has taken unnecessary risks. Although the usual working pressure, around 50 psi, is low by modern standards, it is that used on the first 'high pressure' steam engines of the early 19th century, when it was regarded, with good cause, as extremely dangerous. Unfortunately, the overall level of technology of the usual modelmaking (as opposed to model engineering) workshop is, apart from the introduction of electric motors for certain tools, on a par with the best practice of that period.

Boiler testing

Boilers must have an initial hydraulic test to twice the working pressure, and this test should be repeated at regular intervals while the boiler is in regular use and before it is steamed after a lengthy period of disuse. The test is quite simple, but requires a special rig incorporating a powerful hand pump and a large, accurate pressure gauge. Model engineering societies and other groups catering for live steam operation have this equipment and it can be made available, together with experienced assistance, to any member.

Tests are not carried out using steam for a very simple reason. Water is incompressible, therefore if a hydraulic test reveals a flaw, the pressure drops almost immediately after the casing ruptures. Generally there is no more than a crack that weeps a little water. Steam is a gas and is compressible, so if there is a failure you get an explosion. Agreed, a small model locomotive boiler will not create a very big bang, but it is sufficient to cause damage and, in the not improbable situation where someone has his or her head close to the boiler at the moment of disaster, serious injury or even death cannot be ruled out.

The gas containers for butane firing also need a hydraulic test. The Gauge 1 Model Railway Association, whose members have considerable experience with this form of firing, recommends that they should be tested to 250 psi, considerably more than the requirements for a boiler. This is because the pressure of butane gas rises very abruptly when heated, and anything on a live steam locomotive does get hot. The Association also warns against the practice of using a mixture of propane and butane, as well as the use of propane itself. This gas is even more sensitive to heat.

Despite all I have said, the risk of injury from live steam models is low – less than the risk you run when you cross a busy road. But just as one reduces the risk of being hit by a motor vehicle by observing a set of rigorous rules, so one needs to exercise the same degree of prudence when operating a device which is both hot enough in places to cause second-degree burns and contains gases at high pressures.

Simple steam locomotives

The simplest live steam locomotives employ a pot boiler and oscillating cylinders (Figures 16.1 and 16.2). The best-known example today is the Mamod, which is unusual in its class in that it can pull the skin off a rice pudding. Most of its predecessors had difficulty in moving themselves, let alone hauling a train. Although the boiler is

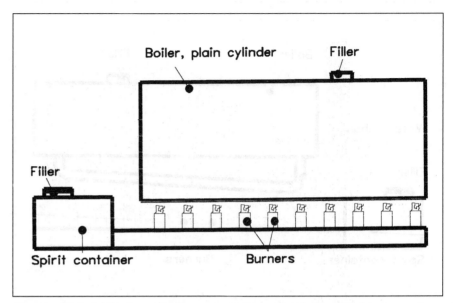

Figure 16.1 *A simple pot boiler, externally heated by a spirit burner and used on 'toy' steam engines. Baffles are essential for outdoor use. Steam pipes and safety valves are omitted for simplicity.*

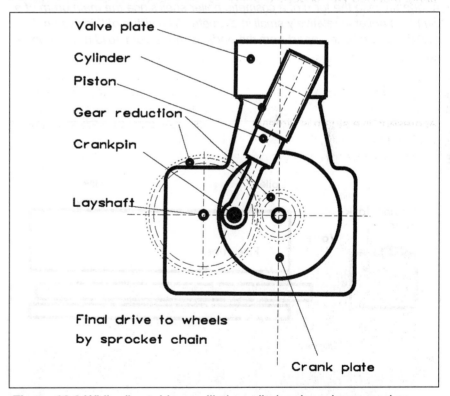

Figure 16.2 *While direct drive oscillating cylinders have been used on simple steam locomotives, this type of prime mover works best at high speeds. By interposing gearing the performance is enhanced. This type of drive is available under the trade name Osmotor. In conjunction with a purchased boiler and lubricator, the Osmotor allows an experienced modeller to build his own steam locomotive without the need for an extensive workshop.*

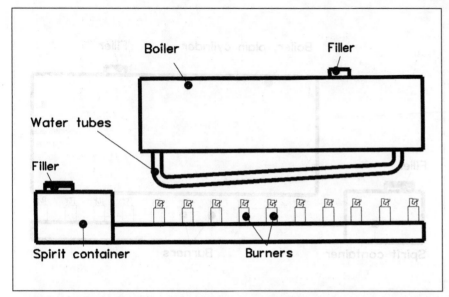

Figure 16.3 The Smithies pattern boiler is a development of the pot boiler, the addition of water tubes under the boiler but inside the flame area of the burner increasing the steaming capacity. Baffles are still needed; these frequently take the form of a cosmetic boiler shell since the main drum of a Smithies boiler is relatively small in diameter. The virtue of this system is that the entire boiler, apart from the ends, is made from solid drawn copper pipe.

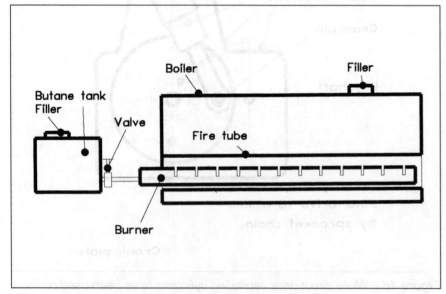

Figure 16.4 The internally fired, single-flue boiler is a modern development which utilizes the flexibility of the gas burner. As the flame is totally enclosed, steam raising is good, while the larger size of the flue simplifies construction.

inefficient, it does produce enough steam, though the main problem with all small oscillating engines is that they prefer to run at high speeds and really need a flywheel to help them get over the dead centres. The most successful small-scale oscillating cylinder locomotives follow the basic design of the full-size Sentinel road and rail units, the drive being taken through reduction gearing to the wheels.

Types of boilers

Most modern model steam locomotives have internally fired boilers and double-acting cylinders. The design of small boilers has been greatly improved by gas firing, since this allows the burner to be inserted in a large boiler tube, ensuring that as much of the heat as possible is used for raising steam. Spirit firing usually employs the Smithies boiler (see Figure 16.3), a very simple form of water-tube boiler with a large header, which is more effective than the simple pot boiler employed on the earliest small-scale steam locomotives.

A 'proper' locomotive pattern fire tube boiler with a coal-fired firebox is certainly practicable in Gauge 1, and many such models have been seen in operation at exhibitions. Coal firing is more demanding than gas or spirit and is generally accepted as being better suited to the larger scales used for passenger-carrying railways. This I suspect is as much due to the fact that it is not merely easier to fire a solid fuel locomotive when sitting behind it on a carrying truck, it is infinitely more fun as well. I will have more to say about this in the final chapter.

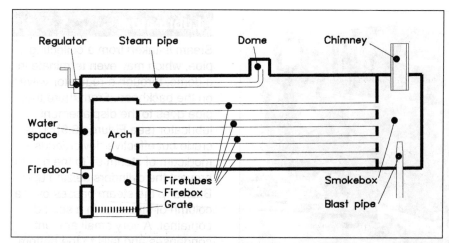

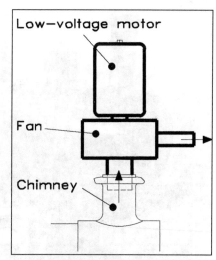

Figure 16.5 *Small-scale water tube boilers for coal firing are well established in model engineering circles. Although doubts have been expressed as to their suitability for small-scale models, they are routinely used in Gauge 1 and have even been found in Gauge O. Their main handicap lies in the need for frequent stoking, disposal of ash and, above all, the problems of raising steam.*

Figure 16.6 *In order to get a good draught on a model fire tube locomotive boiler, it is necessary to fit a blower to the chimney. This consists of a small low-voltage electric extractor fan which sits in the chimney.*

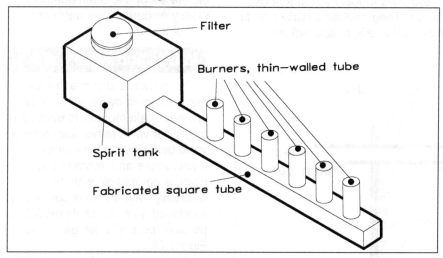

Figure 16.7 *Isometric sketch of a spirit burner for a pot or Smithies boiler. Construction in tin plate or sheet brass is well within the capacity of a simple modelmaker's workshop. The only part which might present difficulty is the screw-top filler, but this is frequently improvised from a pipe fitting. A small hole is needed in the cap to prevent air lock.*

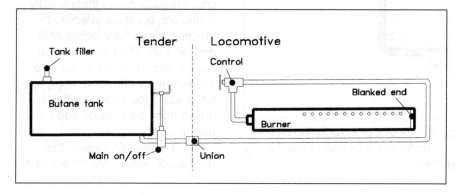

Figure 16.8 *Dick Moger's arrangement for butane firing, where the gas is pre-heated before combustion. Because of the high pressures involved, butane burners are not so simple to make as the spirit burner. All joints need to be silver-soldered or brazed and a well-equipped workshop and a good deal of experience are necessary.*

Argyle is a model of one of the two 0-6-2 locomotives built by Andrew Barclay & Sons for the Campbeltown & Machrihanish Light Railway, the only narrow gauge public railway in Scotland. This model by Roundhouse is, like their standard range, provided with gas firing, modified Walschaerts gear and optional radio control, and can be built to either 32 or 45 mm gauge. (Roundhouse)

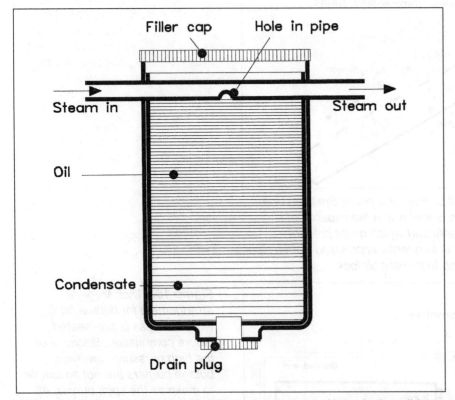

***Figure 16.9** The displacement lubricator is a means of introducing oil into the steam flow to lubricate the cylinders. Mechanical lubricators are the province of the large-scale steam locomotive.*

Lubricators

Steam is taken from a collecting pipe, which may even terminate in a dome, through a regulator valve on the backhead. From there the pipe goes to the displacement lubricator (see Figure 16.9). This crude but effective device adds a modicum of steam oil to the gas to prevent the cylinders seizing up. Basically, the steam passes over a column of steam oil in a sealed container. A very small amount condenses and falls to the bottom of the container, displacing a tiny amount of oil which is carried into the cylinders. The lubricator is provided with a screwed plug top and bottom, the first to fill it with oil, the second to drain out the messy mixture of oily water at the end of the run.

Valves and valve gears

At the cylinders steam entry and exit is effected by the valve. This, in small-scale models, is frequently a cylinder valve rather than a slide valve because it is simpler to manufacture and, more to the point, is compatible with the reversing valve which is commonly employed on small-scale models in place of 'proper' valve gear (see Figure 16.10).

The reversing valve operates by swapping the connections between the valve chamber inlet and outlet ports and the steam and exhaust pipes. It can also function as a crude regulator. It is theoretically inefficient, but quite effective in practice, since the niceties of lap and lead and the virtues of early cut-off, vital in full-sized practice, are extremely difficult to apply to a small-scale locomotive which is driven from the lineside and not from the cab.

With a reversing valve, the distribution valves are driven by a

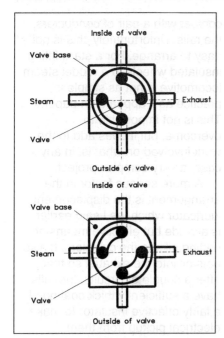

Figure 16.10 *The reversing valve operates by swapping over entry and exit ports to the cylinder. It is the only way an oscillating engine can be reversed and is additionally widely used on low-priced locomotives with double-acting cylinders.*

simple return crank, in the case of outside cylinders, or from fixed eccentrics. Alternatively, the valves

can be driven by a slip eccentric (see Figure 16.11). Here the sheave is free to rotate on the driving axle, but constrained by a simple stop to a 180˚ movement. Slip eccentric-driven locomotives need an initial push in the right direction; this is generally done when the regulator is opened.

Although full Stephenson (see Figure 16.12) or Walschaerts (Figures 16.13 and 16.14) valve gear is more generally associated with 2½ in gauge and upward, it has been used on 7 mm (1:43) scale steam models. However, where valve motion is fitted to a small-scale locomotive, many designers adopt Hackworth gear (Figure 16.15), which is less complicated though in theory less efficient. In practice the difference is negligible, since the difference in valve movement on a full-sized locomotive would amount to less than 10 mm (⅜ in) at the crucial point. While this is very significant at this size, when scaled down it is less than the inevitable slop in working valve motion.

The main reason the small-scale locomotive is generally equipped with a very simple valve gear, offering no opportunity for

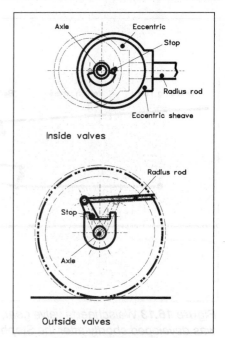

Figure 16.11 *The slip eccentric is the simplest form of true valve gear. The eccentric sheave is free to rotate half a revolution on the main shaft, being restrained by a pin in the shaft. It needs to be pushed to change direction and is mainly confined to models, though the Webb compounds also used this gear on the centre low-pressure engine. The lower diagram shows how a return crank on an outside-cylindered locomotive can be made to function in a similar way.*

varying the cut-off to the cylinders, is that until comparatively recently, small-scale steam locomotives were uncontrolled. They were set going and allowed to run as they would until stopped by extremely crude methods. The most sophisticated of these was an additional cut-out valve which had an operating stalk projecting well above the highest point on the locomotive, but which was short enough to clear any signal gantries, bridges, footbridges and tunnels on the layout. The train could then be brought to a halt by

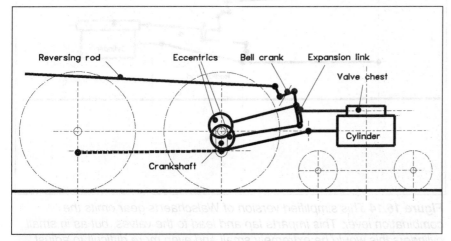

Figure 16.12 *Stephenson valve gear requires two eccentrics off the main shaft. This can be a squeeze even in full size, and it is generally reckoned that its use on inside-cylindered locomotives is limited to the larger scales.*

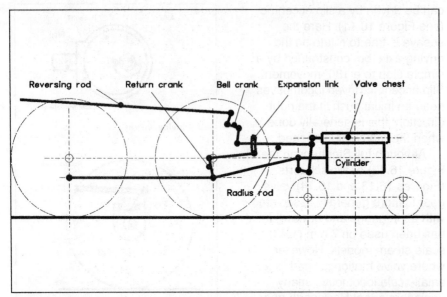

Figure 16.13 Walschaerts valve gear, while regarded as a modern device, was developed shortly after the Stephenson gear. Although normally seen outside the locomotive on three-cylindered machines and on all GWR four-cylindered engines, inside Walschaerts was used extensively.

holding a stick above the track. You could also use your hand, but this was apt to be painful.

Control of steam locomotives

Victor B. Harrison developed a control trailer which incorporated a governor mechanism which opened or closed the regulator through a hydraulic linkage to maintain a more or less constant speed, making it feasible to run steam over an undulating track and improving the overall effect. This was usually fitted into a bogie van.

While various arrangements of lineside trips and contacts have been tried, they were rarely reliable enough to permit effective operation. Remember, a mechanism with a 90 per cent reliability will ensure that one in ten trains runs into the buffers at full speed. True control of small-scale live steam came with radio control.

Many years ago colleagues in

the R/C field asked why we went to all this trouble when the locomotive was in permanent

contact with a pair of conductors, the rails. Unfortunately, this is not easy to arrange. For a start, fitting insulated wheels to a model steam locomotive is not as simple in practice as it appears on paper. This is not impossible to overcome, but it does add to the work involved on what is, in any case, a very complex project.

A more serious factor in the arrangement is the displacement lubricator which, as I said earlier, is a crude but effective means of getting oil into the cylinders. It also gets oil into the exhaust so that, after a couple of circuits, the rails have a sufficiently thick coating of a fairly effective insulator to make electrical pickup from them unreliable. An unreliable system of locomotive control is worse than no control at all since it usually fails at the worst possible moment.

The most telling argument against direct control through the rails is that radio control is in

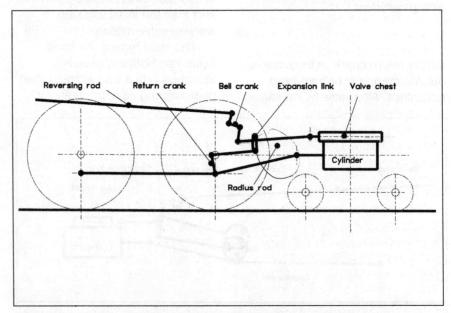

Figure 16.14 This simplified version of Walschaerts gear omits the combination lever. This imparts lap and lead to the valves, but as in small cylinders this would be extremely small and even more difficult to adjust correctly, its omission actually improves the performance of the gear due to the smaller number of joints involved which, on the model, have a disproportionate effect on the valve events.

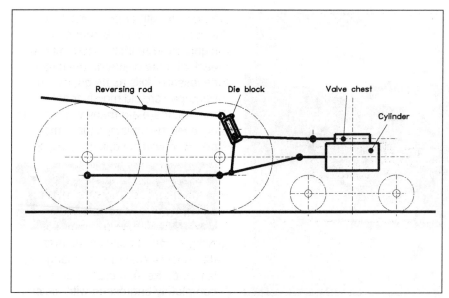

Figure 16.15 Hackworth valve gear converts the motion of the connecting rod into valve movement by means of a die block, sliding up and down in inclined guides. Henry Greenly used a slight variant for many of his designs and it remains popular to this day.

practice much easier to arrange on a locomotive. It uses readily available, reasonably priced and extremely reliable equipment since the first users of R/C, aeromodellers, ironed out the major bugs because, for them, a control failure usually produced a spectacular but very expensive crash. An additional virtue is that not only will a R/C steam locomotive run on any track of the correct gauge, but the control arrangements are locomotive-specific. In other words, there does not have to be a wholly standardised arrangement, since each locomotive has its own controller. Despite this, it is not a good idea to try to run two trains on the same stretch of line: sooner or later one will run into the other.

Manufacturers

There are now several manufacturers of narrow gauge steam locomotives for 32 and 45 mm gauge; frequently the same

model is available for either size to order. Prices range from £250

(1994) upwards. Standard gauge live steam is not so readily available: the main supplier is Aster, offering excellent models at prices which soon pass the £1,000 mark.

The construction of a small-scale steam locomotive is well within the capacity of a small home workshop. Gauge 1 models have been built using the versatile Unimat lathe, which can double as a drill and milling machine. For the newcomer the Gauge 1 Model Association's 'Project', a basic 0-6-0 for 45 mm gauge, with a single inside cylinder and slip eccentric valve gear, is a sound starting point, whilst Norman Dewhirst's *A Steam Locomotive for O Gauge*, recently reprinted, provides details of another basic engine for 32 mm gauge. Thankfully, the *Model Engineer* has at last shaken off the belief that any locomotive for less than

This model of the Welshpool & Llanfair Countess *built by Pearse Locomotives is supplied as standard with radio control, and is built to the highest specification to 16 mm scale for 32 mm gauge (also adaptable to 45 mm gauge to order). Although in every respect a well-detailed scale model,* Countess *has been designed and built to withstand the wear and tear associated with hard work on the garden railway.*
(Pearse Locomotives)

Auric *is a freelance live steam 0-4-0 for 32 and 45 mm gauges by Pearse Locomotives, based on British industrial practice. As with all locomotives by this firm, gas firing and radio control are standard. (Pearse Locomotives)*

3½ in gauge is only a glorified toy and is now featuring Gauge 1 in its pages, while *GardenRail* has already serialised one narrow gauge steam locomotive project.

Live steam locomotive modelling has always been encouraged by blow-by-blow constructional articles and frequently supported by commercial kits of parts, though one is not supposed to say that. This is understandable, since the manufacture of a live steamer in this fashion bears no resemblance to the assembly of a plastic airplane. It calls for a basic familiarity with engineering tools and their correct use, though the highly detailed instructions make it easier for the builder to acquire the necessary skills as he goes along. Perhaps I should modify that last remark: there are many women who have invaded this nominally male preserve with conspicuous success.

Model engineering societies and evening classes

Although the traditional picture of the modelmaker or model engineer is that of the lone craftsman completely engrossed with his craft in his own workshop, the newcomer will benefit from the help and advice of more experienced workers. Nowhere is this more true than with live steam, for there are certain tasks, notably boilermaking and testing, where an experienced tutor is a necessity rather than a convenience. A lively local model engineering society is the best place to find such help, with evening classes at a local adult education centre a close second, since the excellent equipment available there, whilst simplifying many tasks, is frequently a far cry from the more spartan facilities of the home workshop.

The value of the home workshop lies, not in its equipment, but in its availability. Where you only have access to machine tools for a couple of hours a week, progress will inevitably be slow. When you devote 20 or 30 hours a week to a project, as many model engineers do, progress is fast enough to keep the all-essential flame of enthusiasm alight. Be under no illusion, the home construction of even a simplified 32 or 45 mm gauge live steam locomotive from basic materials will occupy over 100 hours' work.

Tuppenny Pup, *a live steam narrow gauge locomotive for garden railway use built by Finescale Engineering Co. (Finescale Engineering Co.)*

Chapter 17

Outdoor Operation

Whether it is located indoors or outside in the garden, operating a model railway follows the same principles. There is just the one important difference which I will come to later. As I have already taken an entire book (*Model Railway Operation in Accordance with Prototype Practice*, Patrick Stephens, 1993) to deal with the subject, I will confine myself here to a brief summary of the underlying principles.

Tailchasing

There is one very important aspect of full-sized operation which is extremely difficult to simulate indoors except on a basic train set-type oval layout, namely travelling at speed over a stretch of main line under clear signals. As this accounts for over 80 per cent of prototype operation, it should have some part to play on a model railway.

The garden railway has room to develop a system where unencumbered plain track predominates, where the train is not brought to a halt almost as soon as the tail lamp has passed the first station's advanced starting signal. By providing plenty of room for trains to run, one gets the benefit of being able to watch them running from different viewpoints.

The main objection to tailchasing is that when you've seen the same train pass the same point on the layout for the third time, the novelty has worn thin. On an indoor railway, or even at an exhibition, the viewer is necessarily watching from a very limited number of locations, often just the one. In the garden, he or she can move around and get a different slant on the same train. Indeed, on a well-developed ground-level system, there is much to be said for allowing a train to make several circuits of the same continuous circuit so that every visitor has a chance of seeing it pass through every feature on the layout.

Steam operation

Where live steam is the main motive power, the business of raising steam, gauging supplies of water and fuel and the subsequent tidying away take up a significant amount of the operator's time. Indeed, for the true steam *aficionado* this is the whole purpose of an operating session; the bit in between, where the locomotive is set off at the head of its train, is very much a secondary consideration. A simple oval circuit with a couple of holding loops together with a large steam raising centre is all that is needed for complete satisfaction.

At a steam meet the track's owner is host to friends and fellow steam buffs, each of whom brings along one or two locomotives for the event. At such meetings the sole purpose of the trains is to provide a tail load for the locomotives. Generally speaking, everyone is content with a rake of

A corner of Graham Colover's Gauge 1 garden railway. The live steam loco is getting a lot of attention.

passenger coaches and another of goods stock for a single-track circuit, whilst for a double-track circuit, a third set of coaches is frequently regarded as sufficient.

A near essential adjunct of the steam meet is a blackboard and ample supply of chalk, so that the roster can be written down and clearly displayed. The usual arrangement is to allocate a fixed time for each operator to run his locomotive. A quarter of an hour is ideal: this allows about ten minutes' actual running, the balance being taken up getting the locomotive onto the train and off again at the end of the session. Clearly steam has to be raised beforehand and the fire put out and boiler emptied afterwards. This leaves ample time for watching the other locomotives in action, chatting to friends, many of whom one has not seen since the last meet, and taking refreshment.

Driver operation

For many years the small-scale steam locomotive suffered from the fact that, once set in motion, it was effectively out of control. Although the same consideration applied to clockwork drive, the big difference was that the steam locomotive, even the simple Bowman and Mamod types, had considerably greater endurance and could make several circuits of a garden railway without running short of water or fuel.

The arrival of radio control has changed the situation. It is now possible for the operator to walk around the track with a transmitter in his hands, driving the train almost as if he were in the cab. This not only allows the speed of the train to be controlled, it also permits shunting to take place. Although radio control is mainly thought of as a steam accessory,

Bert Groves demonstrates two snags of the straightforward ground-level line, that stock often needs to be placed on the line before operation can begin, and that it is necessary to crouch whilst attending to the models.

radio control of battery-powered locomotives has been around for a good many years, though it is only recently that much headway has been made.

This, I suspect, is mainly because simpler methods of driver control are available. So long as the locomotive is suitably geared so that it runs at a sedate pace, it is very easy for the operator to position himself so that he can reach out and throw the loco-mounted control switch. As

The provision of an operating pit makes operation of a ground-level line much more comfortable. This picture was taken in 1955 on Peter Denny's first garden railway, when I persuaded my wife to pose.

modern sub-miniature switches are not very obtrusive even in 7 mm scale, this simple means of control has a lot going for it.

Agreed, this brings the great big over-scale hand into the picture, but the fact that the majority of garden railway operators favour manual uncoupling means that the hand is going to come into the picture anyway. More to the point, in the garden the over-scale hand is less obtrusive, since the high-level raised system is, in general, very much devoid of scenic treatment, whilst the ground-level railway is surrounded by plants and flowers which are clearly out of scale.

Clockwork drive

Although I have not discussed clockwork drive in any detail because it is virtually unobtainable today, the fact that an enormous number of O gauge clockwork locomotives were manufactured between the wars means that some workers are still using this system.

Clockwork locomotives have a relatively short run; furthermore, they normally set off like the proverbial bat out of hell, only to lose speed a few yards down the line. A governor of sorts was fitted to inhibit this characteristic, but it was only cured when the more sophisticated governor fitted to the old-fashioned dial telephone was applied. To a large extent the development of a decent governor was delayed because the serious garden operator arranged his layout with an up grade out of each major station. This not only cut out the rush, it added a good 5 ft or more to the length of the run, since there was a down grade on entering the station to gently nudge the train along with the last dying urge of the spring.

The technique for driving a clockwork locomotive involved a fine appreciation of the power of the actual model, the rolling resistance of the train and the distance between two stations. These factors were translated into 'x turns plus y clicks', in other words, the initial winding was finely judged to allow the train to coast to a halt. This was particularly satisfying since a clockwork locomotive driven in this fashion came to a most realistic halt. At the time of writing, all this is fairly academic, but I have not lost hope that a true toymaker (probably in Nüremberg) will one day remember that not only was it not necessary to print 'batteries not included' on the box, but that the quality clockwork model needs no accessories to get it to work.

Block working

The high-level garden layout with its stations located in sheds is usually operated in much the same fashion as an indoor layout. There is one significant difference: the operators are like prototype signalmen, out of sight and earshot of one another. As a result it is absolutely essential to provide some means of letting the operator in the nearest shed know that it is safe for him to send the next train.

The simplest method is to arrange for the starting signal at station A to be worked by the operator at station B. While this bears no resemblance to prototype working, this is only because, at the dawn of railway signalling, there was no means whereby this could be done. Since the shorter distances involved on a model railway mean that it is a practical proposition for us, this elementary system whereby the 'all clear' is given in an unambiguous fashion is still worth considering.

Alternatively, the message can be given by an indicator light. This is definitely easier to arrange, since the connection is just a length of insulated wire; furthermore, the indicator can be placed on the control panel.

The weakness of this arrangement is that the operator at A has no means of telling the operator at B that he has a train ready to depart. For this we must resort to some system of telegraph operation. This need be no more than a simple bell system, moving up through the various permutations to the use of prototype block instruments. This was very popular some 30 years ago, but then after the collector value of these magnificent examples of late-Victorian hi-tech was recognised, cost became a serious bar. I have described the principles of block operation, modified for model railway usage, in my book *Model Railway Signalling* (Patrick Stephens, 1990).

Timetable working

Block working, even in its most elementary form, is usually closely associated with a working timetable. This introduces a significant design factor which is of considerable importance on the garden railway. Whether it takes the form of a chart, or is set out with flip cards, operating to a timetable implies that the operators must be able easily to read the necessary documentation.

With an indoor railway on raised baseboards this is rarely a problem. Admittedly, one needs a fair-sized, near flat surface to take the tabular timetable, but the flip card is commendably compact and very easy to use. Similar procedures can be followed inside a shed, but outside we have the possibility of rain to consider. If a timetable or a set of flip cards gets wet, the ink will probably run, and the paper or card will certainly be damaged.

Probably the best solution is to print timetables on A4 sheets and hold these in a clipboard. This can be laid down in any convenient position and quickly closed should there be a shower.

Weather

We have not so far considered the effect of weather on operation, yet it can be a very significant factor for the garden railway. Indeed, the fact that on most lines, operation ceases in the autumn and does not restart until the following spring is a clear indication that for many enthusiasts, there must be limits to one's enthusiasm. There are of course those who maintain that as the full-sized railway runs in all weathers all the year round, anyone aiming for the ultimate in realism should do the same. There is, I feel, a little of the 'real men don't bother about such things' in this outlook, but it is none the worse for that.

On the face of it, getting soaked to the skin is something to be avoided. This, I feel, is oversimplifying the situation. Modern all-weather clothing is proof against all but the most severe of downpours. The 'anorak brigade' jibe about trainspotters overlooks the fact that the anorak is designed to keep out the rain and deal with the most provoking feature of having to stand in a rainstorm, the slow trickle of cold water down the back of your neck. With a cosy, dry house close to hand, a short sharp shower or a slow, steady drizzle is not a serious handicap provided everyone is properly equipped.

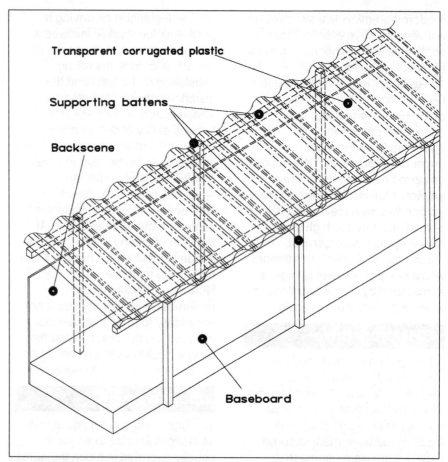

Figure 17.1 *John Anning's method of enjoying all-weather operation is to cover the outdoor sections of the line with a roof of corrugated transparent plastic sheet, carried on a lightweight timber frame. This provides sufficient protection to allow fairly elaborate lineside structures to be permanent features on these parts of the railway.*

Of course, a railway which has its main features housed in weatherproof sheds provides considerable protection for its operators, but it clearly has no such facilities for the trains. As most modern model locomotives and rolling stock will not be seriously affected by anything but the most severe of downpours, some operators are content to carry on regardless. However, the lightweight cover shown in Figure 17.1 is a tried and tested way of ensuring that an outdoor railway with its stations under cover can be operated during anything short of a major storm.

Combatting the cold

Cold is a more serious handicap. Once again proper clothing is essential, but as operating small-scale models when wearing thick gloves is next to impossible, it is very difficult to keep your hands warm enough. This is at best uncomfortable. Although the worst scenario, severe frostbite, is highly unlikely, chilblains are another matter. It is very easy when engrossed with something as fascinating as a live steam locomotive to ignore the fact that most of the feeling has gone from your toes. The repercussion only comes an hour or so later when the intolerable itching begins. More than anything else, low temperatures are the real reason for suspending outdoor operation during the winter months.

The wrong sort of snow

Fortunately, snow is a rare and short-lived phenomenon in much of Britain. This is part of the reason why model snowploughs do not feature largely on garden layouts, even though they appear to be a practical proposition. Two factors are at work. The first is that it is rare to have the opportunity to test a snowplough: if it doesn't work this time you could have to wait two or three years before another good opportunity presents itself. The second is that, for the most part, we have the wrong sort of snow – too wet and too easily turned into mush.

There is a relatively simple answer – the snow can be scooped off the track manually with a small version of the usual snow scoop. This gives the same effect as a snowplough, allowing the trains to run through banks of more or less virgin snow, which can be very effective in photographs. It isn't difficult to knock up a scoop from scrap wood and the effort is well worth while. With any luck you can get the ideal picture for next year's Christmas card.

Leaves on the line

From 'the wrong sort of snow', we move naturally to 'leaves on the line'. A garden railway is usually surrounded by shrubs and the occasional tree that shed their leaves in autumn. This is one reason operators stop running in early autumn – it's too much bother keeping the tracks clear.

Although the comparatively new garden vacuum cleaners could be an answer to this problem, they will most certainly lift loose ballast as well as leaves. On the whole this problem can only be solved by manual removal of all debris. Although I've only mentioned leaves so far, small stones and twigs also end up on the track and have to be taken out by hand. There are two approaches: you can go round before a running session and clear all obstructions, or you can wait for a derailment to show you where the trouble is.

Sunburn

Sunburn is very unpleasant and is not confined to the annual pilgrimage to a sun-soaked beach. Nor is the fact that you are fully clothed going to protect you, since your hands, arms, face, neck and, if like myself you have grown too tall for your hair, the top of your head will be exposed during operating sessions. In any case, you can get sunburn through a light summer shirt.

Model railway operation creates the conditions where one can all too easily get sunburnt without realising anything untoward is happening. While you are concentrating on running trains and revelling in the fact that it is a lovely day, your skin can be absorbing punishment. Whilst soothing creams have their uses, prevention, in the form of a shady hat and a sunblocker, is the best course.

Maintenance

The secret of trouble-free operation is regular maintenance. With the seasonal pattern of the garden railway, most of this takes place during the winter months. There are two factors to watch. The first is the possibility of becoming so engrossed in a major construction programme that runs over time that maintenance is carried out hurriedly at the last moment. It is therefore best to carry out essential repairs immediately after the line has been taken out of service. This will have the added advantage that you might remember the minor faults you noticed during the running season.

The second can best be described as the 'it's been overhauled so it can't go wrong' syndrome. During the running season odd little troubles will occur. Mostly these are of a minor nature and do not immediately affect running. There is, particularly in late August and September, the temptation to ignore these, promising oneself to attend to them later. It never hurts to correct a minor fault before it develops into a major breakdown.

Finally, as with any model railway, it pays not only to make a regular inspection, looking for possible sources of trouble, but to note these down in an orderly manner so that you have a record of what needs to be done. On a garden railway there is the added problem of accelerated weathering. A heavy thunderstorm is best followed by a careful inspection of the line, just to see if any weak places have been revealed.

Chapter 18

Pests and Problems

Unlike the indoor layout, which can be kept in a controlled environment, the garden railway is open to forces over which we have little or no control. Some are predictable: we know that by mid-October at the latest it is almost certainly going to be cold and wet. We can also anticipate the probability of a torrential downpour on any Bank Holiday weekend and arrange our open days accordingly. However, not only were bank holidays fine during 1994, November was also exceptionally mild. Nothing is wholly reliable, but most difficulties can be anticipated.

Wildlife

Wildlife comes high on the list of unpredictable problems. I have already mentioned that tunnels are a favourite hideaway for many animals, but this really falls into the category of a predictable occurrence and can easily be countered by placing a secure cover over each tunnel mouth as shown in Figure 18.1. A piece of board held in place with a stone will not deter the animals too much, but it has been established that British mammals cannot unscrew a wing nut. A pair of hook bolts will hold the cover in place, yet are quite easy to free before running sessions.

Although some writers tend to class all wildlife as pests, I consider that, moles and rats apart, these little folk who share our gardens should be, at the very least, tolerated. To me they are friends. For many years I felt that there were many birds who looked on me as a kindly provider of worms, since I had only to appear with spade or fork for them to flock around. There was one robin who almost became one of the family. The garden railway owner has an excellent opportunity for getting to know the wildlife of his immediate locality.

Whether this is a friendly encounter depends on individual circumstances. An old friend is apt to wax lyrical on the actions of squirrels, which seem to have taken a particular dislike to his O gauge outdoor line. Guerilla warfare is still in progress, yet others tell me these animals cause little if any bother.

Figure 18.1 Tunnels require a secure cover if they are not to become living quarters for wildlife. A wooden cover secured by two hook bolts and wing nuts is a simple and effective barrier.

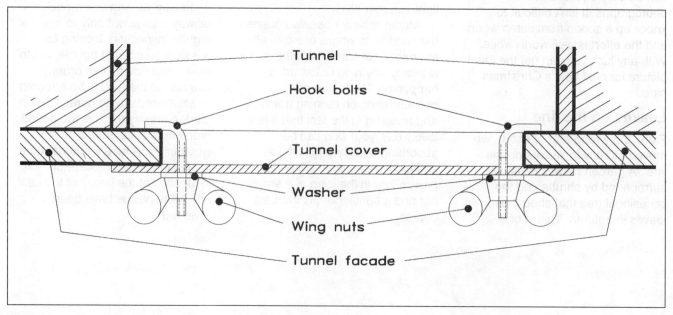

- Tunnel
- Hook bolts
- Tunnel cover
- Washer
- Wing nuts
- Tunnel facade

Large mammals can do accidental damage to more delicate parts of the model, which is one reason why most garden railway builders beef up the more delicate detail or omit it altogether. Fortunately, dogs are not a serious problem, partly because they seem content to keep to their own territory, partly because current legislation, both national and local, has the effect of making dog owners more responsible for their pets.

Cats!

Cats are a special case. After a long study of the subject, I have come to the conclusion that they share our interest in model railways, as no other theory can account for the fact that you will usually find at least one sitting comfortably on the permanent way. Unfortunately, they have a totally different outlook on the hobby and appear to regard rolling stock in general, and model locomotives in particular, as legitimate prey.

Furthermore, once a cat has decided that a particular spot is its own personal domain, it is extremely difficult to convince it otherwise. An extreme example of this occurred some 50 years ago on Alex Jackson's 110v Bridgewater Railway. One of the local cats adopted part of the main line as his personal sun lounge and was regularly turfed off before operation could begin. Unfortunately he was a persistent animal and, as often as not, the moment the operators had gone into the shed to start trains running, he resumed his perch. If this was not spotted and someone sent hotfoot to constrain him, power-up was accompanied by a loud feline complaint as the cat shot vertically some 3 ft off the track. In the main, cats are intelligent animals and learn from their mistakes. This one was exceptionally stupid and remarkably resistant to high-voltage current.

There are several repellent powders on the market which, if sprinkled on the ground, definitely deter cats and dogs (and, presumably, other small mammals). Many use organic products, with peppers as the principal ingredient, and can be assumed to be relatively harmless. I know they work well in flower beds, so I see no reason why they should not be equally effective when applied to the trackbed.

In rural areas the possibility of cows, sheep or deer breaking into a garden must always be accepted and special attention paid to the strength of the boundary fence. Foxes, both rural and urban, will go where they please, though in general they are mainly seeking food. The biggest danger is not from the fox, but from the hunt, should it be possible for the chase to pass across your railway.

Vandals and thieves

Unlike wildlife and pets, which have their rights, the individual who delights in wrecking other people's property is an unmitigated pest with no rights whatsoever. This is not a modern phenomenon, for vandalism was known before the Second World War; the idea that everyone behaved impeccably when the police could clip a youngster around the ear is just another urban myth. The problem is not so much one of curing the individuals concerned (most do become good citizens without any special treatment) as of catching them in the first place.

Prevention is better than cure. In the 1930s, when outdoor railways were kept behind the garden fence lest the owner was accused of childishness, the vandal did not know there was something special to wreck. Modern open plan gardens are not so secure.

Theft is another risk, but as the main target for thieves is the

Cats like model railways, but seem to regard them in a slightly different light. The Dennys' cat is clearly interested in the vans, but is probably debating whether or not they'd make good prey.

locomotives and, to a certain extent, the rolling stock, good security between operating sessions is advisable. Very valuable models should be kept indoors and the provision of an alarm system is worth considering. Insurance is essential.

Wind and rain

In recent years the frequency and strength of winter storms has increased. While the media attribute this to global warming, gaps in the ozone layer, air pollution and other current theories, I have my doubts. Climatic changes occurred long before the Industrial Revolution; indeed, a rough pattern of stormy '90s emerges from the records. This could well mean that we are now past the worst, and that the next 80-odd years will be relatively free from hurricane force winds, but I wouldn't bet on it.

The truth is that, even before the severe storms of recent years, fences blew down, and there was always a distinct possibility that a fence panel could come adrift. For this reason you should make a point of giving any fences close to the layout a careful inspection every autumn and keep an eye on them throughout the winter. Check

that wooden posts are free from rot, inspect any arris rails and make sure that metal fixings are not rusted. A little work with a hammer and nails can save a lot of heartache. It is important to deal with both fences, for the fact that your neighbour is technically responsible for one of them does not mean that he will necessarily have the same concern as yourself. However, it is highly unlikely that he will complain if you keep his part of the boundary in good order. Well, would you if the situation were reversed?

Even without the severe damage a storm can bring, weather has a significant effect on the garden railway. I have already spoken of the need for regular maintenance, painting, oiling and adjusting to keep the ravages of rain and wind at bay. This has its beneficial side, for no-one has to spend time painstakingly weathering a building. A more troublesome hazard is frost, which can give ground-level operators a lot of bother. Its effects fall into two distinct areas: ground movement and damage to masonry. We have already considered the effect of frost on masonry.

To a certain extent, ground movement is self-righting, since

the lifting caused by the swelling of ground water as it freezes subsides when the ground thaws. Unfortunately, the track does not always fall conveniently back into its original position and so a certain amount of adjustment is needed before running can recommence. Again, I have spoken of the need for regular track inspection in what is essentially an uncontrolled environment.

What is less obvious is that even under balmy conditions a lot of grit and dirt is picked up by the wind and deposited elsewhere. This means that outdoor tracks will inevitably get smothered in fine particles. This can cause trouble even with large-scale models, but when one is working in the smaller scales, these problems are magnified. There are two schools of thought here. One maintains that every centimetre of the line should be carefully scrutinised before running; the other waits for derailments to pinpoint the problems. The best approach is a quick preliminary check, paying most attention to the points on the line where a derailment could lead to serious trouble, whilst accepting that the odd bit of grit can remain to cause problems.

Chapter 19

Garden Railways I Have Known

This is a very personal chapter, where I give my impressions of several outdoor railways I have had the pleasure and privilege of visiting. Indeed, had I ever owned a garden which was sufficiently level, any one of them could have converted me to the delights of an outdoor railway.

I first encountered outdoor railways in 1939, when I was evacuated with my school to Weston-super-Mare. By chance, I met a fellow enthusiast who introduced me to two excellent garden railways. One, the Heddle Valley Railway, was worked almost exclusively with Hornby equipment and laid with Hornby tin-plate track. Although in theory this was totally unsuitable for outdoor use, providing everything was smothered with thick paint before laying, it could serve for three or four years before rusting through. This brings home the transient nature of so many pre-war outdoor systems, which were built quickly with little thought for the next five years. The object was to have fun, and there is no doubt that the Heddle Valley Railway provided that in abundance, for it was worked to timetable by a group of young enthusiasts who openly enjoyed playing trains with a purpose. Unashamedly freelance, its principal express class was the Hornby No. 2 special 4-4-0 'County', repainted in blue and named after birds.

Mort Street

The other layout was owned by Mort Street. A more substantial system, it used the best techniques of the day and was laid with solid-drawn rail, the so-called 'Scale Permanent Way'. In addition, it boasted a rake of good-quality, scratchbuilt Southern coaches made by a professional modelmaker in Cheddar, whose name escapes me. Mort had a small but well-balanced stud of scratchbuilt locomotives built on commercial clockwork mechanisms. His line was based on the Southern, despite being firmly in GWR territory.

Mort's garden sloped slightly, so that shortly after leaving the raised main terminus by the house the tracks reached ground level and the further station was laid directly onto the ground. After the war, the remnants of the Heddle Valley group joined up with Mort and the centre of the garden was excavated so that there was a pleasant sunken lawn surrounded by an extensive out-and-back system.

However, when a school friend and I helped run the railway this was all still in the future. Initially, we took turns to operate the main terminus or handle the outer station. The latter soon palled, since the operator at the far end had to spend much of the time in an uncomfortable crouch and,

compared with the main terminus, the layout was rudimentary and offered little in the way of shunting movement. I forget who first realised that an active teenager could outpace a clockwork locomotive on a 60 ft (18 m) run.

John Anning

The O gauge line built by John Anning, President of the Model Railway Club (Figure 19.1), is an excellent example of the old idea of a railway which is in the garden because it is too large to fit inside the house. The three stations are housed in sectional sheds, very much modified from the conventional garden shed to serve their new purpose. The major difference is that each shed is really two sheds bolted end to end, whilst the farther shed has been enlarged sideways to hold the branch terminus. The garage is wholly taken over by the fiddle yards, and also houses a well-equipped workshop where the extensive stud of scratchbuilt locomotives and coaches are built and maintained.

The layout is based on Southern Railway practice in the outer London area, complete with a third rail and four-car EMUs. The main stations are almost completely enclosed in the sheds, and have a full selection of railway structures together with a little scenic treatment, mainly consisting of hand-painted backscenes. There

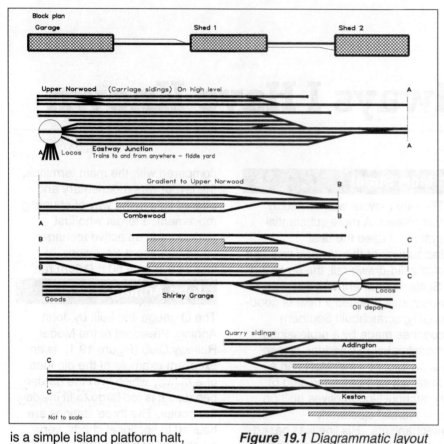

Block plan
Garage   Shed 1   Shed 2

Upper Norwood   (Carriage sidings) On high level   A

A   Locos   Eastway Junction
Trains to and from anywhere – fiddle yard   A

Gradient to Upper Norwood   B

Combewood   B

A   C

B   C

B   Goods   Shirley Grange   C

Locos

Oil depot

Quarry sidings
Addington

C   Keston

C

Not to scale

is a simple island platform halt, Combewood, on the outdoor section between the principal station, Shirley Grange, and the fiddle yard, behind which a fairly steep incline leads to a set of high-level storage roads known as Upper Norwood. The original intention was to concentrate the EMU services here, but the grades proved a little too much for the relatively light power coaches. This section is permanently protected by the light cover described in Chapter 17 (Figure 17.1), but the section between Shirley Grange and the further termini has lost this protection. Although this effectively prevents all-weather operation over the full layout, this is less serious today since the majority of the regular operators are now retired and it is much easier to arrange an operating session at short notice.

The layout requires at least five operators to maintain a full service, following a detailed timetable. Even

Figure 19.1 Diagrammatic layout plan of John Anning's O gauge outdoor Southern Railway layout.

with this number, the single man at the fiddle yard end is kept very busy. Two are needed at Shirley Grange, which is the busiest part of the line, forming the junction of the two branches and additionally as the turning point for short EMU workings from the fiddle yard. Control between stations is maintained by a simple train describer system, using LEDs to indicate the type of train on offer. This is supplemented by block bells for offering and accepting the trains.

One distinct advantage of basing the layout in the Southern outer suburban area is that an intensive service with trains dashing up and down the line at frequent intervals is strictly in line with full-size practice. There never has been any difficulty in finding operators, the layout demonstrating a fundamental, if little known, rule of the hobby, which is that any layout capable of being operated intensively in a railway-like fashion is sure of having enough operators on hand to keep it working to capacity.

John Anning consults the timetable to see which train should be next to arrive at the fiddle yard. The start of the covered section of outdoor line can just be distinguished through the glass. The difference between the clocks is easily explained: the one under the high-level section shows railway time, the other real time.

A Southern 0-6-0 heads a ballast train out of Shirley Grange, bound for the fiddle yard on John Anning's O gauge line. The wooden struts supporting the corrugated plastic cover can be clearly seen.

Barry Harper and Ivor Lindsell are fully occupied operating Shirley Grange, the main station on John Anning's layout.

A 'King Arthur' 4-6-0 heads a five-coach express out of Shirley Grange, en route to Addington. The track in the immediate foreground is the single-track branch to Keston. This shot shows the construction of the baseboard: outdoor grade ply bolted to Dexion angles which in turn are supported by a timber strut bolted to a concrete spur set in the ground. Note that the line is some distance from the fence panels.

Geoff Bigmore

The Bigston Railway of the late Geoff Bigmore (Figure 19.2) is another example of a shed-based outdoor railway, again with a fine stud of scratchbuilt locomotives and rolling stock. Based on LNER (Great Northern) practice, the line began at Bigston, located in a large shed adjacent to the house, and originally terminated in a reversing loop at Archway. Later, a second shed housed Westbridge, a smaller terminus, and finally Westbridge High level was added. This was provided as a terminus for a service of North London Railway trains, represented by a pair of this line's 4-4-0 tank locomotives and a rake of four-wheeled coaches.

In its final condition two operators were needed to maintain the timetable. Geoff normally took Bigston whilst the visitor was ensconced at Westbridge. Communication was primarily through prototype block instruments with a standby telephone. Points and signals were worked by a miniature lever frame housed in the signal box, which was provided with a hinged roof to allow access. It was all very railway-like with the operator as signalman, but as Geoff had thoughtfully provided a very detailed set of instructions, once the first four trains had been successfully piloted to their correct platform road, one could relax and enjoy a bout of serious operation.

Geoff made no attempt to keep strictly to a specific time slot, although most of the stock fitted the Gresley years. There were some pre-grouping intruders. I have already mentioned the North London train; there was also a Tennant 2-4-0, straying up the East Coast to North Eastern territory, while a Class 25 diesel shifted the period into modern times. The railway was operated on a seasonal basis, giving Geoff ample time during the winter to add to the range of fine locomotives and coaches that were his life's work. His most productive period came after his

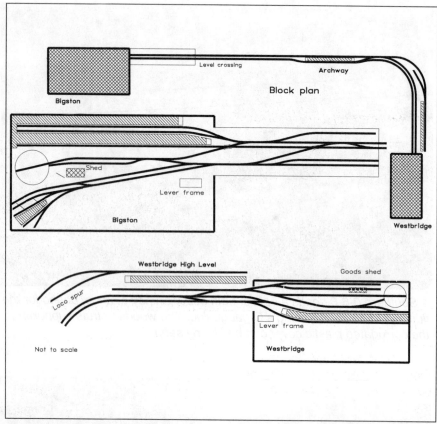

Figure 19.2 Geoff Bigmore's Bigston O gauge LNER garden layout.

The departure end of the platforms at Bigston on Geoff Bigmore's O gauge garden railway.

The storage roads at Bigston are located in the open beyond the shed. The breakdown train is in the nearest road, with a five-car express rake on the high-level carriage siding.

This level crossing marks the break between the ply-topped section of baseboard carrying Bigston sidings and the main line section, laid on a slatted top framing.

retirement, when construction continued throughout the year.

One feature of this layout was the way its impact on a very pleasant garden was softened by the planting of rose bushes under the main line proper. These needed frequent pruning and trimming, but provided a pleasing splash of colour around the otherwise stark raised sections.

Westbridge High Level with a train of North London Railway four-wheelers. The N7 is heading a triple-art suburban set out of Westbridge.

Green Arrow at the head of a five-car Pullman train waits for the clear at Archway. The signal box is purely cosmetic: points are controlled from Bigston.

Westbridge, the further terminus of Geoff Bigmore's O gauge layout, is, like Bigston, situated in a timber shed.

Bob Ledger

I have to confess that although I know Bob's layout well (Figure 19.3), I have never seen it in its garden setting, but rather at several exhibitions in the North West. Unlike the other layouts in this section, Manchester Central began life as a demountable layout, the initial idea being to take everything inside during the winter months. Before long it was realised that this made it equally suited for exhibition work, and in this form it was a very popular feature of the Northern exhibition circuit.

The setting is London Midland Region circa 1960, when diesel traction was running side by side

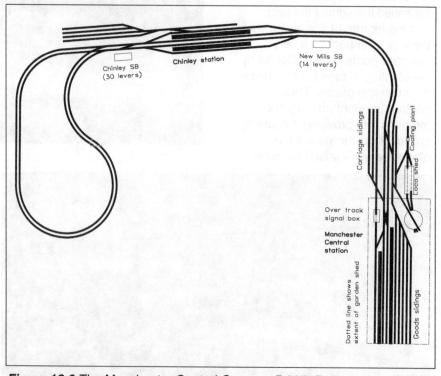

Figure 19.3 *The Manchester Central O gauge British Railways layout built by Bob Ledger.*

New Mills South Junction on Bob Ledger's layout in the autumn of 1993. (Bob Ledger)

In its latest incarnation, Manchester Central is permanently housed in a shed, with most of the throat, storage roads and loco depot outside. Only Chinley is fully transportable and available for exhibition display. The legs rest in proprietary steel fence spurs, which are fairly expensive but do make it easy to dismantle the line for winter. I queried their use with Bob, since I have had a steel line post socket rust away inside ten years, but he assures me that as they are heavily enamelled and, unlike the socket, cannot collect water, they appear to be standing up to their duty well.

with steam on what was still a traditional railway network, Dr Beeching having yet to pronounce the death of a thousand cuts. Again the great majority of the stud is scratchbuilt. Operation is strictly to timetable and, when enough operators are to hand, very intensive, as befits a layout based on what was, at the time modelled, an intensively worked section of main line railway.

An ICI limestone train at Chinley on Bob Ledger's layout. (R.A. Loynds)

Peter Denny

While it might be thought that the rigours of the British climate keep the fine scale modeller indoors, this view must be tempered by consideration of the work of one of the great pioneers of what we now know as finescale modelling, my old friend Peter Denny. Unfortunately we live too far apart for it to be more than a rare delight to visit him and to enjoy a morning's relaxed running over his 1:32 scale garden railway, where trains run at random and end up

Diesel power is very much in evidence on Bob Ledger's O gauge layout. Here we have old and new Metro-Cammell sets passing outside Chinley. (R.A. Loynds)

A Class 45 passing though Chinley station on Bob Ledger's O gauge layout. (R.A. Loynds)

wherever the operator's whim takes them, to be followed after lunch by a more serious session on Buckingham, where every move is made according to strict railway rules and a detailed timetable.

Stage 1 – Harrowbarrow

Originally, Peter's ideas for a garden railway centred around Gauge 1, but when he arrived in Cornwall, he had the garden but balked at the cost of Gauge 1. Instead, whilst retaining the size, he was able, using Hornby O gauge mechanisms and wheels, to work to ⅜ in scale on 1¼ in (32 mm) gauge track to arrive at 3ft 6in gauge narrow gauge. The TVLR was, and still is, a strictly freelance system, though everything is based closely on an actual prototype.

The Harrowbarrow line (Figure 19.4) was known as the Tamar Valley Light Railway, a fairly obvious choice considering its geographical location. The layout was simple, a U-shaped line, mainly on a rockery foundation, with access to the central path over a lifting bridge. Motive power was clockwork, and no turntables were provided, so that the hole for the winding key was always on the operator's side. For most of his stay in Harrowbarrow, the TVLR was his principal interest, for although the then dismountable Buckingham branch, slightly cut down from its former size, was stored within the confined space of a very cramped house, it made too great an impact on his family to be erected very often.

Rockery Tunnel on Peter Denny's original TVLR.

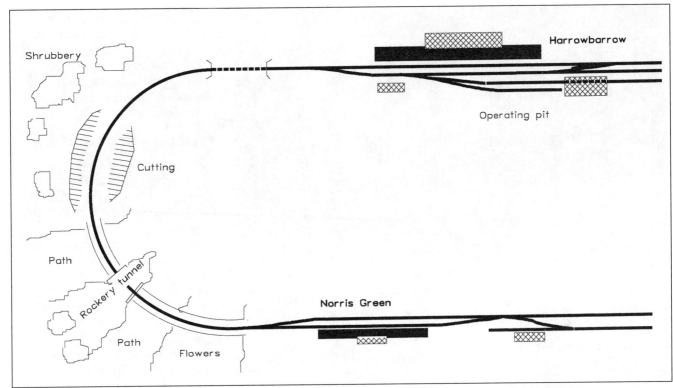

Shrubbery

Harrowbarrow

Cutting

Operating pit

Path

Rockery tunnel

Norris Green

Path

Flowers

Figure 19.4 *The first incarnation of Peter Denny's Tamar Valley Light Railway (TVLR) narrow gauge ground-level garden railway at Harrowbarrow.*

Harrowbarrow, the principal station on Peter Denny's first garden railway.

Norris Green on the first TVLR.

Peter Denny (left) and Nick Freezer discuss the finer points of operation at Lawnton at St Newlyn East. Trepolpen is at the rear.

Stages 2 and 3 – St Newlyn East

When he obtained a living at St Newlyn East, Peter had a large, rambling Georgian vicarage where he had space to erect Buckingham in its own room. He also had an extensive garden which included an old, but reasonably watertight greenhouse which contained an ageing grapevine and precious little else of note. This seemed the ideal location for a new terminus for the TVLR, but it soon proved unsuitable for two reasons. For a single-handed operator, the walk around the large greenhouse to the door and then to the station took too long – one got there well after the train had arrived. When

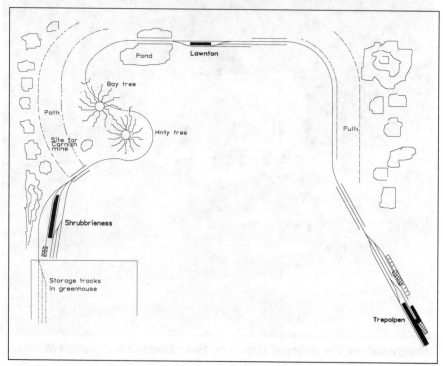

Figure 19.5 Stage 2 of the TVLR, now the Trepolpen Valley Light Railway, as first erected at St Newlyn East.

The battery-electric railcar set at Lawnton on the St Newlyn East line. Photography was shortly to be brought to a sudden stop by the start of a torrential downpour, possibly the most prevalent hazard of the garden railway.

Figure 19.6 *The third, improved, version of the TVLR at St Newlyn East.*

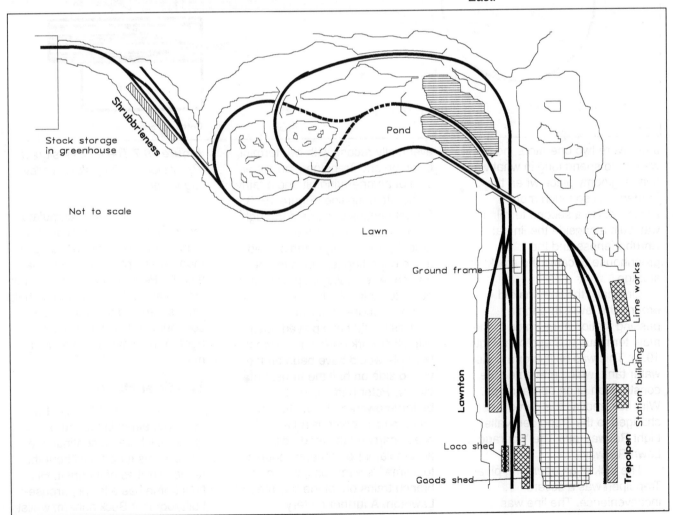

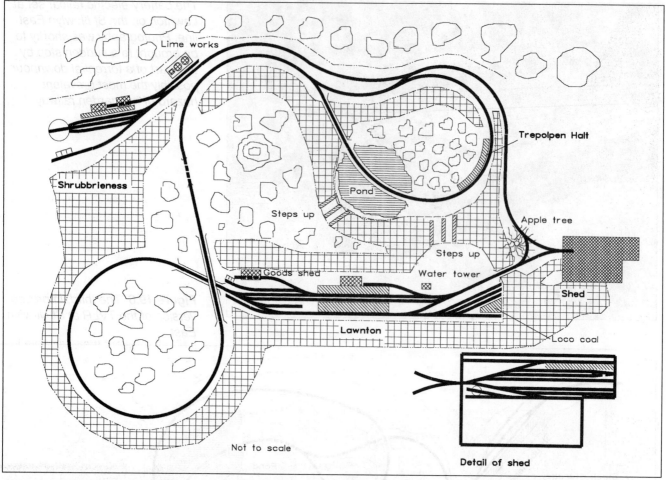

Lime works

Trepolpen Halt

Shrubbrieness

Pond

Steps up

Apple tree

Steps up

Goods shed

Water tower

Shed

Lawnton

Loco coal

Not to scale

Detail of shed

Figure 19.7 The final version of Peter Denny's Trepolpen Valley Light Railway.

there were two operators, no-one wanted to spend long in what was a fairly gloomy place when the garden was so much more attractive. So a second terminus was built alongside the line at Shrubbrieness and the greenhouse became the stock storage.

Originally the line snaked around the lawn, through a passing station at Lawnton to the main terminus at Trepolpen (Figure 19.5). This was built over a buried water tank, which prevented the construction of an operating pit. With its removal, the name was changed to the Trepolpen Valley Light Railway, aka The Vicarage Lawn Railway.

The lack of an operating pit at Trepolpen was a severe inconvenience. The line was

eventually recast, with two termini, Lawnton and Trepolpen, on either side of an operating pit and a fairly elaborate main line (Figure 19.6). Shrubbrieness became a through station on the way to the greenhouse storage, and served as an operating terminus for the branch. A reversing loop was later put in to make single-handed operation more practical.

This would have played havoc with clockwork operation, since the key hole would have been on the wrong side on half the turns, but by now Peter had moved to battery-powered electric traction and a railcar, comprising a bogie coach carrying the lead-acid accumulator permanently coupled to a small 'steam' loco, worked the branch trains out of the bay road at Lawnton. A further battery

locomotive, with the accumulator in the tender, joined the locomotive stud. In this form the railway gave many years' pleasure until it was time for Peter to retire from his full-time ministry. Even though he held vicar's freehold and could have continued indefinitely, he felt it right to hand over to a younger man.

The final stage

When he left St Newlyn East, Peter remained in the Truro diocese, where he continues to exercise his ministry without the responsibilities of a parish. His final home has a large purpose-built room for Buckingham, whilst

Lawnton station on the final (?) version of the TVLR. The shed housing the unnamed terminus can be discerned in the background.
(Photo courtesy Peter Denny)

Another view of Lawnton, TVLR. The station buildings are wooden with a covering of roofing felt, scribed to represent stonework.
(Photo courtesy Peter Denny)

the garden has been transformed to house the TVLR (Figure 19.7). The value of covered storage for the trains had been learned, so a small shed was erected at a low point and provided with a terminus which has never received a name, since although the shed door is so arranged that it is no bother to follow a train inside, everyone prefers to go outside to enjoy the garden.

The main station, Lawnton, is on timber baseboards and easily worked without stooping. The small terminus at Shrubbrieness, which is reached by wandering around the paths that flank the railway, is at ground level. It was provided with a turntable so that clockwork locomotives could be turned to present their key hole to the operator, but by then not only were the ageing mechanisms

Shrubbrieness is difficult to photograph, being all but buried in a shrubbery. The lime works, built to an Edward Beal design, have just caught the sun. (Photo courtesy Peter Denny)

beginning to flag, the development of the electric drive, using a German-made geared motor which was once supplied in the Meccano system, had rendered this system obsolescent. All traction today is battery-electric, making operation extremely easy. Every locomotive is geared down to run at a very sedate pace indeed, the driver following it around the route on the strategically located paths.

Unlike the previous layouts, it is not operated to a strict schedule. This is mainly because it is used to complement Buckingham, where every train movement is made according to a very detailed timetable. Normal operation is driver-oriented; everyone is allocated an engine and proceeds to run it according to his own inclination, the only rules being that railway-like practices should be adopted and one must check that the road is clear before sending a train out onto the main line. The more experienced visitors prefer freight operation: it's more fun shunting the yards at Lawnton and Shrubbrieness. With its combination of point to point, out and back and continuous running, there is plenty of variety to keep three people busy. Were this the only railway, it would be possible to devise a 'proper' timetable, but whether this would be more fun is open to question.

Chapter 20

Passenger-Carrying Lines

This 'double-headed' train on H.W. Franklin's 10¼ in gauge line is clearly a posed photograph, since neither engine appears to be in steam and it is highly unlikely that a boy would be allowed to drive the lead locomotive. (Author's collection)

the highly practical miniature railway which is today an essential feature of any theme park worthy of the name. With his sights set on 15 in gauge, he offered 10¼ in gauge as an alternative for the private user, believing that anything smaller would be unstable. Much of his own work was for 15 in gauge, the two best-known examples, still operating to this day, being the Ravenglass & Eskdale and the Romney, Hythe & Dymchurch railways.

Small gauge passenger hauling today

Today, we know that even with 'ride in' coaches, 7¼ in gauge is perfectly safe, whilst the straddle

In Henry Greenly's pioneer handbook on the hobby, *Model Railways*, published in 1924, he makes several references to passenger-carrying lines, a particular interest of his. Indeed, I doubt if many readers have not at some time toyed with the idea of owning such a line, only to dismiss it on the grounds that whilst it might be the ultimate in garden railways, you need a very large garden.

Certainly the type of railway Greenly discussed did need a private estate, for he had taken Sir Arthur Heywood's original concept of the 15 in gauge minimum-sized estate railway and converted it into

A well-filled train of 'ride on' coaches on the mixed 7¼ in/5 in gauge passenger-carrying line at Swiss Vapeur Parc, Le Bouveret, Switzerland.

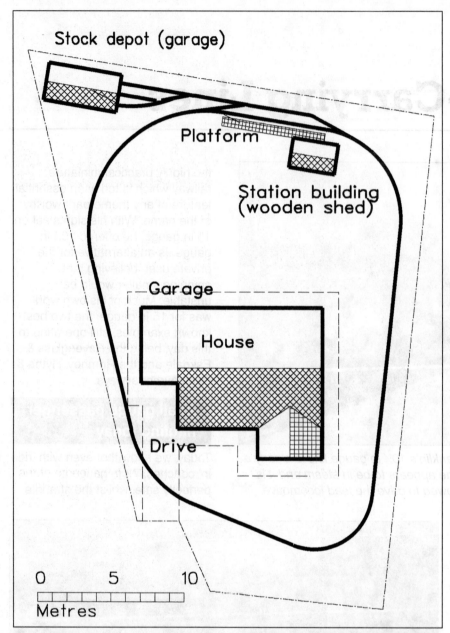

Stock depot (garage)

Platform

Station building
(wooden shed)

Garage

House

Drive

0   5   10

Metres

Figure 20.1 Plan for a passenger-carrying line around a detached chalet bungalow.

pattern vehicle can be used on as small a gauge as 5 in, with the line laid on the ground. Raised on trestles, passenger hauling by 2½ in gauge locomotives has long been established, though such tracks are normally multi-gauge concepts with the monorail-type

vehicles running on 5 in gauge for improved stability. Such tracks are usually owned and maintained by model engineering societies, though many live steam locomotive builders have a test track in their own gardens.

The idea of a personal ground-level passenger-carrying railway received a boost when Triang produced a 10¼ in gauge system in the 1970s, using electric traction with a locomotive based loosely on

the then current Southern Region electric locomotives accompanied by ride-in coaches which purported to be 'Golden Arrow' Pullman cars. It was not a success, for it proved too light for commercial use and a shade too large for home use. There was also the feeling that while it was great fun for the children, really it was too much to let them loose with so big a toy. The traction system – low-voltage two-rail supply – no doubt had an effect on many buyers; it sounds dangerous though in point of fact it is not.

It did however set several individuals thinking, one result of which was the realisation that, with the right sort of house, a ground-level passenger-carrying loop was a wholly practical proposition. All it needed was a detached property with at least 1 m (3 ft) clearance at either side. This I found interesting since I happened to own just such a property, though the ground levels ruled the idea out of court before I even considered the cost. For what it is worth, I include a plan based on the site (Figure 20.1), where a sectional garage is used for stock storage.

The main objection to this design is that the railway is very visible. There could be some objection from neighbours, though where there are plenty of youngsters in the vicinity and one is happy to provide rides, most of the opposition will evaporate once the fun starts. An intractable problem is that of vandalism – not merely the attention of destructive louts, but the more worrying case where the local children, led by a good-hearted but irresponsible teenager, break into the stock lockup and start giving unsupervised rides which almost always end up with someone getting badly hurt.

Traction choice

Three forms of traction are possible: steam, internal combustion and battery-powered electricity. For this type of system, internal combustion is not advised, since on this very short circuit there is not time for the exhaust fumes to disperse before the train comes round again. After four circuits, only the foolhardy persist in travelling through what is rapidly becoming a lethal concentration of toxic fumes. Steam is definitely for the dedicated, experienced individual, preferably with some engineering training, but battery-electric drive is a good all-round system that is instantly available so long as you remember to plug in the charger.

Gauges for passenger hauling

Although passenger haulage is just feasible on 5 in gauge, the preferred amateur size is 7¼ in, since the vehicles are more stable. This consideration is even more important on a private passenger-carrying line than on a commercial system, since the chances of children getting access to the equipment are considerably higher. Clearly this is a major project, and one such locomotive is as much as most individuals can consider. In most cases, any private individual working in 7¼ in gauge tends to confine his personal system to a long straight test track running the length of the garden. Often this is a portable system that can be taken to a local exhibition or fete and laid out on any level stretch of ground to provide rides for the children. However, most such attractions are provided by model engineering societies and specialist associations.

Clearly, we have passed at this point from pure railway modelling into the field of model engineering, since the construction of even a 5 in gauge locomotive calls for a very well-equipped engineering workshop. For 7¼ in gauge one is really into light engineering! Nevertheless, many individuals have built locomotives of this size, whilst even more have purchased their motive power from one of the specialist builders who cater for this field. While we are talking

Although this looks like a halt, Chablais Village at Le Bouveret is really a sheltered seat for visitors. The train is one of the visiting 5 in gauge models seen in action on the line's festival in June 1994. Part of a regular passenger train can be seen on the high level at the back of the shot.

A diesel-hauled train emerges from the tunnel on the Beer Heights Light Railway, the 7¼ in passenger-carrying line at Pecorama.

No. 4, Thomas II, *one of the Beer Heights Light Railway's stud of narrow gauge locomotives. By adopting narrow gauge proportions the locomotives are roughly 1:3 scale and extremely powerful. The main divergence from prototype is the provision of a tender, which is essential to provide the driver with a comfortable seat.*

serious money, the cost of a passenger-hauling locomotive is by no means unattainable, whilst the running costs would be considerably less than for a canal cruiser. You don't have to be a millionaire, but it certainly helps if you are.

Large passenger-carrying lines

Some joint ventures are quite large, and are usually open to the public every weekend during the summer months. There is normally a hard core of locomotives and stock kept on the site, supplemented by the occasional visiting locomotive and its owner/driver. A successful line will organise at least one open weekend each year. This is not open in the sense that anyone can turn up unannounced, since each locomotive must meet certain minimum requirements and be fully insured, and visitors' credentials have to be checked beforehand. The idea is to provide a chance for responsible owners of large gauge model locomotives to give their prized possessions a good run.

While most lines of this nature are amateur based, a growing number of permanent miniature railways are owned by individuals who happen to be in a position to create an attractive passenger-carrying line which they then run commercially in order to defray the costs as well as making the whole enterprise more fun. It gets rather dull trundling a train of empty stock round any miniature railway – much better fill it with happy

The loading ramp on the Beer Heights Light Railway. This short spur is aligned so that it is roughly on a level with the trailers used by 7¼ in gauge locomotive owners to transport their models around the country, thus eliminating much of the manhandling needed to offload and reload the heavy machines. It sees intensive use at the weekends when members of the 7¼in Gauge Society visit the railway to enjoy intensive operation over a very elaborate scenic system.

holidaymakers. Increasingly, such lines play host, at least once a year, to responsible societies such as the 7¼ in Gauge Society.

S. C. Pritchard - An Outdoor Enthusiast

As this book was being prepared, my former employer and good friend, S. C. Pritchard, died. To most railway modellers he is best known for his involvement with model track; indeed with Peco Streamline he set the standard that other OO/HO track manufacturers have followed.

What is less well known is his great interest in garden railways. During the immediate post war years, when garden lines were in

eclipse, he insisted that they must have a regular place in *Railway Modeller* and, in particular, the August issue had to feature garden railways. Not that I needed any instruction on that point, it was another case where our ideas and inclinations coincided.

With the development of Streamline track, he seized on its weatherproof potential. Unwilling to rely solely on theory, he had several lengths outside to be exposed to sun, rain, frost and snow – not that we had much of that in East Devon. Only when he was satisfied that nothing would deteriorate did he allow us to say openly that it was suitable for outdoor use.

The introduction of O gauge Streamline track owed a great deal to his own plans for a garden layout at his own home. Indeed, when members of the staff once queried whether the production of turnouts for O gauge would be commercially justified, he asked whether they wanted to stop him building his railway! That he was proved right in the long run was quite immaterial, he was going ahead regardless.

The home layout slowly took second place to the outdoor tracks at Modelrama. At the same time, he conceived the Beer Heights Light Railway, ostensibly as a tourist attraction but in reality to satisfy a long held desire to get as near as possible to a "real" railway. The line is conceived on the grand scale; that extensive excavation was needed to create a level trackbed was part and parcel of the fun. Although the initial line was quite adequate for its ostensible purpose, within a couple of years he purchased more land, had another battle with the planning authorities and created an exciting extension that opened up fresh vistas of the countryside, skirting an artificial lake and nature reserve, the wild nature of which provided a contrast with the neatly tended grounds on the other side of the tunnel.

He lost no opportunity to walk around the line, delighted to see the visitors enjoying their rides. However his greatest pleasure undoubtedly came when he hosted a week-end meeting of the 7¼in Gauge Society. The Beer Heights Railway would be thronged with visiting steam locomotives driven by their delighted owners. In the middle was one man, getting more fun than anyone else, Sydney Pritchard.

Appendix I

Further Reading

Very few books have been published which deal specifically with small-scale garden railways, and of these, half are out of print. References are made to the subject in Henry Greenly's *Model Railways* (Cassell), first published in 1924, but probably more readily available in its revised version by his son-in-law, Ernest Steel. Edward Beal also refers to garden railways in his rare pre-war book *The Craft of Modelling Railways* (Nelson). However, only the bibliophile need bother to search for either volume; for the curious, copies are to be found in the Model Railway Club's extensive library.

The classic work is Ray Tustin's *Garden Railways*. This was originally published by Percival Marshall in 1949 and is one of the rare PM books to be dated. A recent reprint as a booklet has been published using the original setting. A more recent book by Don Neal, *Railways in the Garden* (Peco, 1978), is currently out of print. Both books deal with the author's own O gauge layouts and the methods employed to build them, and both are worth the trouble of tracking down.

A less well-known book, *Chronicles of a Garden Railway* (MAP, 1968) by W.A. Strickland, deals with the trials and tribulations of a pioneer worker in OO gauge. Its value lies in demonstrating that OO out of doors is not only practical, it allows long trains to be seen in a railway-like setting. Still on the theme of OO gauge outdoors, Peco publish a pamphlet called *OO Gauge in the Garden* by B.F. Burchell, which briefly summarises his extensive experience in this area.

Jack Ray's *A Lifetime with O Gauge* (Pendragon Atlantic, 1992) not only deals in full with his famous Crewchester outdoor O gauge layout, but has a good deal to say about other O gauge layouts as well. It is an extremely readable account with ample illustrations. Although more about a garden railway than garden railways in general, it contains a wealth of information on this branch of the hobby.

I should mention two books I have not read. One is *Railways in the Garden*, published by GardenRail in 1994, which appears to be a good summary biased towards ground-level layouts, mainly narrow gauge. I shall doubtless be adding this to my library, but have refrained from reading it to avoid any hint of plagiarism. Another book which I have had recommended is *Live Steam Model Locomotives, 16mm Scale Vol.1* (Nelson & Saunders Ltd) by Peter Dobson.

Of specific interest to live steam loco construction are the Gauge 1 Association's *The Project*, describing a basic Gauge 1 0-6-0, and Norman Dewhirst's *A Steam Locomotive for O gauge*, originally published by Percival Marshall but recently reprinted, both of which provide a good deal of information for the beginner.

Finally, the magazine *Garden Rail* (GardenRail, PO Box 42, Skipton, North Yorks BD23 5SU) is essential reading for anyone even remotely interested in the subject. Apart from the excellent articles, the advertising pages provide a wealth of information about products for the outdoor operator.

Appendix II

Specialist Societies

Most scale/gauge combinations have their own associations, which exist for the mutual help and assistance of members. Most publish a magazine or newsletter, the quality of which varies from society to society and in many cases is liable to change with the editor. This is more marked with the smaller groups which are frequently run by three or four dedicated enthusiasts working in their spare time. Despite these handicaps, a surprising number manage to achieve standards which any professional would be proud of.

While you do not have to join any of these societies, membership of the appropriate group will undoubtedly simplify many problems. One of the recurring features of the hobby is that, every decade or so, someone reinvents the wheel and then tries to establish patent rights.

The following list is not guaranteed to be complete and no reference is made to Society Officers. You should consult either *GardenRail* or *Railway Modeller* for up-to-date information:

O Gauge Guild
Gauge 1 Model Railway Association
3 Gauge Society
16 mm Model Railway Association
16.5 gauge Narrow Gauge Association
G Scale Society.
7¼in Gauge Society

Appendix III

Useful Addresses

The following addresses and telephone numbers were believed to be correct at the time of going to press. However, as these are subject to change, particularly telephone area codes, no guarantee can be given for their continued accuracy.

Please note: It is important to telephone or write in the first instance since many firms only accept visitors by appointment.

Argyle Locomotive Works (M.D. Wright)
Burnside
Aboyne
Aberdeenshire AB34 5ES
Tel: 013398 86494
Live steam

Aston Scale Models
Lorne House
The Green
Aston Rowant
Watlington
Oxon OX9 5ST
Importer of US products

Brandbright Ltd
The Old School
Cromer Road
Bodham
Holt
Norfolk NR25 6QG
Tel: 01263 588755 Fax: 01263 588424
16 mm scale and G gauge locos, coach and wagon kits, track

Chalk Garden Rail
25 Harmer Street
Gravesend
Kent DA12 2AP
Tel: 01474 351672 (evening 01474 332038)
Retail stockist

Elgee Hobbies
16 Thomas Street
Portadown

Co. Armagh BT62 3AL
Retail, LGB

Fairwind Garden Rail
60 School Road
Wales Village
Nr. Sheffield S31 8QJ
Tel: 01742 692604 (evening 01909 772751)
Importer of US products

Finescale Engineering Co.
Unit 10, Victoria Business Centre
Neilston St.
Leamington Spa, Warks.
Tel: 01926 335123
16 mm scale live steam

Friog Models and Electronics
New Inn
Friog
Fairbourne
Gwynedd LL38 2NX
Tel: 01341 250071

Garden Railway Specialists
Station Studio
Princes Risborough
Bucks HP27 9DT
Tel: 01844 345158 Fax: 01844 274352
Retail; stockist, electric train control

Highland Signals
Harmony
Caroline Place
Wolfhill
Perth PH2 6DA
Tel: 01821 650454 or 01850 600225
Retail stockists

Ivydale
37 Farfield
Kidderminster
Worcs DY10 1UQ
Tel: 01562 829702
G gauge

JD Models
10 Rogate Road
Luton, Beds
Tel: 01582 20711
16 mm scale battery locomotives

John Prestcott Engineering
Penkridge
Staffs ST19 5QJ
Tel: 01785 712452
Live steam

Kent Garden Railways
28 Multon Road
West Kingsdown
Kent TN15 6DB
Tel/fax: 01742 852586
Mail order

Lionel Pike
32 Keswick Drive
Lightwater
Surrey GU18 5XE
Tel: 01278 474021 (mobile 0831 113200)
Survey, design and installation of garden railways

Locomotion
88 Berrington Road
Nuneaton
Warwickshire CV10 0LE
Tel: 01203 392277
Live steam

Longhedge Locomotive Works
19 Cakwell Close
Stansted
Essex CM24 8JF
Tel: 01279 815571
Gauge 1 electric power locos

Martins Models
Llanbister Road
Llandrindod Wells
LD1 5UW
Tel/fax: 01547 5503646
Retail stockist

Maxitrak Ltd.
4 Larstore Park
Lodge Road
Staplehurst
Kent TN12 0QY
Tel: 01580 893030
Live steam

Mike Chaney
116 Vicarage Road
Chelmsford
Essex CM2 9BT
Tel: 01245 260096
Retail stockist

Pearse Locomotives
The Brow
Clive Avenue
Church Stretton
Shropshire SY6 7BS
Tel: 01694 723806
Live steam

Pemberton Models
12a Springvale Mill
Waterside Road
Haslingdean
Lancs BB4 5EN
Tel: 01706 211841
Gauge 1 live steam

Peter Chandler
19 The Cravens
Smallfield, Surrey
Jigstones building construction
system

Priory Carriages
20 Priory Lane
Kents Bank
Grange-over Sands
Cumbria LA11 7BH
16 mm scale carriage kits

Pritchard Patent Product Co. Ltd.
Beer
Seaton
Devon EX12 3NA
Tel: 01297 21542
Peco track

R&J Feather
15 Der Street
Todmorden
Lancs OL14 5QT
Tel/fax: 01706 8144042
U-mould modelling system

Ross Harrison Designs
The Glen
Eithnog Lane
Llanfair Caereinion
Powys SY21 9EB
Tel: 01938 810937
Working designs, model construction

Roundhouse Engineering Co.
Unit 6, Churchill Business Park
Churchill Road
Wheatley
Doncaster DN1 2TF
Tel: 01320 328035
Live steam locomotives

Samson Engineering
14 Fairfield Avenue
Ruislip
Middlesex HA4 7PH
Tel: 01895 634738
Live steam

Severn Valley Models
240 Westbourne Street
Wribbenhall
Bewdley
Worcs DY12 1AG
Tel: 01299 402192
Layout building service

Tenmille Products
18 Thorney Road
Capel St Mary
Ipswich
Suffolk IP9 2LQ
Tel: 01206 299006
Gauge 1 and 16 mm scale rolling
stock kits and accessories; track

The Engine Shed
Freepost BR792
Arundel
West Sussex BN18 9BR
Tel: 01903 88488 Fax: 01903
884377
Retail stockists

TME
87 Ardgowan Road
Catford
London SE6 1UY
Tel/fax: 0181 693 3085
Live steam

Trackworks
PO Box 58
Welshpool
Powys SY21 7AA
Tel: 01938 554728 Fax: 01938
55586
Track bases and concrete moulds

Transport Models
Kew Bridge Steam Museum
Green Dragon Lane
Brentford
Middlesex TW8 0EN
Tel: 020 8748 4319

Welshpool Pottery
The Glyn
Cyfronydd
Welshpool SY21 9ER
Tel: 01938 83303 Fax: 01938
83383
16 mm scale buildings

Wolverhampton Models & Hobbies
1 Meadow St.
Chapple Ash
Wolverhampton WV1 4 NZ
Tel: 01909 26709
Scratch building service

Index